Pilot, Prisoner, Patriot

An autobiography by

Air Vice Marshal Hugh Slatter

Published in the Republic of South Africa by
Ex Montibus Media
26 Caledon Street
Darling, 7345

ISBN: 978-0-620-76975-4

Cataloguing-in-publication data is available from the
South African National Library.

Printed and bound in the Republic of South Africa by:
ABC Printers
21 Kinghall Avenue
Epping.

For a complete list of 'Ex Montibus Media' titles contact:
admin@exmontibusmedia.co.za
or visit:
www.exmontibusmedia.co.za

Dedication

I dedicate this autobiography to my family, to my wife Jayne, and children Mark and Lee, and grandchildren Sean and Kaylee, and to their mothers, Denise and Chelsie. And to my friends and other family worldwide without whose support these life-changing events would have been much tougher to handle.

I am grateful to have been able to witness the growth of my loving family and the gift of grandchildren, and I hope that future generations of my family and my friends` families will find some interest and enjoyment in this story about Africa and America in years to come.

God`s blessings are on all of us.

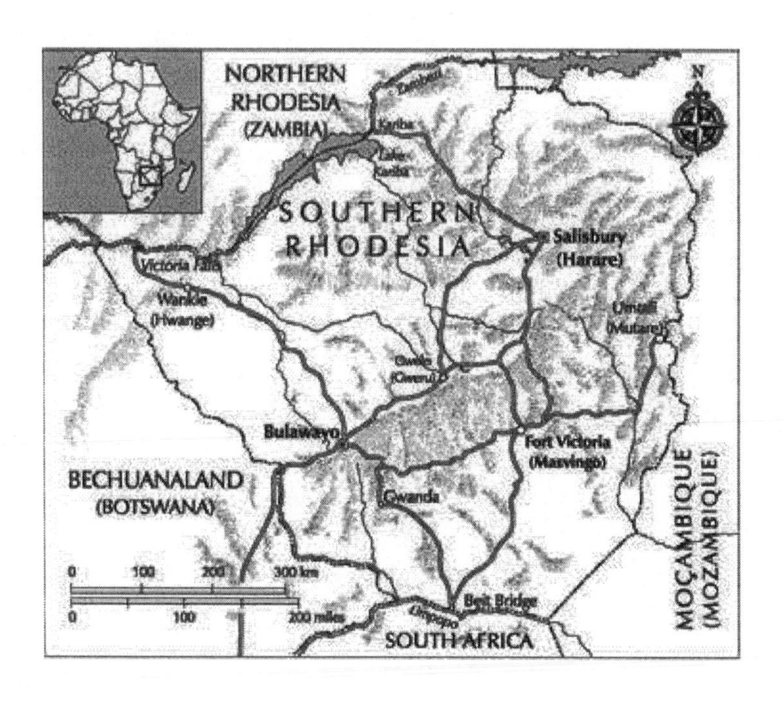
NORTHERN
RHODESIA
(ZAMBIA)
N
SOUTHERN
RHODESIA
Salisbury
(Harare)
Victoria Falls
Wankie
(Hwange)
Umtali
(Mutare)
Bulawayo
Fort Victoria
(Masvingo)
BECHUANALAND
(BOTSWANA)
Gwanda
0 100 200 300 km
0 100 200 miles
Beit Bridge
SOUTH AFRICA
MOÇAMBIQUE
(MOZAMBIQUE)

NOTES FROM THE AUTHOR

Any profits that I may receive from the sales of this book will be donated to select Wounded Veterans Associations in the USA and Southern Africa in recognition of their service to the Free World – thank you all and may God bless you and your families.

I gratefully acknowledge the assistance and encouragement provided by many friends in compiling this book.

I particularly acknowledge the help, patience and perseverance of our friend, Al Stroh, without whose astonishing computer skills I would probably still be penning the first chapter and gluing pictures onto pages! Al also spent a great deal of time conducting a first edit of the script and offering valuable criticism and thoughtful suggestions. Thank you, Al.

Thanks to my wife, Jayne, for her undiplomatically frank but always helpful comments and suggestions. And thanks to our friend and neighbor, Emily Rumiano who offered useful early analysis of style and content.

Thanks are also due to my friends who provided or allowed the use of their photographs; Al Stroh, Roy and Bobby Neep, Senator Tom Eagleton, Vera and Hal Balo, Merilyn Walsh, Tol Janeke, Granny Frazier, Phil Condit, Warren Mandy, Daan Retief, Nick Price, Jean-Marie Saget, Garth Wensley, Patty Bamber, Pete and Paddy Briscoe, Joe Sutter, Chelsie and Lee Slatter, Denise and Mark Slatter.

Foreword

by Group Captain F.D. `Tol` Janeke

THIS IS THE TRUE STORY *of a remarkable man. A story full of excitement, comradeship and fun. But also of incredible hardship, great fortitude and perseverance.*

Hugh Clarke Scudamore Slatter, airman and business leader of great distinction. A man who was wrongly accused of sabotaging the very aircraft that he had worked so hard to acquire for the Air Force of Zimbabwe. Hugh Slatter has a name as interesting as his history. Born in the heart of Africa, in the most interesting time in modern history, he has lived an extraordinary life. It is recorded here in his own words in vivid clarity.

His grandfather, Clarke Slatter, was a soldier with General Lord Chelmsford at the famous battle of Isandlwana in January 1879. This was the pioneering heritage and spirit that was to shape his later life. It was the foundation of the qualities of leadership that were to mark him from an early age, and the very qualities that were to guide him to become the Chief of Staff at the age of just forty in the Air Force of Zimbabwe.

Having joined the Royal Rhodesian Air Force in 1962 as a youngster, he had served his country through the changes in name to the Rhodesian Air Force and lastly as the Air Force of Zimbabwe. He had risen to the rank of Air Vice Marshal and held the appointment of Chief of Staff in this new structure. This meant swearing loyalty to his erstwhile enemy. It is a not only a story of success, betrayal, torture, and imprisonment, but also of enduring courage and determination to succeed under the most difficult conditions; to rise again to the very highest level of management in business in a new country and a fresh career in civilian life.

In the late 1970's dramatic changes were taking place in the political landscape of Africa, south of the Equator. Portugal was abandoning its colonies; the Federation of Rhodesia and Nyasaland had been broken up, and Britain was anxious for Rhodesia to be handed over to majority rule. I first met Hugh in 1962 when he was an officer cadet and I was instructing at the Advanced flying school. After qualifying for his 'Wings' and getting commissioned we became friends at work, on the sports field, and socially. He rose rapidly through the ranks in justification of his strong qualities of leadership – qualities that were to become very evident during the protracted Rhodesian Bush War.

His integrity and strength of character was clearly demonstrated in an operation in support of Portuguese forces operating against Frelimo, in Mozambique. While doing an evacuation of civilian refugees, one of the helicopter pilots, having landed, indicated to the Portuguese soldier on board the chopper, that they were being overloaded. The soldier's response was to open fire on the group of refugees awaiting uplift. When this was reported back at the forward base, Hugh was so alarmed at the indifferent attitude of the local commanders to this flagrant abuse of authority, that he submitted his resignation. This resulted in the incident being reported at the highest level of command and an assurance given that it would never happen again. Only then could he be persuaded to withdraw his resignation. He had made it clear the he would not be party to the killing of innocent civilians and that this was not what he had signed up for. He was prepared to resign his commission, as a final resort on this principle.

The Rhodesian Air Force was, for fourteen years, heavily engaged in what became known as the Bush War. Inevitably Hugh found himself at the sharp end as a pilot, Squadron Commander, and Officer Commanding Flying Wing. After fourteen years of operational flying it had become apparent to officers like Hugh and myself that the protracted war that we had been engaged in, was drawing to a weary end. This would result in dramatic change in the governing structure of the country. It would almost certainly mean that the very enemy we had been fighting, in a long and terrible conflict, would now become our new masters.

Sadly, this resulted in some painful decisions for those career airmen who would have to choose to either remain in the country they loved, or seek pastures elsewhere. The small, closely knit and highly professional team was to be torn apart. Some believed that if they stayed on they would help to make conciliation work. Others immediately decided to abandon everything that was dear to them and start afresh. There were convincing arguments for either choice. Hugh chose to stay on. I decided to leave the Air Force and Rhodesia. There really was no right or wrong decision as the future was to demonstrate in the years ahead.

Losing people like Hugh with all his talent and experience from Africa where the leadership qualities are so desperately needed, was tragic. That it should have happened through false accusations, imprisonment, and torture, makes the whole sorry saga so much worse. There was then, and still is to this day, a mistrust and an inability to forget the legacy of colonialism in Africa, an inability to forge a new future, using all available talent and skills. These skills were as abundant as all the natural assets of the land. That this mistrust should finally result in his relocation to the United States, adds to this fascinating story.

Following the trumped up charges against him and his fellow officers, they were all subjected to the harshest cruelty in prison. Beatings, electric shock treatment and constant deprivation were the order of the day. Notwithstanding this he showed enduring courage, while constantly under threat of death in prison. His friends in Zimbabwe, and all over the world, were aware of the dire situation the Air Force officers found themselves in during the incarceration. Various plans were discussed to assist in securing their release.

Having heard on the South African news that United States Senators Tom Eagleton, Paul Laxalt, and Mark Hatfield were doing a whistle-stop, human rights tour through Southern Africa, I contacted General Peter Walls, ex-Military Supremo in Rhodesia. The General had by then retired in South Africa and was aware of the Air Force officers' predicament. He in turn used his good offices to arrange a private interview for the parents of one of the incarcerated officers, Peter Briscoe, to meet Senator Eagleton. This meeting duly took place in a Johannesburg hotel where the senator was briefed in detail about the background. This resulted in the Zimbabwe government and President, Robert Mugabe, being put under direct pressure by the USA for the immediate release of the Air Force officers.

Following his final release from prison and flight to London, he never let up on doing everything possible to achieve the release of his fellow officers, who were still in prison. He kept up the pressure notwithstanding the fact that he had still to be united with his own family.

Starting a new life with a young family in the USA proved both challenging and exciting. It required that he devote much time to his new career, while studying for a degree. This was done with the solid support of his wife Jayne and two boys, Mark and Lee. Inevitably his employer, General Electric, was to recognize his abilities and from a relatively late start in his life he was to rise to the position of Vice President of the GE Aviation/Boeing programs.

His move to the USA meant adjusting back into civilian life in a strange country, with his family, that he had almost lost touch with during his long imprisonment. The pressure of work, study and domestic life never deterred him from his personal goals. It was no surprise that his ability soon became apparent. During these years of his advancement my wife and I were fortunate enough to visit them several times.

Travelling to the UK and USA from South Africa, we were privileged to meet some of his colleagues and friends. It was wonderful to see how well they were being accepted by the senior management of both GE and Boeing. Clearly Hugh was held in high regard. So much so that, having retired fifteen years ago, he continues to work for these two aviation giants in a consulting role. After 56 years in the aircraft world he remains committed and is still involved. One must wonder if he would have reached these heights had it not been for Mugabe's ill-fated decisions.

In the final analyses Mugabe failed his people, his country and sadly, the whole of Africa as a leader. Ridiculed and despised by those that put him into power, he has become a sad and lonely old man. It is estimated that as many as three million Zimbabweans have fled the country into South Africa. In stark contrast, Hugh has risen from the depths of darkness and humiliation to become one of the global captains of industry. A pillar of strength to his family, admired by his contemporaries and a true friend amongst friends. Ironic justice has found its mark.

Preface

A Life-Changing Event

"YOU WILL TALK!" *he screamed. The voice was maniacal. "No one can stand this for long. I promise we will make you talk soon!"*

The scene was surreal. I was lying stretched out and face down, with two heavy hoods covering my head and face, making it difficult to breathe normally. I was on the hard, back seat of what seemed like a Jeep or similar vehicle, with someone sitting on my back and legs so I could not move. My shackles had been moved from my hands behind my back, to my hands in front of me, with layers of cloth wrapped around my wrists, and the shackles tightened as far as they could go without cutting through the cloth wraps. The thin cotton shirt and pants that I had been wearing since the secret police had picked me up two weeks ago, offered no protection from the cold, or from what was about to happen to me.

Suddenly, my shirt was lifted, and I felt needles being pushed into my back, first at the base, and then at the top of my spine. Later I would learn that these were advanced methods of electric torture, whereby breaking the natural resistance of the outer skin to allow the electric current to enter the fluids of the body, provides much more effective shock, resulting in significant spinal contortion and pain.

How had it come to this? At the time of my arrest, I was the Chief of Staff of the Air Force, and confirmed for promotion to be Commander of the Air Force in a few months. How could anyone be Chief of Air Staff one minute, and a prisoner in shackles the next minute?

Well things had changed. The recently elected government had brought the most significant and far-reaching change in the 100-year-old history of the country. Rhodesia had become Zimbabwe, Robert Mugabe was the new prime minister, but he had promised us an era of reconciliation and an opportunity to work towards a successful multi-racial democracy.

But these people, who seemed intent on doing me harm were supposed to be my co-workers, helping the fledgling Zimbabwe get on its feet - not the enemy we had been fighting for some 15 years in a vicious and ugly war.

In an effort to understand this more fully, I have to go back in time to earlier days in Africa, in Southern Rhodesia, and in Rhodesia particularly. Yes – those earlier times were very different times, a different country, a different government, and a different life for all.

Contents

PART ONE

Growing up in Africa

GROWING UP AS A YOUNG BOY *in Southern Rhodesia during the 1940's and 1950's, as the grandson of pioneering stock, I was never fully aware of the almost idyllic lifestyle we enjoyed. Salisbury, the capital city, sat at an altitude of 5,000 feet and enjoyed a good rainy season from November through April. Summer temperatures could get quite warm, often reaching into the upper 80's and occasionally into the 90's, while winter temperatures were relatively mild but brought with them an occasional frost. The city was home to some 100,000 residents in those days, with wide, treed avenues and attractive parks.*

My father was the headmaster of a renowned junior school, Highlands, situated some four miles to the north-east of the capital, Salisbury. His students were primarily the children of farmers who, generally speaking, lived great distances from the city. As such, the school was a boarding school too, where a lot of the children lived during the academic term and went home for the holidays.

I have a favorite memory of my father, which is still as clear as the day it happened. Late one afternoon, I saw him walking across the playing fields from his office, coming to the boarding school accommodation where we also lived. There were four or five young girls, aged about seven-eight years, all fighting to hold his hand as they walked. It was a constant struggle to see who among them could keep hold of his hand the longest as they all jostled for position! He was a caring father-figure to all of them - they loved him and he loved them. I understood at that moment why the school children adored him and why their parents loved him too. That memory will stay with me forever. He was a very good man.

My mother taught at a prestigious private school, Chisipite, also in the northern suburbs of Salisbury, and occasionally gave lectures on Greek and Latin at the local University. She was an intellect with a photographic memory and could be quite intimidating because of her own strict upbringing and mores. However, she was a very generous woman with a heart of gold, once you got to know her.

My life revolved around school, my fellow classmates and classes during the mornings, with sports during the afternoons. The academic standard was high and was based on the British system of schooling; sports activities followed the similar British pattern of cricket, rugby, soccer, tennis, swimming and other popular sports of the period. With homework in the evenings, our days were full and rewarding.

Holidays were occasionally spent on the coast in South Africa, Mozambique or at the fruit farm that my father started in the mountainous area of the Eastern Districts where he spent considerable time teaching my brother and I how to shoot and to fish. It may come as a surprise to younger generations that I had my first rifle and shotgun at age 10, but I was only allowed to shoot in competition and for 'the pot' (to put food on the table) or for protection.

In the late 1940's, my father had purchased approximately 160 acres of virgin land in Juliasdale, just past the hotel and store. It was a beautiful piece of land with a natural spring in the top western most corner of the property. It was completely undeveloped but over the years, my father and one helper planted 40,000 pine trees and 1,300 fruit trees (mostly apple).

He also built a wooden cabin, complete with running water, but with no electricity. The toilet was the classic `long-drop` for many years and was some distance from the cabin itself. This necessitated a visit at last light and first light, since there was too much wildlife in the early years to guarantee a safe visit!

Year after year, my father improved the accommodations, including an indoor toilet, although we still had to rely on lamps for lighting, fire for cooking and hot water and paraffin for a very old and inefficient refrigerator. This in itself was a vast improvement over the previous practice of bagging the perishables and submerging them in the icy waters of the spring. Since the farm was at some 6,000+ feet above sea level, the climate was usually cool and the air invigorating.

In the early days, it was a full day`s drive from Salisbury to the farm over strip and dirt roads, but was reduced to some four hours as the roads were improved. Initially, my father had somehow bought a very large Chrysler, especially fitted out for safaris for an eccentric American millionaire. This vehicle was a convertible and we loved to drive to Inyanga (Juliasdale) with the top down, begging my father to keep it down even when we encountered isolated rain storms!

My father loved the land, the style of life and we spent many happy holidays with him, 'helping' as we got older. When my father died in 1974, we tried to keep the farm viable, but after my brother moved to South Africa in 1978, and after my imprisonment in 1982, it was impossible. My mother had to sell the farm to someone who could maintain it and also to help pay for the ever-increasing legal costs of my lawyers, for reasons that will become clear later in this book.

Those were the early days in Rhodesia and wildlife was still plentiful. Leopards, baboons, wild pigs and small antelope, usually duiker were abundant and would come right up to the cabin. Fortunately, the more dangerous wildlife, such as lions and elephants, were further away and we were not at risk.

My father had Army experience, served during World War II and was a strict disciplinarian and teacher; especially when it came to handling guns. He spent many hours instructing us on all the safety features of our weapons and many more hours on the finer aspects of shooting. Consequently, I became a decent shot and to this day remember clearly my father's lessons. Little did I realize how valuable those lessons would be later in life or how the fundamentals would remain the same, whether on an official weapons range or delivering ordinance from an aircraft.

Our schools were a mixture of boys and girls until age 12 or 13, but the high schools were either all boys or all girls. Most schools had a sister or brother school and in one's senior years, there would be evening dances held for socializing with the opposite sex. I attended Churchill High School and our sister school, Roosevelt High School, was a couple of hundred yards down the road. Since most students rode bicycles, there were ample opportunities to mingle on our way to and from school.

My Grandfather, on my father`s side, was a very interesting man. At 97 years old, he was still tending a garden of some seven acres, all on his own. Sadly, he died when he was 99 years old; not from any illness but from a fall he suffered that broke his hip. There was no remedy in those days and once he realized he would basically be bedridden, he decided to let go.

He had fought in the Zulu wars in the late 1800's and had survived the well documented Isandlwana massacre of 1,250 British soldiers by a Zulu *Impi* (army) of some 40,000 warriors. He and a handful of others who had been out on patrol had returned to camp to discover the massacre, managed to escape to the equally well known Rorke`s Drift outstation and survived. He had come to Southern Rhodesia with the Pioneer Column in 1890 and he was a true pioneer.

In 2012, Jayne and I were able to visit Isandlwana and Rorke`s Drift, courtesy of our great friends, Tol and Anne Janeke, under the expert guidance of the well-known and respected South African authority on the Zulu wars, Ron Lock. Ron was able to re-trace my grandfather`s route that fateful day and showed us how he and a handful of others managed to escape. It was an eerie experience, standing in the same places as my grandfather and trying to imagine his excitement and fear.

My brother, Don, and cousin, Anthony, were both four years older than me. When they were about eight, we would play games on our seven-acre property; usually involving some sort of hide and seek. If I was found and could not escape, they would capture me and `punish` me. On one occasion, they had finally caught me, pinned me to the ground and said, "We are going to torture you!" Unaware of the meaning of the word, I asked, "What`s torture?" Their ominous reply was, "You`ll find out!"

Their form of torture was to cut thorns from a nearby bush and stick them into me. Apparently, this caused them much delight, although they obviously could not do too much damage or my parents would ask questions. The session would end with dire threats of more torture if I told my parents. This only happened once that I recall, but it gave me an early understanding of the word. Ironic that the practice would reappear later in life, under more skilled hands!

After four years of high school, we could take the Cambridge Overseas Examination. I chose another option though, which was to spend an extra two years in school and take the Cambridge Overseas Higher Schools Examination. This was deemed the equivalent of one year of university and allowed one to enter any South African University of one's choosing. Not too surprisingly, my final grades indicated that I had spent more time playing sports and enjoying some professional acting with a local theatrical company, than time spent studying my academic subjects.

With no distinctions, but with all first-class credits, I chose a good university in Durban, where I decided to study for a Bachelor of Arts degree. At least two of my good friends would be attending the same University; one to study architecture and the other to study accounting, which would decide the next phase of our lives. Our Higher School Examinations had been completed in December, and we were required to report to University in the middle of January. That short schedule didn't provide much time to prepare, but my parents had already laid the groundwork. At 18 years of age and being blessed with good parents, I didn't have to worry too much about preparations!

The 1,000-mile (1,609 kilometers) journey to Durban was by train and took a couple of days and nights. Leaving home and leaving my family was not overly stressful, and while we were certainly a caring and loving family, we were not given to outward displays of emotion. And so, with the usual farewells, I climbed aboard the train with my friends and we were on our way.

The start of university life was uneventful, with the usual initiation rites and general acquaintance with the campus. I found the Bachelor of Arts program boring, but I was fascinated by the Architectural program that my friend was pursuing. Following some discussion with my parents, I enrolled in the Architecture program. That change was instantaneous, with new subjects that excited me, but along with that excitement came long, long hours of studio work and late studies. Gone were the opportunities to play baseball and participate in athletics in the evenings, but it all seemed worth the effort.

As the year progressed, I found myself increasingly frustrated with the Dean of the faculty. We were at odds several times during the year and I found myself becoming despondent over what I interpreted as his preconceived ideas. I was not the only student disillusioned with his approach, and it was disturbing to discover later that a particularly creative student by name of Paul Mikula had also decided to leave because of the rigidity of thought. Many years later, I discovered that Paul had actually become the Dean of the architectural school and was highly esteemed by his students for his creativity and freedom of expression in design! Finally, and towards year's end, I decided I had had enough. At the end of the final term, my friend and I rode motorcycles home to Rhodesia and I arrived on my parent's doorstep unannounced. To this day I am grateful for parents who understood the unpredictable behavior of teenagers.

While they were disappointed that I felt I could not continue with the program, they were supportive of my plan to get a temporary job while I figured out what to do in the future. My temporary job was performing clerical and administrative duties at the Rhodesian National Archives, surrounded by row upon row of interesting historical files and notes. When I was not busy responding to requests for data, I was able to research subjects of interest to me, quietly and on my own. My work colleagues were older than I and looking back, they must have wondered what they had done to deserve trying to train this polite but persistent teenager.

While working at the archives, I saw an advertisement in the local newspaper, soliciting applications for the Rhodesian Air Force. I had taken a serious interest in flying since I was a young boy and I could see no harm in applying. I found out that some 600 others had also applied for pilot training with the Air Force, and I was under no illusion that this would be an easy path. Little did I know at the time that this decision would lead to so many challenges, happiness and sadness and would be life changing in the extreme. My trouble-free schooldays in Africa were over!

PART TWO

My Life in the Air Force

Pilot Training

After weeks of tests *and examinations, which included strict medicals, aptitude and co-ordination tests, as well as pre-requisite academic results in mathematics, science and English, we were further narrowed down to some 30 candidates to undergo final interviews. Those final interviews and medical tests, which were conducted over a few days at Air Force Station New Sarum, near Salisbury, further reduced the number to 12 finalists who received offers to undergo pilot training in the Rhodesian Air Force. I was delighted to receive the offer and accepted immediately!*

So, the die was cast. I was to report to Air Force Station New Sarum at the end of January, 1962, for onward transport to Air Force Station Thornhill, near Gwelo (now Gweru) in the Midlands, where all flight training was to be conducted. Unbeknownst to me at the time, the next 21 years of my life would be the most satisfying and rewarding that I could ever have imagined and lead me to the joys and the sorrows of flying in the service of one's country; both in peacetime and during war.

The common bond of this small group of aspiring pilots was that we all had an interest in flying. However, we had signed up as "Officer GD," (General Duties) which meant that we could be required, not only for flying duties, but for any other duties that the Air Force deemed fit. Our training started in a regular Boot Camp. For the Initial Training School of four and a half months, we were drilled, shouted at, trained in weapons handling, studied all the subjects necessary as a pilot, ran many miles daily, polished our boots, kept our own bed spaces immaculate, suffered hazing from our senior pilot course instructors, drilled some more, performed daily gymnastics and drilled some more again!

Sleep was just a word and after finishing our studies late at night, we'd have to prepare the barracks for inspection, very early in the morning. Sometimes our senior course instructors would decide to 'help' us by visiting us late at night, after we had completed our preparations for inspection. They would rearrange all our preparations by tearing apart our bed packs and throwing gravel on our polished cement floors, necessitating another cleaning and polishing prior to inspection.

Inspections were always interesting. Our drill instructor was a tough and extremely fit man who had served in the Irish Guards. He was also the regimental boxing champion of the Irish Guards, as we were to find out when we displeased him. However, and although he was very tough, he was scrupulously fair and demanded increasingly lofty standards of drill, discipline and fitness. He grew to be highly respected by our course because if we were unable to meet his standards, he would persist until we got to the required standard.

During the initial weeks of training, we grew to hate the man, and after one particularly long and arduous drill day, we found ourselves discussing what we would do if we found him alone in an alley somewhere. Somehow, word or suspicion of this must have reached him because the very next day, we were invited for boxing training in the gymnasium. While the boxing training turned out to be only amongst ourselves, our instructor, by his presence and demonstrations, made us aware that WE would be the ones in trouble if we found him in an alley somewhere! And so, he climbed another step on the ladder of our respect.

Early morning inspections during Initial Training School phase were always a trial. Inspections were scheduled for 5 am, while it was still dark. We were accommodated in old World War II, corrugated iron buildings with cement floors, which had to be polished to a gleaming shine. This was extremely hard work at the best of times and made harder when our senior course instructors would walk across the floors late at night with gravel on the soles of their shoes.

We would be up and getting ready at around 4am every day, showering, shaving, getting uniforms ready and putting the finishing touches on cleaning the barracks. Each student was allocated his own 12' x 12' bed space and was responsible for his area to pass inspection, with the communal areas of study rooms, toilets and showers being the responsibility of the whole course. Inspections were carried out with all lights on and windows open.

One particular inspection remains vivid in my mind. It was a Monday morning and we had all spent the entire weekend studying and making a super-human effort to get the barracks in perfect shape. As we were putting the final touches, we heard the command from the adjoining room to "Stand by your beds," as our drill instructor arrived to start the inspection. Since I was in the second communal room to be inspected, we had a few minutes to check each other's uniforms and areas, and then we were ready and standing at attention for inspection.

Suddenly, to our horror, a large moth flew in through one of the open windows and began to circle the room. We could do nothing but remain at attention and wait for our inspection to begin. The moth, however, was clearly unwell and after a few somersaults, flopped onto the bed space of the student, Chris, next to mine, just as the drill instructor marched through the door. He stopped dead in his tracks as he caught sight of the moth, flopping around on the floor.

Marching over to the unfortunate victim, and as only a drill instructor can, he put his face a half an inch from my fellow student's face and yelled, "What is the meaning of this disgusting mess on your floor space?!" Before a reply could be made, he continued with, "I refuse to inspect a barracks where I am up to my knees in filth. You are confined to barracks for three weeks!" With that, he stormed from the room.

We all commiserated with Chris (Dixon), who later became better known as 'Green Leader' when leading a major external operational attack against ZIPRA forces in Zambia in 1979. Confinement to barracks for three weeks was not as bad as it sounded because we had little or no time to leave the camp anyway. However, failing an inspection set the tone for a tougher and longer drill session than normal, and we would all be punished. While it seemed harsh at the time, it's clear that our drill instructor was merely establishing his total authority over all disciplinary aspects and looking back on that experience, we could all see the humor in the situation.

The transition from Initial Training School (ITS) to Basic Flying School (BFS) was an exciting time for us all. No one was expected to be scrubbed from training during ITS, but the fitness and academic standards were tough and everyone was learning new subjects, including aerodynamics and the technical aspects of piston engines, jet engines and airframes. One week before the completion of ITS, we were taken up to the squadron, issued with Pilot's Notes and shown around the aircraft in which we were scheduled to complete 110 hours of basic flight training during a six-month period.

The aircraft was the Percival Provost, a solid, low wing, fixed undercarriage, side by side two-seater with a large, nine-cylinder, radial engine. While this was a pretty simple aircraft that behaved well in spins, stalls and aerobatics, it had a narrow main undercarriage with a small tail wheel that demanded some skill and attention when landing, especially with significant crosswinds. The instrumentation was basic but adequate for all types of flying.

During the basic flying school phase, we would be instructed in general flying, instrument flying, night flying, low-level flying, formation flying and navigation, along with the corresponding academic subjects. Navigation aids were non-existent – 1:250,000 scale maps and dead-reckoning using the eyeball was the basis for all cross-country flying.

Generally speaking, flying was carried out during the mornings and academic training occupied the afternoons. Evenings would be occupied with studies and maintenance of our barracks to the required inspection standards. Our senior course eased off on us slightly and our drill instructor seemed to give us some credit for getting this far, although there was no change in the required discipline or standards we had to achieve.

After inspections, we were required to double time up to the drill area on the eastern side of the airfield, and hard standing. Drill would usually last one hour, unless there was a penalty to pay for some infringement of discipline. Such was the case on one particular day, and although it was the middle of winter, all we wore were uniform trousers, short-sleeved shirts and drill boots. We were soon perspiring freely as we drilled at double pace. Our drill instructor would check our physical state frequently by standing behind each one of us and running his 'pace stick' down the middle of our backs. Once everyone's shirt stuck to the back, one could usually expect the session to start winding down.

On this particular day though, it seemed that our drill instructor was not satisfied that everyone's shirt was showing enough perspiration and we went on and on and on. It finally became clear that there was only one individual left without perspiration showing through his shirt. After running his pace stick up and down this individual`s back numerous times, he thrust his face in the victim's face and demanded an explanation. It transpired that this individual had decided to put a sleeveless sweater under his shirt, because of the cold. The sweater was simply soaking up the perspiration, which was NOT a good idea!

Furious, our drill instructor returned to the front of the squad, informed us in no uncertain terms what he thought of us and what his remedy would be. The remedy was simple; no one left the drill square until everyone`s shirt was wet. We drilled and drilled some more and drilled some more and drilled some more until finally the culprit`s shirt showed perspiration, which ended a two-hour drill session! While our colleague had the decency to apologize to the rest of the course, this lack of discipline sadly reared its head again during training. His training was terminated almost at the completion of the BFS stage when a farmer reported him for unauthorized solo low flying, and he was thrown off the course immediately. It was a salutary lesson for us all.

Towards the end of ITS, we had been given an introductory flight in the Provost as a carrot to help us keep our eye on the ball. We had been given the opportunity to meet our flight instructors and now, as we started BFS, we were all excited and wondering which instructor would be paired with which student. We had learned from our senior course something about each instructor's training methods and we all had our preferences, of course.

I was extremely fortunate and was assigned to Flying Officer Bill Galloway, a motivated, careful and patient pilot to whom I owe much. He was not the type of instructor to take the crowbar from the inside of the cockpit and bash you on the side of your head if he thought you weren't trying hard enough. And I appreciated that! It seemed that he realized I really wanted to learn to fly and that I would try my best, regardless of the outcome. Later, when I became a flight instructor and was sometimes tempted to become impatient or to feel that the student was not trying hard enough, I remembered his example. Flying Officer Galloway steered me through the BFS successfully and I was grateful. The other students, with the exception of one, also passed the BFS successfully.

A few weeks before the end of BFS, we were all taken for a familiarization flight in the aircraft we would be piloting during our advanced training; the Vampire T 11, a twin seat jet aircraft. During the familiarization flight, I was instantly struck by the quietness and lack of vibration as we took off and climbed away. The rate of climb was impressive, compared to the Provost, and soon we were above 30,000 feet where we did some basic handling and some aerobatics before returning to base. We carried out a couple of circuits and landings and it was evident that things happened much quicker at the circuit speeds and approach speeds of the Vampire. Overall, it was an exhilarating experience that left me with the motivation to rapidly complete Basic Flight Training and move on to advanced training in this aircraft.

With Advanced Flying School (AFS) came new academic subjects, as well as continued drill, fitness and discipline training. Although we could sense a slightly more relaxed attitude, we were no longer required to double time (run) everywhere we went. The flying syllabus for advanced training followed the same basics as before; general flying, instrument flying, night flying, formation flying and navigation, with great emphasis on speeding up our thought processes and the hand/eye coordination required. The Vampire enjoyed better instrumentation than the Provost, with newer versions of the basic instruments and a radio compass, although with only a very few radio beacons in the country, this was not quite as useful as imagined.

Much emphasis was still placed on map reading for the navigation phase of training. The aircraft had a decent top speed of almost 500 knots, or more than 550 mph and had generally reliable handling characteristics. I am only aware of a couple of unpredictable events, both of which involved spin training. In the first, Tol Janeke, the instructor, and Bill Buckle, his student, were forced to eject when the airplane refused to respond to any known technique to exit the spin. I had a somewhat similar experience with a student, but fortunately did not have to eject because the aircraft finally and suddenly responded and we were able to exit the spin. This phase was scheduled for six months and 110 hours of flight time.

As much as I loved the jet, I found the cockpit cramped and the ejection seat uncomfortable during a one-hour sortie. I am six feet, two inches tall and it seemed this aircraft was not designed for my body type. Years later, during a flying medical with a particularly meticulous doctor, he took some extra leg measurements and told me that if I were to eject from the T11, I would have my kneecaps removed by the front canopy support on the way out of the cockpit! I never complained about discomfort again and flew the T11 many more times during operations.

Notwithstanding that adventure, I progressed at a satisfactory rate through AFS, despite a four-week forced absence from flying due to a serious knee/cartilage injury. My course-mates really stood by me, kept me current with the academic requirements and helped me get back into flying as soon as possible. The instructors, after some discussion, decided much to my relief to keep me on this course, rather than put me back to a later course. Since the AFS phase of training was allocated to be a six-month period, I had basically lost one of those months and I was very grateful to be allowed to continue.

Survival Course

About half way through Basic Flying School, we were all loaded into a transport aircraft and flown to Binga Airfield on the shores of Lake Kariba. At that time, Kariba was the largest man-made lake in the world, some 150 miles in length and 30 miles in width, formed by the great Zambezi River, running across the bottom half of Africa and emptying into the Indian Ocean. We were to conduct a one-week survival training exercise in the adjacent Matusadona area, starting from the southern shores of the lake and moving further south into a remote and rugged wilderness full of dangerous game, including lion, leopard, elephant, buffalo, rhino, hippo and crocodile.

Our party compromised our course commanding officer, our drill instructor, several helpers and all of us students, along with a senior Ranger from the National Parks. We were taken by truck to the pre-assigned drop-off point and then had to walk some 20 miles further inland. We were dressed in old flying overalls and could carry one blanket and water.

By the time we reached our resting spot for the night, it was already starting to get dark. We made small fires in the four corners of the resting area, ate some rations and lay down for the night. After a few hours of fitful sleep, there was a disturbance just outside the edge of the camp. Some of us got up and moved over to that side to try to see what was happening and to make sure that the fires were stoked. Our Game Ranger was up as well and he explained that rhinoceros were often upset by fires. He suspected that there were one or two rhinoceros just outside the Camp and warned us to be prepared for a charge through the Camp.

After some time and with no further disturbance, we all went and lay down again for a few more hours of uneasy sleep. What woke me was the ground shaking and a mad scrambling of bodies as two rhinoceros charged through our camp. I remember leaping up and starting to run for the nearest tree, some 25 yards away. As I started to run, I noticed our course commander still lying down and I shouted at him to get up as I continued to run past him. The ground was shaking more and more and sparks from the fires, which the rhinos had disturbed, flew everywhere. My sight, however, was fixed on my safety tree, which was getting closer by the second.

As I passed the tree and swung behind it, I was surprised to find two others already there, including my course commander whom I had just passed on the ground a few seconds before! The wonder of adrenaline! The two rhinos continued to charge right through our camp and then disappeared into the night, leaving a group of shaken humans, dust and sparks. The rhinoceros did not reappear again that night nor did they disrupt the sleep that we all desperately needed!

We had several encounters with wildlife during the rest of the exercise, including being chased by an elephant down a hilly game trail. Miraculously, we managed to avoid falling down in its path. We had no encounters with lions, although they were known to frequent the area. We always made sure that we were covered by the leader with a high-powered rifle to protect us from crocodiles when fording the many estuaries of the lake. This break from the pressures of flight training was welcome and certainly helped in the team bonding process.

Wings Parade

Finally, the glorious and long-awaited day of our 'Wings Parade' arrived. Having successfully completed the Initial Training School, Basic Flight School, and Advanced Flight School phases of our training, we were awarded our commissions as officers, in addition to receiving our 'Wings'. The parade and fly-past performed by our instructors was memorable. Friends and families filled the stands to witness the results of eighteen months of hard work by all concerned and my own proud parents joined me for the celebration. As the reviewing officer pinned our new 'Wings' badges on our uniforms, we could scarcely contain our pride and joy.

Perhaps the most memorable moment was when our drill instructor met us as we came off the parade route, stood smartly in front of us, saluted each one of us and said "Congratulations, Sir". It was an emotional moment for us. Here was this amazing man who had drilled us, disciplined us, got us flying fit, badgered us at every opportunity and here he stood; the first to congratulate us! We had grown to know this man for over 18 months and to recognize his dedication to getting us through the course to his standards. It was a great credit to his ability that even in the last few months when he would come down hard on us, we understood what he was doing and why. He had earned our utmost respect and I, for one, will never forget him. Thank you, Warrant Officer Paddy Molloy.

Of course, we were grateful to our flying instructors and our academic instructors as well, and at the 'Wings Ball' that evening we were able to share a celebratory drink with them. Girlfriends joined us for the evening of fun and the really good news was that we had one week's paid leave, starting the very next day.

Weapons Training

The next phase of our training would be the Operational Conversion Unit (OCU) where we would learn to use the aircraft as a weapons platform. While we now had the basic and advanced skills of flying under our belts, the addition of weapons work would allow us to be posted to operational squadrons. This phase also was scheduled for six months and approximately 120 hours of flight time.

Personally, I enjoyed this phase of training the most. A new aircraft, the single seat Vampire FB9 jet, was added to our training. I loved this little aircraft; it had plenty of cockpit room and wonderful visibility through a bubble-type canopy. The main disadvantage was that the aircraft was not equipped with an ejection seat. No problem, unless you needed it! Be that as it may, it was an excellent platform for weapons, especially cannon, rockets and bombs.

Firing weapons from the air and measuring the results on the Air Force range gave one a good idea of one's handling of the aircraft. Smooth, clear weather conditions made site control much easier, while bumpy or bad weather conditions complicated handling and usually had an adverse effect on one's results. We were a competitive bunch and as soon as we would return from the range, we would get together in the crew room and compare results, with the predictable banter and ribbing.

Our instructors were operational pilots and while we enjoyed some camaraderie with them, we really held them in awe as they demonstrated the necessary skills on a daily basis. Again, there were new academic subjects, technical aspects of gunnery, rocketry and bombing, Gyro sights, fixed sites, various projectiles and flying/handling aspects to improve weapons delivery accuracy. This phase was more comfortable too, from an accommodations aspect. Gone were the barracks, daily inspections and drills, and in their place, we had our own individual quarters and could use our own cars, instead of having to double time everywhere. Life was good!

My fellow OCU pilots decided that a belated 21st birthday celebration for me was in order, and so, on a random Friday afternoon we congregated at the pub. I seem to recall buying my friends the first round of drinks, but after that, things started to get a bit hazy. There was no flying for the next two days and so we continued happily drinking and chatting about flying; the usual topic around pilots. At some stage, I recall walking outside into the parking lot for some fresh air. The next thing I knew was I was lying flat on my face with an empty beer bottle next to me. Then I felt someone shaking me by the shoulder and on looking up, saw that it was Squadron Leader Norman Walsh, the Officer Commanding 1 Squadron – a hero in every young pilot's eyes.

"Are you alright?" he asked.

I was embarrassed, but determined to make some sort of recovery and I tried to stand up.

"Thank you, Sir. I`m a bit unsteady, but if I can make it to the bar, I would love to have a beer with you."

Norman helped me up, but instead of heading for the bar, he turned around and started walking me to the nearby car park.

"I`m taking you back to your quarters," he said. "You are in no condition to drive."

Norman had a tiny little FIAT 500, which would have been difficult enough to get into when sober, but proved a bit of a problem when inebriated. However, I managed eventually. It was only a short drive to our officers` single quarters, and Norman offloaded me and told me to get some sleep. I mumbled my thanks and promptly fell asleep on top of my bedcover.

I awoke with a start some time later. Looking at my watch, I had been asleep for about an hour. I felt surprisingly well, and decided that I should not miss the opportunity to thoroughly enjoy my 21st with my friends and perhaps have a beer with the OC 1 Squadron. I swallowed some headache pills as a precaution and made my way back to the bar.

The gathering was still in full swing and my friends welcomed me back – I`m not sure that they even knew I had left! OC 1 Squadron joined those of us who were left and we all enjoyed a beer together. I don`t think any of us young pilots could believe we were actually having a beer with this great man., but as life moved on and we all followed Norman`s stellar career, we all realized that this was the real Norman – unaffected and sincere and a great Air Force team player. I was fortunate enough to share paths with Norman on many occasions throughout our careers, and consider myself lucky to have worked alongside this extraordinary man.

By the end of the year we had completed our OCU training and were ready to be posted to operational squadrons. After almost two years of training, I personally had amassed 333 flying hours, covering the full spectrum of Air Force flight training to prepare one for full duty. Our pilot course, Number 16 Pilot Training Course, members were about to be sent on separate journeys; the first time we would be broken up as a group in two years. I was posted to Number 4 Squadron, based at Thornhill Air Force Base. A couple of my fellow course members were also posted to Number 4 Squadron, while our remaining members were posted to different squadrons at Thornhill and New Sarum, our country`s two main Air Force bases at the time. The next phase of my flying career began.

Number 4 Squadron. 1964-1966

Number 4 Squadron was responsible for counter insurgency operations and had a separate responsibility for basic flying training. The aircraft used was the Provost, the same airplane we had trained in during basic flight school, but now we would use it as a weapons platform. And so, it was back to the range to learn and practice weapons delivery from the Provost aircraft. Our weapons training in the Operational Conversion Unit had been in jet aircraft, but the Provost required much more attention to the use of rudder, because of the large, radial engine and propeller wash.

The political situation in Rhodesia was unsettled. Britain had already granted independence to Northern Rhodesia (Zambia) and to Nyasaland (Malawi), prior members of the Federation, on the basis of majority rule. Quite different to South Africa and its policy of apartheid (separate development along racial lines), Southern Rhodesia had been a self-governing colony of Britain since 1923 and enjoyed a qualified franchise, resulting in a prosperous and generally peaceful citizenry.

However, in 1965, as a direct result of Britain`s interference in the affairs of the country and its insistence on early majority rule, Rhodesia decided to declare its political independence from Britain. In turn, this caused Britain to plead a case at the United Nations to impose total sanctions against Rhodesia. This encouraged the Communist countries, China and Russia to provide direct support to the extreme African nationalist factions inside and outside the country, and lead to the start of an ever-increasing war, first inside Rhodesia and later spreading to the neighboring countries of Zambia and Mozambique.

The two main African nationalist factions determined to overthrow the elected government were ZANU (Zimbabwe African National Union), led by Robert Mugabe and ZAPU (Zimbabwe African Peoples Union), led by Joshua Nkomo. ZANLA was hosted in Mozambique and supported by China, while ZIPRA was hosted by Zambia and supported by the Soviets.

They each formed their own military force. ZANU called their military wing the Zimbabwe African National Liberation Army (ZANLA) and ZAPU called their military wing the Zimbabwe African Peoples' Revolutionary Army (ZIPRA). These forces became the main adversaries of the Rhodesian Security Forces and received ever increasing political support from the United Nations and material support from China and from Russia. There was, however, no love lost between these two political factions and this became more and more apparent as the war intensified.

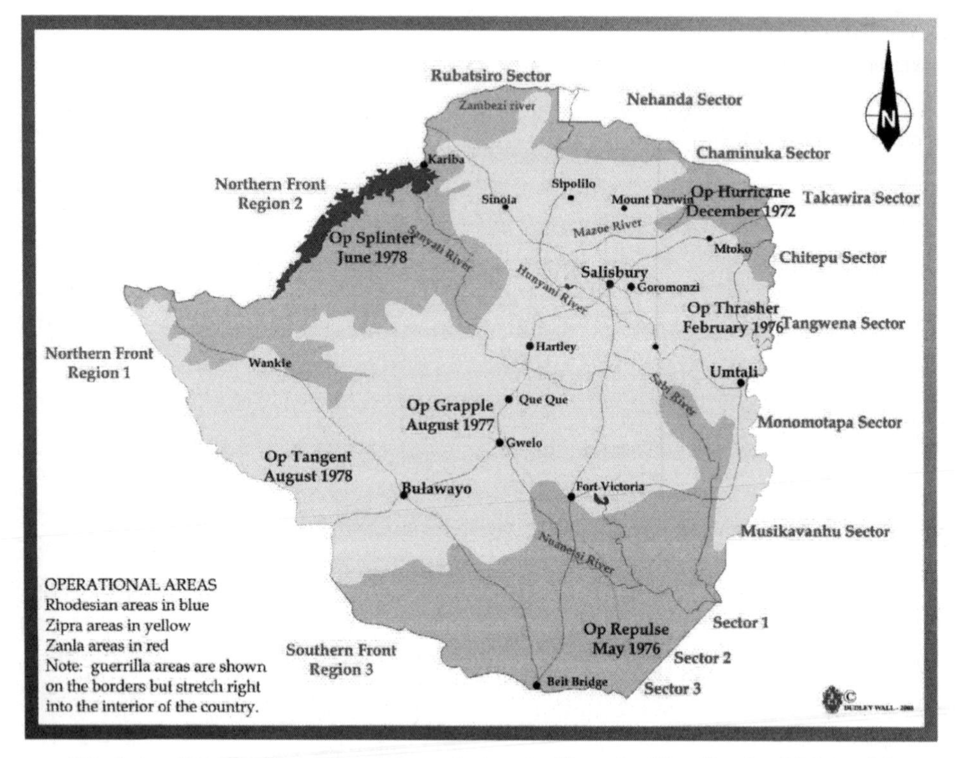

Rhodesian Combat Operational Areas during the Terrorist War (Credit: W. Mandy).

The counter-insurgency (COIN) role of the squadron was important, since there was intelligence indicating the presence of terrorists on Rhodesia's northern and eastern borders. While the Western World, especially the media and some politicians, seemed to prefer the name "Freedom fighters" that the terrorists had given themselves, we were under no such illusions. Those who would murder farmers, their wives and their children in their beds at night did not fit the term 'Freedom Fighter' in my book, and never will.

Navigation and visual reconnaissance played an increasingly important role in the squadron's daily activities. Lengthy border control flights were routine and co-operation with our army and police ground forces were the order of the day. The more we worked with our army and police counterparts, the closer the relationship became, and in the process, we laid the platform for the 'Joint Operational Command' (JOC) that was to be the main feature of the extremely efficient Rhodesian anti-terrorist operations in later years.

One of our anti-terrorist duties was to carry out long border patrol flights. These were of limited value in the early days but did serve to teach us the geography of the entire country. They were of maximum fuel duration (and toilet maximum) of some 4 plus hours. There were always two pilots on these missions and on one particular flight,

I was accompanied by an experienced operational pilot who admitted that he found little excitement in a four-hour flight on an uncomfortable, hard parachute and seat.

We had been flying for about three hours and were in the south-eastern area of the country, at low-level and a theoretical 250 feet above ground level, but sometimes it was necessary to get lower, for more detail, when Bruce decided that he needed to stretch his stiff muscles. I was piloting the aircraft and Bruce unwound the canopy, undid his seat and parachute harness and stood up, holding the front frame of the canopy as he did.

The flying conditions had been fairly good and although it was very warm, it was relatively smooth. However, within a minute of Bruce standing up, we encountered a major air pocket, which almost threw him out of the aircraft! But for the fact that he had a grasp on the canopy rail, he would have flipped out of the aircraft, low-level and without a parachute!

It was a moment of reality for both of us and in one rapid movement, Bruce was sitting on his parachute and firmly strapped back into his harness with the canopy closed. I continued flying while we both sat in silence for a while, contemplating the consequences of what might have happened. After a short while, we could communicate and we had no difficulty in agreeing that was a very foolish action, with hard to imagine ramifications. We further agreed that we had both dodged a bullet. Lesson learned!

After about a year, I was offered the chance to be trained as a Pilot Attack Instructor, an opportunity I readily seized. This valuable qualification involved more weapons work and academic study. I loved the work and the flying and thrived in the environment. Normal squadron duties continued and I now had the added enjoyment of passing along what I had learned to the new pilots who joined the squadron. It struck me that the satisfaction I gained from helping new pilots gain these skills must have been similar to the satisfaction my parents gained from educating school students; a rewarding job indeed.

Shortly after completion of the Pilot Attack Instructor course, I was offered the opportunity to participate in the Flight Instructor's School. While this was not my first choice, it was an opportunity that might not have been presented again. This course offered plenty of flying and more detail of the associated academic subjects. It was fascinating to experience all the different types of flying I had learned in Basic Flying School (BFS), but from a different perspective. This time, I would be the instructor demonstrating the exercise. The challenge was learning how to "patter" the demonstration. In other words, how to explain every handling move required while one flew the aircraft. After a while, this became second nature and I found it more enjoyable as my skills progressed. I wondered as we instructors took new students on their familiarization flights, whether they all got together later to discuss their preferences for an instructor, as we had done after our first flight! I found instructing a full BFS to be extremely rewarding as my students achieved the required milestones of first solo followed by the essential steps of instrument flying, night flying, formation flying, navigation, low flying, and general handling.

My remaining years in Number 4 Squadron were spent on Squadron duties, instructing on a couple more Basic Flying Schools, as well as instructing on Flight Instructor School courses. As time passed, I found this flying more and more enjoyable; not only did it improve one's own skills, knowledge and handling, but the reward of seeing one's students being awarded 'Wings' at the annual 'Wings Parades' was the icing on the cake, so to speak.

After three years on the Squadron, I found myself posted to Number 7 Squadron, based at New Sarum, in Salisbury, the capital of the country. This squadron operated helicopters (Alouette 3s) in close support of our Army and Police.

A Life-Changing Event

During my second year serving in Number 4 Squadron, I experienced what was to become an unexpected, life-changing event. I had driven up to Salisbury for a weekend off and to visit my girlfriend. We decided to go out on Saturday evening and started our evening at a folk singing nightclub. Shortly after we had settled down with a drink, a longtime friend of mine came over to say hello and to introduce his date for the night. It was good to see my old friend, who was a renowned Game Ranger, by the name of Kerry Fynn, who spent most of his time flying around the country in his Piper Cub airplane, working with wildlife. We spent the rest of the evening together and while I did not know it at the time, I had just met the young lady, Jayne, who would become my wife a few years later. Jayne`s parents were farmers and had opened up a virgin farm near the town of Macheke, right after WWII, when they had pioneered the land.

Number 7 Squadron. Dec 1966-April 1970

I was lucky enough to have an excellent instructor for my helicopter conversion. Flight Lt. Peter Petter-Bowyer was already making a name for himself, especially in the reconnaissance role. He was knowledgeable, skillful and patient! After my conversion was complete, I was assigned to squadron duties and flying.

The squadron flying was interesting, varied and included assignments supporting our Army and Police activities. Terrorist actions within our country were soon to challenge us as the ZANLA (Zimbabwe National Liberation Army) and ZIPRA (Zimbabwe Peoples Liberation Army) exiled nationalist factions sought increasing military support from Russia and China. The Western world too was becoming increasingly hostile to our situation. Britain had already invoked the support of the United Nations in the application of full sanctions against our country.

Rhodesia was a self-sustaining country, with the exception of oil. Cut off from our normal supply through Mozambique, we turned to South Africa who bravely agreed to supply us with the fuel necessary for the country. It was during these joint Army and

Police operations that the unique cooperation between our forces was developed and indeed became a hallmark of the success of our joint operations as the terrorist war grew over the years.

Strong bonds of friendship and respect were formed over these times and proved vital as the intensity of operations increased, with the inevitable and sad loss of lives.

The flying was serious but the bonds of friendship were strong, both within the Squadron and between the services. I believe we had the finest fighting soldiers in the world at that time, which included the Rhodesian Light Infantry, the Special Air Services, the Rhodesian African Rifles and the Rhodesia Regiment, along with special units of the British South African Police. While we had no 'fancy' equipment, our forces were more than adequately equipped and especially well trained. A lot of our country's fine young men gravitated towards the services because of the increasing seriousness of the terrorist threat to our country.

While it was inspiring to work alongside them in operations, it was always heart-wrenching to have to CASEVAC (Casualty Evacuation) our wounded, or worse still, our dead warriors during or after particularly fierce battles. Such experiences however, served to make us emotionally stronger and more determined than ever to defend our country and all its citizens.

After a year of squadron flying and operations, I was assigned to helicopter flight instructor`s school and spent four months before qualifying as a helicopter flight instructor. The flight handling was demanding but satisfying and I enjoyed the rewarding aspects of training new pilots to fly a helicopter. Fixed wing pilots transitioning to the helicopter found the sensitivity of control, especially in the hover, to be particularly demanding. Watching new pilots learning to hover was always exciting, as the helicopter would act as though it had a mind of its own. It would zoom from one edge of the large training area to the other side, with the pilot struggling to avoid the normal over control typical of new helicopter pilots.

After five or six hours of practice, the knack of hovering was usually acquired and the rest of the flying training could continue. Another problem for fixed wing pilots was getting used to seeing the airspeed indicator falling below usual fixed wing comfort levels – 90 knots, 60 knots, 30 knots, and then transitioning into the hover instead of stalling into the ground!

Amongst the serious aspects of flying were some amusing and surprising incidents. Tracking was an essential element of finding terrorist groups who were infiltrating our country from the northern and eastern borders. We were especially fortunate to have an excellent tracker by the name of Mawire, a local who had been a tracker with the Game Department for many years. Mawire was getting on in years and my guess is that he was in his 50's, although pretty fit. Although he was not Air Force, he was especially proud of an Air Force cap which he had acquired over the years and which he wore proudly.

On one particular occasion, I was tasked along with a second helicopter to drop some of our troops and Mawire at a point close to a known but occasional terrorist infiltration route to check for any activity. We were tasked to position our troops at sunrise and since the drop-off point was no more than 20 minutes flying time from our base, we decided to leave our engineer/gunner at the base so that each helicopter could carry another soldier.

There was no prepared landing zone, so we had to find a suitable place to off-load our troops. The terrain was not friendly and we finally decided to drop our troops from the hover, above a fairly rocky hill top. This was never ideal, especially considering our troops were carrying weapons and packs, so we hovered as low as we safely could and gave the signal to the stick leader to deplane. I focused on keeping a steady hover while the troops left the helicopter one by one, adjusting the hover as the helicopter got lighter and lighter as each soldier climbed out and dropped to the ground.

Since I had no engineer/gunner to tell me when all the troops were safely out, I checked over my shoulder from time to time and when I saw there were no more troops inside, I transitioned from the hover into forward flight and started heading for base at low level.

Skimming above the trees, occasional areas of grass and with the sun rising on my right, I had a wonderful picture of the shadow of my helicopter, racing along next to me, when suddenly horrified, I noticed something hanging beneath the helicopter. Slowing down over a grassy area I could tell that something, or rather someone, was hanging on to the steps of the helicopter!

I had a sinking feeling. Mawire had been the last to deplane from my helicopter and I suddenly realized that he had been taking more time than usual to drop from the helicopter onto the rocky area below. Thinking that everybody had fully deplaned, I had mistakenly started to return to base, along with Mawire hanging on to the step of the helicopter! I immediately landed in the grassy area and Mawire climbed aboard rapidly. I tried to indicate an apology to Mawire on our way back, but he was having none of it. After landing at base, he stalked off while I found another tracker to re-deploy. Mawire was later seen without his Air Force cap, had decided enough was enough with the Air Force and had returned to tracking for the Game Department. I felt guilty but had little time for anything else. Wherever you may be, Mawire, I apologize and I wish you well.

An important aspect of helicopter flying was being able to operate safely in mountainous terrain. Our country had mountains rising up to 7,000 feet on the eastern border and we used this area for training; general flying in mountainous areas and especially casualty evacuation drills. Our helicopters were fitted with cargo slings and hoists to allow stretchers to be lifted aboard. Additionally, we used a simple underarm harness to allow rapid pick-up of those not injured and strong enough to wear the harness.

On one particular occasion, I was in the mountains, along with another helicopter crew, for continuation training. We agreed to meet at one of the small lakes in the mountains after we had finished our respective training and to enjoy our packed lunch together. While the water was cold, it was possible to swim, particularly on a good weather day. My crew and I still had some training to do after our lunch, and I generously offered to hoist the pilot of the other helicopter, who was a very good friend of mine, out of the lake after his swim.

This was good training for my crew and we hovered over him and lowered the hoist, which he put over his head and under his arms, and we lifted him out of the lake. Swimming was typically in the nude; flying suits, boots and underwear off, and then drying off in the sun. And so it happened that this particular pilot and a good friend of mine came to be hanging onto the hoist, some 30 feet under my helicopter and totally nude.

It had come to our attention that the women`s training course was also going on at the same time and that they were also taking a lunch break and swimming at a lake nearby. I asked my hoist operator to keep my colleague below the helicopter and I flew over to the nearby lake where, sure enough, the women were picnicking and swimming. The ladies were delighted to see us as we hovered a few feet above the lake, with my colleague doing his best to cover himself and not fall out of the hoist in doing so.

After a few minutes, we returned to our lake and sat our colleague down safely. Initially, he was really irritated but he soon saw the humor in the situation and we finished our training and returned to the hotel we used as a base. This incident earned my colleague several beers in the pub that evening! The free marketing that I and my hoist operator had provided for our `cargo` did not pay off, because the ladies had decided to camp out in the mountains that night, rather than join us in the pub!

Bill Bailey

Another incident arose on a subsequent mountain flying mission. Over time, we had become friendly with the Director of the Outward-Bound School, a gentleman by the name of Bill Bailey. He was extremely knowledgeable and always appreciative of our help with such tasks as carrying oxygen cylinders and various supplies to different base camps in the mountains. These tasks were not only helpful to the staff of the school but provided valuable training for us in hoisting, cargo swinging and general flying.

On one particular occasion in the local pub, Bill, in a friendly manner, had become teasingly critical of the squadron and we, in an equally friendly manner, warned Bill of potential consequences! This did nothing to stop Bill so we decided on a suitable plan of action.

Early the next morning as we flew off for our training of the day, we attached our hoist to the only 'Porta-Potty' located at the main base camp, flew up the mountain range to the highest peak and carefully and skillfully set the 'Porta-Potty' upon a small, very sheer outcrop. With binoculars, it would be possible to see the new outline of the mountain from the base camp! Having completed this task, we proceeded with the rest of our training for the day, confident that word would spread quickly amongst the mountain training courses and that Bill would soon be aware of the situation.

It was customary for us all to meet in the bar of the hotel before dinner and I was confident that Bill would be there too! Sure enough, Bill arrived, much chagrined and just as we were ordering our first beer. His usual good humor had returned and we enjoyed a few beers together and agreed we would recover his 'Potty' the very next day. This we accomplished, the outline of the mountain returned to its natural state and a good laugh was enjoyed by all concerned. I also noticed more respect and gratitude from the Director for other helpful tasks we performed for the school!

My flying instructor, Peter Petter-Bowyer, insisted that if his student was to learn the full capabilities of the Alouette helicopter, not only would he become proficient in all aspects of flying, but he also needed to fully understand the operation of the rescue hoist. This is well illustrated by the accompanying photo showing the instructor flying the helicopter while his student (that would be yours truly) swings below.

Wonderful Willy

One of the great characters on Number 7 (Helicopter) Squadron in my day was an engineer/technician by the name of Willy Jervois. Willy and I were often crewed together and we were nicknamed the 'Skraal' (skinny) crew because I weighed about 160 lbs in those days and Willy weighed no more than about 135 lbs. We used to joke that because of our sleight weight, we could carry an extra troop or additional cargo!

On one occasion, we had been carrying Mawire, our famous tracker, and Lieutenant Bruce Snelgar, with a couple of other soldiers trying to track a group of terrorists whose presence we had discovered the day before and were now following up on their tracks. This involved flying low and slow and confirming their direction of travel whenever they crossed a grassy area and Mawire could confirm their movement.

We landed from time to time so that Mawire could get on the ground and ascertain how old the tracks were and gather more information about whether they were lightly or heavily loaded and any other useful information to give us a better idea of what we were up against in this particular instance. We had done this a couple of times and Mawire had informed us that the tracks were some 12 hours old, and so we pressed on. When we next landed in a grassy area on a bit of a plateau, and believing we were still some considerable distance behind the group of terrorists, I switched off the engine of the helicopter and Willy and I stood aside while Mawire and the others examined the tracks. The level of excitement increased instantly when Mawire announced that the tracks were now only one-hour old!

Bruce and Mawire and the other soldiers moved forward on the tracks with their weapons cocked, and within about 30 yards, disappeared from sight over the edge of the small escarpment. I did not like this. It takes about 45 seconds to start a helicopter, it`s noisy and during that time, you are a sitting duck. If the terrorists had set up an ambush, we could already be in the sights of one of their rockets.

Almost immediately, Willy and I heard the sounds of gunfire, just over the edge of the escarpment, and then everything went quiet. We waited and looked at each other. Still nothing happened. I had to make a decision – had our guys been ambushed? Were they alright or had they been wiped out? Did they need reinforcements? I was not hearing anything on the radio and so I said to Willy, "Take your rifle and go to the edge of the escarpment and see if you can discover what has happened. I`ll get the chopper ready for an immediate take-off, if necessary."

Willy looked at me as if I was mad, but obediently moved off to the edge of the escarpment, and then, with a last look in my direction, disappeared over the edge. This was not in my plan, and now I was back to total ignorance of the situation. I was strapped into the helicopter and ready to start at a moment's notice, if only I knew what was going on.

Suddenly, Willy appeared over the top of the escarpment, his rifle in his one hand and giving me the sign with his other hand to get the helicopter started. Right behind Willy was Mawire, doing his version of a sprint towards me. The start cycle seemed to take an eternity, while we sat expecting a rocket to destroy us at any second, but nothing came. We lifted off and immediately I could communicate with Bruce.

Our guys were safe but pinned down and needed some help, since the group of terrorists appeared larger than expected. We had no weapon mounted on the chopper at the time, so we started a series of troop movements which Bruce directed to be dropped in cut-off positions. This took most of the rest of the day, with the help of another helicopter from Kanyemba, piloted by Randy Du Rand.

The upshot was the elimination of some eight terrorists and the capture of most of the rest of the group over the next few days – excellent work by Bruce and the stop groups with no loss to our forces! One more group of terrorists that would not be carrying out its murderous task of killing innocent farmers and their families. I`m not sure that Willy has forgiven me for expecting him to act as infantry for a while, and there was an uneasy truce between us until our next call-out.

Refueling one`s helicopter in the operational area required one to pump fuel from pre-positioned 44-gallon drums in many locations. One drum would give one about an hour of flight time and we could carry about 1 ½ drums of fuel (about 600 pounds) when trooping. Before we had learned to use the helicopter engine to pump fuel from the drum into the chopper, we used to carry a small petrol-driven pump which did the job. This small pump had a regular fuel discharge nozzle on one end, to fit into the fuel tank of the chopper, and a telescoping pipe that went into the drum. This pipe was stored in its most fully retracted position, so that it would fit into the side storage compartment on the side of the helicopter, and one would then physically pull the pipe into its extended position so that it would fit all the way to the bottom of the drum and allow all the fuel to be transferred. The drums were obviously heavy and it was always preferable for both pilot and technician to move them into position for refueling.

On one particular occasion, Willy and I needed fuel and on landing at an outlying base, I had to make a report to an Operations Officer in a tent nearby. Willy said he would get on with the refueling in the meantime.

The report took a bit longer than expected, but I could hear the small refueling pump running and assumed all was well. To my great surprise, when I exited the tent, I saw Willy flat on his back with most of the weight of the fuel drum lying horizontally across his chest. I rushed over to help, but Willy was determined to finish the refueling. "Sir", he said with great difficulty, "this bloody stack pipe is only about 18 inches long and it won't go all the way to the bottom of the drum, so I've had to tip it over to get all the fuel!"

I dragged the drum off Willy and he was able to stand up.

"Willy, this is a telescoping pipe – you have to physically pull it out to its full length. Then it will reach the bottom of the drum!"

We finished the refueling in silence. Willy was new to the squadron at that stage, and I was becoming an old hand. Willy swore me to secrecy, as I remember, but that was almost 50 years ago, so forgive me, Willy.

We had started the practice on the squadron of allocating a particular helicopter to a particular crew. It was a good practice that encouraged pride in one`s own aircraft, and for a while, Willy and I were crewed together. Willy was particularly proud of keeping our helicopter in immaculate condition. As soon as we returned from an operational stint, he would thoroughly clean and service our machine with almost loving care. He was less than impressed when I was instructing new pilots on engine-off landings one day and had a mishap.

Helicopters are pretty safe machines and carrying out a landing without an engine running requires only some very prompt action to maintain the energy of the main rotor while descending, and then to use that conserved energy in one brief and carefully judged burst, just above the ground. To create and use this burst of energy requires putting the helicopter into a steep nose-up attitude at the end of the descent, which obviously puts the tail even closer to the ground – this is one of the reasons that the tail rotor has a protective guard underneath. This guard is a simple aluminum tube extending a few inches beyond the rotor – enough to protect the rotor in all but the most severe situations.

We had completed some twenty of these flying training maneuvers that morning and I was aware that we had scraped and probably bent the tail rotor guard on some of them. Knowing that Willy would not be happy with this development, I decided to confess immediately after landing, rather than pretend I knew nothing about it.

"Willy," I said," I`m afraid there`s some damage to the tail rotor-guard." Then hoping to appeal to his gentler side, I added, "New pilots, you know."

Willy surveyed the damage carefully and then turned to me and said,

"It's alright, Sir. To err is human, to forgive is divine."

Bless you Willy.

Falling In Love

When I moved to Salisbury at the end of 1965, to take up my posting to Number 7 Squadron, I was able to contact the young lady I had met a year or two before when Kerry Fynn had introduced us at a folk singing club one evening. We started dating almost immediately and although our schedules were very different, we were able to see each other quite frequently. Jayne was working shifts at the airport with the local airline and I was often away on flying duties with the squadron. However, we always enjoyed each other's company and before long, we were in love.

Not one year later we decided to get married. My father, Roland, had loved Jayne from day one while my mother, Eve, was like most mothers; not sure that ANY young lady was good enough for her son! I was delighted to meet Jayne's parents, who were farmers and lived about 60 miles from Salisbury. Jayne's father, Leslie, was a giant of a man, around 6 feet six, 230 pounds with an athletic frame and strict disposition. Her mother, Barbara, was petite and delightful and we all got along extremely well.

While Jayne and I definitely wanted to get married, it was customary in our country and in those days to show the parents the courtesy of asking for their daughter`s hand in marriage. And so, we went to the farm for a weekend to do this and to make any necessary arrangements. Jayne`s mother had an inkling of what was happening, but did not let on, and I found myself procrastinating while waiting for the right opportunity.

Finally, on Sunday afternoon, I broached the subject with Jayne's father, who promptly invited me to join him in his study for a discussion. Knowing Leslie, this was not entirely unexpected and I spent the next hour answering his questions about my ability to support his daughter and any family that might arise from our marriage, including pay, promotion prospects and so on. I had always been confident about my career in the Air Force, had established sensible but challenging goals and I felt that with Jayne's support, I could be even more motivated.

I'm sure that Leslie realized that an Air Force officer would never be a millionaire, but fortunately, this was not his criteria and he gave me his blessing to marry his daughter. Barbara was delighted and did not give me the same inquisition! And on 16th December, 1967, we were married in a small church in Avondale, a suburb of Salisbury, amongst family, friends and fellow Air Force members. We had a reception at the Officers Club where, by tradition, any officer and member of the Club was automatically invited.

With families, friends and fellow Air Force members, the celebration began. When it was time to leave, we went outside to our car, only to find it had been suitably decorated and lifted onto the top of the entrance steps to the mess! With much fun and no damage (luckily!) our car was placed back on the driveway to shouts, cheers and laughter. We left for our honeymoon hideaway at Mermaids Pool, a favorite spot with locals and a welcome break from the rigors of squadron operations and war.

Tragedy On The Zambezi

A dangerous and sad incident that particularly sticks in my mind, occurred fairly late in my tour of duty on 'Choppers'. I was on standby for emergency call-out and I received a call to report to the Squadron immediately, at about 8:30 pm in the evening. I got there quickly and when I arrived, I noticed the helicopter was already prepared and on the hard-standing. I read the air task signal which directed me to be at Kanyemba on our extreme northern border as soon as possible, to search for a missing Army Officer who had been lost off a patrol boat on the Zambezi River.

Needless to say, this was a very bad situation. The area was teaming with dangerous wildlife and the river was infested with crocodiles. To survive in the river at night-time or even next to the river during the day and without a weapon would be a miracle. I was teamed with a fine engineer, Johnny Ness, with whom I had flown on many operational missions, and we discussed our situation briefly.

Our helicopters were not designed for lengthy night flying sorties in poor visibility, having only very limited instrumentation and no refinements, such as auto-pilot or gyro-stabilization. This would be a flight of more than one hour and although it was night-time, the weather at base was good and we could observe a clear horizon. We decided to leave immediately so that we could be on the ground at Kanyemba and ready to start our search at first light.

We took off and set course, climbing to a safe altitude of a few thousand feet in order to avoid some mountain ranges on route. The first 30 minutes of the flight were uneventful, but soon we started to lose our visual horizon and entered some patchy clouds. This was not what we were expecting, but weather reports and forecasts in those days were not as good as today!

We decided to continue as long as we had occasional reference to the ground, mindful of the fact that one of our army colleagues was in desperate need of our help. However, as we continued, the weather deteriorated further and we decided to descend carefully and find a safe spot to land, since it was already too late to turn around and go back.

The patchy clouds had become solid clouds with rain at times, and I had reduced speed to an air taxi while descending only a few feet per minute. I had turned off the helicopter rotating beacons and lights, to minimize the chance of vertigo, while Johnny was using the helicopter spotlight in an attempt to identify any terrain. We continued like this for what seemed an awfully long time, until we broke through the clouds at low level, around 100 feet, and were able to identify a clear area nearby where we promptly landed, thankful to be on the ground in one piece!

Looking back, I realize this was a poor decision to continue, but I had got us into a position where it was as dangerous to turn back as it was to continue, having made a decision driven more by emotion than sense. As the first glimmer of light arose, we were able to see that we had actually landed next to a set of large, high power lines! Someone had been looking after us that night! We started the helicopter and completed the final 30-minute flight to Kanyemba, where we landed and hurried into the briefing room.

Except for the Army major who was carrying out the briefing, I was surprised to see my friend Rex Viljoen, and it dawned upon me that it was Rex's son who was missing. Rex's wife was a good friend of my wife and had been the maid of honor at our wedding. Charl, Rex's son from a previous marriage, was a Lieutenant in the Army and was a renowned sportsman in the country. He was the apple of his father's eye and had huge potential for the future. I told Rex that we would not rest until we found him. And so we started, Johnny and I in the helicopter, along with a couple of Army observers, so that we could cover both river banks more effectively.

The Zambezi River is a large river, and since this was the rainy season, it was very full and flowing fast. There was mixed vegetation along the river banks, thick reeds in some places and large trees in others. We moved slowly and carefully, searching for any sign that might indicate that Charl had climbed up one of the banks. We also flew just inland of the river bank, in case he was attempting to work his way back to the Camp. There were plenty of hippos and crocodiles to be seen and, no doubt, further inland there were elephants, lions and other very dangerous animals.

Charl, alone, possibly injured and without a weapon, would be in a very vulnerable situation. We refueled the helicopter a couple of times and spent the whole day searching, but without any success. The briefing at the end of the day was a somber affair, but we tried to remain optimistic and I assured Rex that we would start again at first light the next morning. The tension for Rex, waiting all day in the briefing room for any hopeful message from us, must have been unbearable.

We started bright and early on the next day and in a similar fashion, with observers on both sides of the helicopter, as we searched from the camp downstream for several miles. This time we went a bit further, but there was still no sign of Charl or any indication of where he may have exited the river or walked along the bank. By late afternoon, short of searching the river all the way to the ocean, there was little more we could do.

We returned to camp and briefed Rex, who was doing his utmost to control his emotions. When Rex asked if we could do one more sweep and take him along, I agreed and Johnny and I and Rex took off. We had not gone far when in a tragic and bittersweet moment, Johnny saw the body floating in the middle of the river. This was very traumatic for Rex and he became so excited that I told him we would have to drop him off on the river bank so that we could recover Charl.

We found a clearing upstream and out of sight, and put Rex on the bank, telling him to wait there until we returned. Then Johnny and I returned to recover the body. This became quite a challenge, since he was waterlogged and too heavy to drag into the helicopter. We started by hovering next to Charl, and using our rotor downdraft to blow his body sideways towards the bank, with Johnny half out of the helicopter, grabbing hold of Charl`s jacket. This worked quite well, although we were moving downstream at the same time. We were able to co-ordinate our movement downstream and sideways to finally steer ourselves into a relatively small but clear cove.

With Johnny hanging out of the helicopter and keeping hold of Charl`s jacket with one arm and the helicopter frame with the other arm, I was able to slowly inch forward until we had Charl fully out of the water on a relatively clear bit of the bank. We radioed the base camp and asked them to send a patrol boat to our location to recover Charl's body and take it back to the main camp. Since the boat was already on the river, this was accomplished quite quickly and Johnny and I flew off to fetch Rex from where we had left him on the river bank.

Fortunately, Rex was still there and had experienced no problems from hippos, crocodiles or anything else nearby. There was nothing we could do to console Rex and I cursed the irony of the tragedy, which may have been lessened only slightly if Charl`s body had floated earlier when we did not have Rex on board. It seems that Charl may have been knocked unconscious when falling off the patrol boat, causing him to drown and subsequently get trapped, perhaps in some undergrowth underwater and unable to surface. Eventually, the body had released itself and floated to the surface or we would probably never have known what happened to Charl.

Back at the camp, Rex was understandably distraught and concerned about the state of his son's body, especially if there had been damage from crocodiles, hippos or the like. I was relieved to be able to tell Rex that there was no damage to the body, and this seemed to console him to a degree. Rex was to fly back on the transport airplane with Charl`s body and Johnny and I hoped this would allow some closure. We said our sad farewells, thanked our Army and Police colleagues for all their help and then we flew back to Salisbury, shattered by the events of the last 48 hours. This tragedy affected Rex for the rest of his life and I also had to stop a few times to control my emotions while writing this account.

Two years later, in 1969, Jayne and I were blessed with the arrival of our first child – a son whom we named Mark, in memory of my cousin and two other Slatters who had been killed in the tragic air accident near Doula, years before. Mark was a healthy baby and has been a source of great joy and pride to us. In 1996, he and his wife Denise gifted us with a grandson, Sean, continuing the long line of Slatters.

The War Escalates

Meanwhile, anti-terrorist operations within Rhodesia were escalating rapidly, as China and Russia trained and provided material support to the extreme nationalist movements: ZANLA and ZIPRA. As our Army and Police Force became busier and busier, so did our Air Force and Number 7 Squadron, in particular.

Terrorists would cross our borders in small groups, infiltrating weapons and supplies and attacking farms. I became infuriated with the international media that went along with the terrorist propaganda of calling themselves 'Freedom Fighters!' I certainly would not consider anyone who murdered farmers and their families in their beds at night a 'Freedom Fighter!' Along with our Army and Police, we became pretty adept at tracking and engaging these groups and killing or capturing most of them. Tragically, we would lose our own service members in these engagements as our own brave young men and women fought to defend our country.

While welcoming the opportunity to play a meaningful role in the defense of one's country, these deployments were real, live actions with real live weapons, and one could never guarantee returning home alive. These were stressful times indeed for those with families serving in the Defense Forces at the time.

Even in those early days of the war, we were committed to external operations to assist the Portuguese forces and prevent the use of Mozambique by ZANLA terrorists using the country as a safe haven. A particularly tragic event happened on one such operation.

We had four helicopters, which had been deployed for a week conducting reconnaissance and troop movements, to isolate the terrorists. The Portuguese had implemented a system of protected villages, and all locals were required to live in these villages, to further isolate the terrorists; especially from food sources. This also meant that movement observed outside these villages would likely be terrorists, making it easier to follow up, make contact and capture or eliminate them. I was one of the helicopter pilots, and on the last day of our deployment, I was tasked to re-position some troops in an area about a half hour`s flying time from the base of operations.

Having completed the task, and flying back to base at low level, I saw some movement of unidentified people, just under my helicopter. There was no protected village anywhere nearby and my suspicions were aroused. I had little fuel left, no troops on board and when I landed at base, I debriefed the operations officer, as was normal procedure, and mentioned the unidentified people I had seen. It was decided that two helicopters with troops would fly to the grid reference I had provided and investigate.

I seem to remember it was late afternoon and I went and got a cup of tea, while waiting for the helicopters to return. They returned after a while with the troops and some others on board. When the pilots had debriefed, I went to find out what had transpired. The one pilot, whom I knew well, looked particularly shaken. He told me that they did indeed find the unidentified people near the same grid reference and they appeared to be locals, but far from any protected village; very suspicious. The decision was taken to load them onto the helicopters and take them back to the protected village near the base.

However, the helicopters could only carry a limited number of extra people, so John waved off the last one or two, including a female, and tried to indicate to the Portuguese Army troops with him that he would return to fetch the remaining one or two. And then the unthinkable happened. Either due to misunderstanding or language, one of the Portuguese army troops simply opened fire and killed the remaining locals.

John was clearly upset and seemed unable to think clearly. I was enraged and went straight to our commanding officer, who promptly went to the Portuguese General to voice our concerns. Our deployment ended. I wrote my letter of resignation that night and gave it to my Station Commander back at New Sarum. I was not prepared to support such behavior in any way and I did not want my name or my family`s name associated with any such action.

While I knew we were fighting a war, that sort of undisciplined behavior was unacceptable, in my view. The final upshot of this ugly incident was that our Air Force Commander had a discussion with the head of Portuguese forces in Mozambique and received the assurance that such behavior would not be tolerated and that orders would be issued accordingly. I withdrew my letter of resignation. While that alone would never atone for the tragedy, I felt more confident about future operations and indeed, I never witnessed such an event again in several other external operations with the Portuguese.

Jayne`s and my lives were brightened in May 1969 by the birth of our first son, Mark. This welcome addition to our family took all of Jayne's time and allowed her to focus on other matters, rather than my absence on operational deployments. While welcoming the opportunity to play a meaningful role in the defense of one's country, one could never guarantee returning home alive.

My tour of duty in Number 7 Squadron came to an end in the middle of 1970, after three and a half years of flying and operating with the dedicated and brave men and women of our Air Force, Army, Police Force and other government departments, whom I would pit against any other joint forces in the world. My assignment was a promotion to flight commander on Number 6 Squadron (Training), where I would be responsible for basic and advanced training at Thornhill Air Force Base, a very different but still satisfying role.

Number 6 Squadron – Thornhill. May 1970 – Feb 1972

Training students to become qualified Air Force pilots is always rewarding, and it can be exciting too! The next 18 months were spent instructing basic and advanced flying students on Provost and Vampire aircraft, as well as conducting Flying Instructor Schools for new flying instructors. Flying duties also included instrument rating tests and running courses for instrument rating examiners. While I missed the excitement of helicopter operations on a daily basis, it was rewarding to train ab initio (beginner) pilots to full 'Wings' standard, as well as training qualified pilots to become flying instructors. There was always enough excitement, albeit of a different kind, in training students to fly to the standard required by our Air Force. Interestingly, aerobatics never posed any danger because they were practiced at altitude. Things became more interesting close to the ground and especially landings in a narrow undercarriage, tail-dragger aircraft in strong crosswinds.

I remember a student who shall remain nameless who was having difficulty learning to control landings in strong crosswind situations. We must have practiced the skill at least 100 times, but I had to take over the controls every time and at the last second to prevent ground looping the aircraft. Finally, and in desperation, I told my student that he had enjoyed more than enough practice, that he knew exactly what to do, and that I would under no circumstances save him again. Of course, the inevitable happened.

Upon landing, I let the student take too long to correct for the strong crosswind and we must have performed a full 360° turn on the ground, disappearing in a cloud of dust from the dry grass runway. The fire and ambulance crews arrived immediately, finding one very wide-eyed student, as well as one wide-eyed instructor, as the dust cloud disappeared. It's not only student pilots who learn from experiences like that!

As rewarding as qualifying pilots to 'Wings' standard was, there were always occasions when it was necessary to terminate a student. This was a difficult action but one that was not only in the best interest of the Air Force, but in the interest of the student too. The flying syllabus was designed expressly to test the student in all aspects of flying, and no sooner did a student successfully pass one phase of the flying, then he would be pushed directly to the next phase of flying. There was never any let-up in the pressure. A student could be terminated at any stage of training, usually in the early phase of training, although I remember instances of termination in the penultimate stages of the course as well, usually due to a serious disciplinary infraction, such as unauthorized low-flying.

Interestingly, and because of the unusually high standard of flying demanded by the Air Force, most of the students who were terminated went on to successful flying careers in commercial aviation; some by choice, when they completed their military contract, and some because they were not suited to military flying. The syllabus was comprehensive and tried and tested over years of training. When a student completed the course successfully to 'Wings' standard, he could feel comfortable that he was well equipped to start an Air Force flying career.

On the home front, my wife and I were blessed with the arrival of our second child, a healthy son whom we named Lee. Lee was supposed to be delivered by Cesarean section, due to complications my wife experienced during the birth of our first son, Mark. However, Lee had a plan of his own and arrived 30 minutes before the surgeon, who was scheduled to perform the Cesarean procedure! Forty-five years later, Lee still marches to his own drummer!

Selection for Staff Course

One day in early 1972, I was summoned to Air Force Headquarters for a meeting with the Staff Officer Training. He informed me that I had been selected to attend a staff administration course with the South African Air Force in Pretoria. I considered this a good sign for my Air Force career, but on leaving his office, he apologized to me, saying that he was sorry to put me on the course but that he could find no one else!

Thus motivated by this senior officer, I returned to Thornhill to inform my wife of my new assignment. The course was to run for three months, on an unaccompanied basis, and was to start in two weeks' time. Notwithstanding the staff officer training's remarks, I felt sure that the course would be interesting and rewarding. And so, I duly reported to the South African Air Force Officers' Mess at Voortrekkerhooghte on a Sunday afternoon, to find my lodgings and be ready for a course introduction dinner that evening with my fellow students.

In very different surroundings, and after checking in at the front desk of the Officers' Mess at the South African Air Force College, I was shown to my rondavel (a free standing, circular room with a thatched roof and comfortably furnished with a large desk and chair), unpacked my belongings and then walked over to the pub for our introductory dinner. It being a Sunday and late afternoon, the pub was very quiet, with only a few others present. I introduced myself to them and we realized we were there for the same purpose; namely the Staff Administration Course.

There was a fellow Rhodesian from the technical/engineering branch of our Air Force, and the others were South Africans. After a beer and at the designated time, we moved upstairs to a private dining room for dinner. There we found the rest of the other officers who were also designated for the course. We were 16 in total, mostly of major or commandant (Lieutenant Colonel) rank. I was the exception, being a mere Flight Lieutenant (Captain), while my fellow Rhodesian was a Squadron Leader (Major).

We were greeted by our senior officer and Course Commander, Commandant Dan Zeeman, and after a cocktail and introductions, we sat down to dinner. No sooner had we sat down then the wine steward arrived to take our orders. Dan, being our course commander, decided upon red wine, or "osbloed" (literally ox blood), a heavy, Cabernet type of wine made in South Africa. When the wine steward suggested three bottles, Dan snorted and asked the wine steward how many people were at the table. When the wine steward had counted and announced there were 16, Dan said we obviously needed 16 bottles! This caused some consternation with the wine steward, but he eventually got the message and returned with 16 bottles!

I realized then that Dan worked hard and played hard and that fact became more obvious as the course progressed. As course leader, Dan bore the brunt of any misstep by any of the course members, and it became a pattern for Dan to arrive late at the school on Monday mornings, dressed in his number one uniform because he had been required to report to headquarters and explain away some real or perceived misbehavior attributed to our course during the previous week. Dan took this all in stride, never complained and my respect for him grew week by week. There was already considerable pressure on each and every student, without him having to carry the load for us all.

The course work was not particularly difficult, but there was plenty of it requiring long hours and working late at night. My fellow Rhodesian and I experienced a language problem because half the course was in English and half in Afrikaans. I cursed the fact that I had studied French for six years at school, rather than Afrikaans! However, Dan and some of the others whose mother tongue was Afrikaans, took me under their wing and helped me patiently to the extent that after a few months, I had developed enough of an understanding to get by on a very basic level.

As we got closer to the end of the three-month course, there was word that the course might be extended into a full Air Staff Course lasting some nine months, and this indeed did transpire. This was a good news/bad news type of situation. The bad news was that I was missing my wife, my very young sons, and nine months would be a long time. The good news was that successful completion of a full Air Staff Course could put one in line for promotion to General rank, in time. This was the most sought-after and senior course in all of the military and indeed, we had students from the Navy and the Air Force on our course.

This was quite literally a once-in-a-lifetime opportunity.

The situation improved markedly when I was informed that I would be allowed to have my family join me for the duration of the course. I was delighted and enthusiastic to get started and in fact, the transition from the Staff Administration Course to the Air Staff Course was seamless. All of our course members had worked closely together for three months and we felt we were a solid team and ready to tackle the big course!

My family arrived almost immediately and we were able to rent an apartment in town. While I would not be able to spend much time with them, I was happy that they were nearby and I could usually spend time with them on weekends, even though I would be working. Mark was almost three years old now and Lee was nearly one, which meant that Jayne's hands were very full.

The work on the Air Staff course was very different from the administration course, and I found it more difficult to get good grades. The focus was on scenario-based service papers. Typically, at the end of the day on Friday, we would be handed a large document which would outline in detail a situation; usually historical and military in nature, requiring a clear definition of the issue and an in-depth analysis leading to a detailed plan offering the best course of actions to resolve the issue.

The situations presented were never simple and were compounded by large quantities of data and information, and even misinformation, in order to ensure that one had considered all aspects of the situation. While there could be several solutions, there was only one right solution that would get you a successful grade for your paper. These papers were mostly done in one's own time after the usual workday, and usually one per week, although later in the course one could be working on two or even three service papers simultaneously, as a means of creating some work load pressure on us.

The days were spent listening to visiting lecturers of a high caliber, from the universities, major businesses or senior officers from the Services, as well as enjoying visits to industries and businesses crucial to the economy and defense of the country. The Directing Staff of the college were knowledgeable and helpful, with strong military backgrounds and experience. While they seemed to enjoy their duties and went to great lengths to help, I felt sure that most of them would rather have been back with their airplanes or ships!

I had decided to keep a weekly graph of my progress from the start of the course. The grading was so severe that I could barely manage a passing grade in the initial phases. However, and interestingly enough, my grades started to improve significantly after the arrival of my family. Since I had always been a good student, I could only ascribe the earlier difficulties to my considerable concern about being separated from my young family.

My determined and continued efforts to learn Afrikaans brought much mirth to many who bore the brunt of my attempts, but my good Afrikaans friends persevered to the extent that I ended up with a decent vocabulary for service papers and jokes, with not too much in between!

The camaraderie of the course was magnificent, as was to be expected amongst service members. Our group of sixteen included most disciplines within the services and many years of experience. Since my promotion to Squadron Leader had come through in April, I was no longer the odd man out, in terms of rank, and we had a good party to celebrate in true Dan Zeeman style!

With very full days, late nights and busy weekends, time went by swiftly and we were soon at the point of our final papers. Sadly, two of our course members had not been able to make the necessary progress and had left the course; a difficult moment for us all. For my part, my confidence was high as my graph of progress kept moving in the right direction. With each set of papers graded, I found myself enjoying the learning environment and experience and suddenly, it was done.

All lectures completed, all visits completed and all papers graded. All that was left was our final exit interviews and presentation of our diplomas. Our exit interviews would be conducted individually by Colonel Eccles, a fine senior officer, a real gentleman and the head of the college. The interviews were scheduled for the final Friday of the Course and we had unwisely scheduled a party for the Thursday night prior. Needless to say, we partied well into the small hours of Friday morning, not leaving much time to shower, shave, and get dressed in number one uniform for our interviews.

The interviews were scheduled for approximately 10 to 15 minutes each, and I was programmed for the last interview of the day. There was much back slapping and handshaking as each successful student emerged from the Colonel's office with many joking remarks, such as, "The Colonel must have forgotten to tell me that I was the top of the class!" While there was only a pass or fail grade at the completion of the Air Staff Course, it was apparently traditional that the top student, and he alone, would be informed.

My hangover seemed to be getting worse. My good friend, who had helped me so much with my Afrikaans, and I had demolished plentiful supplies of Red Heart Rum at the party, and in the hot waiting area for the interviews, while sitting in my formal uniform, I could smell the rum as I perspired! The waiting area was emptying, one by one, as the interviews were completed, and finally it was my turn.

The adjutant showed me into the Colonel's office and shut the door behind me. It was a large office with the Colonel seated some 20 feet ahead me and facing me.

"Come and sit down, Slatter," said the Colonel. Mindful of the strong smell of rum still emanating from my body, I apologized to the Colonel;

"Please excuse me Colonel, but I think I must stay some distance away from you. I drank a lot at our party last night and I'm sure that I must smell like an open bottle of rum, Sir".

"Slatter," said the Colonel, "I have sat here this morning through 13 interviews, and everyone has brought with them a different smell of different liquor, so please sit down and join me".

It seemed the Colonel was used to conducting exit interviews after a long and difficult course! The interview proceeded with a record of my results, contributions, shortcomings and my position on the Course. It was a very significant step in my life and I felt extremely grateful to have had the opportunity. I thanked the Colonel and his staff for their guidance and help over the long course and took my leave.

I was happy and proud and rushed off to collect my family, since we were leaving for home that afternoon. It was a bitter-sweet time, leaving my fellow course members and the camaraderie we had built over the months on course, but wonderful to be heading home after a job well done.

The value of the Air Staff Course was threefold. First, teaching one to analyze different situations and recommend courses of action in a clear and decisive manner. Second, equipping one to make valuable input to the decision-making process, as a result of the skills and broad knowledge gained regarding the economy, the industries and the Services. And third and probably most importantly, establishing contacts and friendships that would serve me and the others so well in future joint services planning and operations.

Interestingly, and as the war in our country intensified and our services co-operation with South Africa increased, I found several of my ex-Air Staff Course members in key command positions in the South African Defense forces, as Colonels and Generals, making for easier communication, understanding and decision making between us. I had already been assigned to the Joint Planning Staff at Air Force Headquarters on my return, and although disappointed not to be posted back to an operational flying squadron, this was an assignment well suited to the work I had done over the last nine months. I was good to go!

Joint Planning Staff. November 1972 - November 1973

The offices for the Joint Planning Staff (JPS) were situated in Milton Building, on Jameson Avenue in Salisbury, which housed the Prime Minister's offices as well as Air Force headquarters offices. We were required, amongst other things, to prepare staff papers based on scenarios prepared by the chairman of JPS, or provided by government or by the military services. It was a perfect fit for my work on the Air Staff Course.

This was my first opportunity to work alongside Norman Walsh, who at that time was a Wing Commander (Lieutenant Colonel) and who later became the Commander of the Air Force as an Air Marshal. When I was a junior pilot, I had known Norman at Thornhill, where he commanded Number 1 (Fighter) Squadron. Norman was a man of action and was not at all excited to be writing service papers, instead of flying fighters! Little did I know at the time that it would be Norman who would prove invaluable to me, my family and the other officers falsely accused of sabotage by the agents of the new Government of Zimbabwe, but more on that later.

The scenarios for the service papers were varied and interesting. This was a period in world history when terrorism was on the rise and hijackings of aircraft by mid-eastern terrorists were proving popular, which resulted in several papers centered on this theme. Norman had an almost uncanny ability to quickly analyze these scenarios, and he would inevitably have the best courses of action recommended well before the rest of us had acquired the data, analyzed it, prepared different courses of action and could finally come up with the recommended solution!

As the terrorist incursions into our country increased, so did the laying of landmines in our roads, as well as ambushes and farm attacks resulting in increasing numbers of deaths to our service members, and especially our farming community. Accordingly, JPS spent more and more time briefing government officials, including the Prime Minister, Ian Smith, about our day to day operations. The Prime Minister's office would usually request that the briefings be done by Norman, and since they were both men of action, this was a good fit. Our Prime Minister, being an ex-Air Force man himself, spoke a common language and was much admired and respected for his common-sense approach and honesty.

For my part, I often found myself briefing the Minister of Information, and later, the Minister of Defense; the Honorable P.K. Van der Byl. The minister was a great character, always dressed immaculately in business suits and with suitable headwear, either a trilby or a bowler, and always wearing a carnation in his lapel. The carnation became such a part of his attire that no cartoonist worth his salt would dare to omit this essential item of dress!

I seem to remember the Minister getting off a helicopter for a tour of one of the operational areas, immaculately dressed in a safari suit with the inevitable carnation. He was well liked by the Services for his deep and genuine interest and love of the country and its people. I believe he had been educated at Bishops and served in the Hussars, and spoke with the perfect Etonian English accent. I remember this being clearly evident when I was briefing the minister on one occasion, when terrorists had attacked some farms in his constituency and had murdered a farming family. He was incensed. "Dammit, Squadron Leader, this is my Constituency! What are you doing about it?"

I assured the Minister that we already had troops and trackers on the ground, with helicopter back-up, and we were confident that we would have the murderous terrorists dead or alive very shortly.

"Excellent, Squadron Leader! Make sure they feel the heel of the boot!"

With that, he thanked me for the briefing and left the room, but the phrase `heel of the boot` has stuck with me to this day. Thank you, Minister!

Promotion to Squadron Commander. November 1973

Almost one year after starting duties with JPS, I received notice that I was to be posted to Number 2 Squadron, Thornhill, as Squadron Commander. I was ready! It had been almost 2 years since I had performed any flying duties and that, after all, was what I had joined the Air Force to do!

Number 2 Squadron, based at Thornhill, was an operational squadron, flying Vampire dual and single seat jets, as well as conducting operational Conversion Unit weapons training on Vampire and Provost aircraft for 'Wings' qualified pilots, as well as pilots transferring from other squadrons.

My family and I were happy to be back at Thornhill. Although the Air Force Base was only a few miles outside the town of Gwelo, one's life centered around the squadron, the married quarters, the clubs (Messes) and the sports fields. Families were a major element of life on the base, and indeed, Thornhill seemed to operate as one large family.

Flying, unless one was on active operations, was usually from 6 am until 1:30 pm, leaving the afternoon free for sport; an essential part of Air Force life. Several evenings a week would be spent in the pub, with wives and girlfriends joining us regularly. Weekends would often be consumed by sporting events of all types, and indeed, Thornhill teams included several national players, including the likes of Ian Bond, Mike Mulligan, Don Ogilvy, Roy Stewart, and Bobby Knott, to name just a few, as well as many combined services players. Rugby and cricket dominated, but soccer, tennis, squash, baseball, golf and swimming were all popular, and the climate was generally conducive to outdoor activities.

November 11th, 1965, was the date that Rhodesia declared independence from Great Britain, the Unilateral Declaration of Independence (UDI), because of that country`s increasing pressure to hand Rhodesia over to an unqualified majority. Rhodesia already enjoyed a multi-racial government with a qualified electorate, but this was not enough for Britain, who was embarrassed, became angry and belligerent, and invited the Western world and the United Nations to impose total sanctions on this `upstart` colony. Rhodesia, however, remained defiant and found ways to become self-sufficient in almost everything but critically, not oil and ammunition. After fifteen years, political pressure from many biased countries finally led to a political settlement, effectively handing the country over to a Chinese and Russian supported government, and the country became Zimbabwe.

However, during the 15 years of independence, November 11th was a national holiday and was celebrated throughout Rhodesia in different ways. In the Air Force, we would carry out fly pasts over as many towns and cities as we could, timed to coincide with memorial services for those killed on active service, and we would then celebrate in our respective clubs.

Unfortunately, the carefree days were changing. As more and more terrorist groups infiltrated our country, the tempo of operational flying increased steadily. Deployments of aircraft and crews also increased and we started to face the reality of losing our own crews during strikes inside and outside our country. In a tightly knit community, this was always devastating, and while we knew that our fellow Services were also suffering fatalities, this did not make it any easier. I roundly cursed those overseas politicians who had brought this deadly war to our country, with little or no feeling for all its peace-loving inhabitants.

The Vampire was a decent weapons platform, especially for rockets and cannon. On operational sorties, we would usually follow the Hunters and the Canberras, with their more potent weaponry, to soften up or neutralize the target before the helicopters would drop our ground forces in for the pitched battles that would often ensue. In the dive onto the target, the recoil from 4×20 mm cannon was significant and required concentration to keep the gun sight on target as events unfolded at high speed. At this stage of the war, the enemy camps were relatively lightly defended, but this was to change later as the terrorists were supplied with Sam 7 (Strela) missiles and anti-aircraft guns, posing high risk to our crews with several fatalities. While our aircrew losses were small, even the loss of one crew was one too many. We were a small Air Force and every aircrew member literally knew everyone else. The loss of one crew could amount to almost 10% of the squadron strength.

On a lighter note, the old adage about working hard and playing hard could not have been more appropriate. The Clubs (Messes) hosted frequent parties and social get-togethers, Friday nights, in particular, being the most popular night for socializing. The Officers' Mess at Thornhill had a wonderful outside pub, aptly named the 'Grog Spot', where wives and girlfriends would join their men folk to socialize. Those parties could get a little wild and occasionally would involve some `streaking`. This behavior was a definite `no-no` and when word got to headquarters, there was some consternation. Headquarters issued a signal forbidding any streaking, which promptly had the opposite effect!

It was not unknown for squadrons to do formation streaks through the 'Grogspot' and on one particular occasion, my squadron completed an immaculate diamond nine from the mess through the 'Grog Spot' and back to the Mess to get dressed again. The wives and girlfriends always thought it fun to hide the men's clothes and true to form they had done so this time too. After a while, we were able to find our clothes and get dressed and return to the 'Grog Spot'.

We had just sat down in the corner and ordered a beer, when to my horror, I noticed one of the older officer`s mother present at the bar. This was not usual and I decided it would be best if I approached her and offered her my apologies. But before this could happen, she had walked over to me and fixed her eyes firmly on me.

"Young man," she said. "I understand that you have just performed a streak through the bar?"

The room had gone strangely quiet. I was mortified and started to offer my apology, but she cut me off.

"I was busy getting a drink at the bar," she said, "so I missed the whole thing. Would you mind doing it again?"

With that, everyone erupted in laughter and all was well. What a wonderful old lady, I thought, wondering if she had ever been in the Women's Royal Air Force (WRAF). We did not repeat the streak but we did enjoy a drink with her.

Another incident which comes to mind emanated from a joint squadron strike.

Number 1 Squadron, operating Hunters out of Thornhill and Number 2 Squadron, operating Vampires out of Fylde, carried out a coordinated strike outside our country on a particular Saturday morning, and then both squadrons landed at New Sarum Air Force base, in Salisbury, to position for a possible re-strike the next day. It was not often that our two squadrons had a day off in the capital, and we decided to join up for a lunchtime drink in town, at a famous watering hole named 'La Boheme', which was a nightclub and also a popular meeting place on a Saturday lunchtime.

We all linked up and were enjoying a couple of beers and listening to some live music, a welcome respite from the intensity of operations. When the band decided to take a break, one member of our party got up on stage and started an impromptu performance of mime and impersonations. He was a talented entertainer and we were all enjoying his performance when suddenly, the manager of the club appeared and demanded that he vacate the stage immediately.

I happened to be standing at the bar, next to the officer commanding Number 1 Squadron, Rob Gaunt, a highly popular, capable and feisty pilot, who promptly told the manager to get lost. We heard no more from the manager for a few minutes until he reappeared and demanded that the senior officer present order all the pilots to put down their beers and leave the club immediately. Rob, still sitting at the bar, turned to the manager and said, "I am the senior officer here. I told you before to get lost and now I'm telling you to f**k off!"

We were all within a few feet of Rob, he knew he had our full moral support and he obviously did not need our vocal support! The manager disappeared and we continued to enjoy our beers and the performance. Suddenly, the manager reappeared and announced that he had a Mr. McLaren on the phone, who wished to speak to the senior officer present. There was a stunned silence. Air Marshal McLaren was the Commander of our Air Force and a superb officer; strict but fair.

Rob and I went to the office and Rob took the phone. While I could not hear what the Air Marshal was saying, it was a pretty one-sided call with a few "Yes, Sirs" from Rob and a final "Monday morning. Yes, Sir" and the call was over. This was not a good development and we left the phone, walked back to the other pilots and told them to finish up their beers. We all left the club, walking past the smirking manager, resisting the impulse to pour our beers over his head and making a mental note not to frequent his club again!

Back at our Air Force base, Rob and I sat down to write the report that the Commander of the Air Force had requested. The report was brief and factual and while I do not recall all the details, I do remember a particular choice of phrase that Rob had used that I thought was very apt. Rob wrote, "When the manager told me that Mr. McLaren was on the phone, I was dismayed!"

To me that summed up our reaction perfectly. Air Marshal McLaren read the report and, being an ex-fighter pilot himself and understanding the stress of operations, decided not to take the matter further. Just one of many incidents that made me proud to be in an Air Force with men like Rob Gaunt and Mick McLaren; work hard and play hard.

'Operation Virgo'

'Operation Virgo' was a Top-Secret operation, and as Officer Commanding Number 2 Squadron, I was summoned to Air Force HQ in April of 1974 for a top-level briefing on Phase 1. While our fleet of Vampire aircraft was adequate for close support operations, it was no longer in any condition to support the flying intensity of advanced flying training schools. Accordingly, agreement had been reached between our government and the South African government to train an initial batch of flight instructors in South Africa on their advanced jet trainer; the Impala, (Aermacchi MB 326). The next phase would be to train student pilots on advanced flying schools in South Africa.

The final phase would be the purchase of sufficient Impala aircraft to re-establish advanced flying school training in Rhodesia. This final phase would be dependent upon the political climate, and at the time there was sufficient optimism that a suitable political solution could be reached, which would persuade Britain, the Western World and the United Nations to recognize a representative and independent government for our country.

Against this background, in May, I departed for South African Air Force Base Langebaan, in the southern Cape Province. Before driving to South Africa, I visited my father, who was in a good hospital in Salisbury having just undergone surgery the day before, was recovering and was expected to leave the hospital in a few days. I couldn`t tell him the details of my assignment, but being an ex-military man, he understood. He was in good spirits and when I took my leave, we shook hands, not knowing how many months it might be before we could meet again.

To drive from Salisbury to Langebaan is a journey of several days, and I spent the first night in Pretoria with some Air Force fellow pilots and then drove the next day to Bloemfontein, in the Orange Free State, and checked into the Officers' Club on the Air Force Base.

Death of My Dad

No sooner had I done this than I received a visit from the Duty Officer. I was not unduly concerned because personal communications over long distances in those days were not easy. Certainly, there were no cell phones and long-distance calls were expensive and unreliable.

The Duty Officer had a grave look on his face and he informed me that my father had passed away. I was shocked, to say the least. It was only a couple of days since I had seen my father and we were expecting him to be home in a few days. What had happened? When? How? Why? Of course, the Duty Officer could not answer these questions but went on to explain that there was already a booking on the early morning flight to get me back to Salisbury the next day.

I thanked him, grateful for his help, but got little sleep that night, with many questions racing through my mind. I admired my father immensely and we had become closer in the later years, as I became a better son, learning that my dedication to the Air Force and my family were qualities that he understood and admired himself. He was a well-known, revered and loved teacher and headmaster, and I still remember my favorite image of him walking back across the playing fields with three or four young girl boarders fighting over who would hold his hand!

My brother Don, flew from Johannesburg where he was working as a metallurgist in the mining industry, and we both descended upon my mother`s home to stay and make arrangements for my father`s service and funeral. My mother did not have much more detail about what had caused my father`s death, other than the surgeon giving her the blunt news that my father had suffered complications two days after the surgery.

This did not sound like an adequate explanation to me and I arranged an appointment with the surgeon, a well-known and respected man in Salisbury. I explained that I was not on a 'witch-hunt' but that I wanted to satisfy myself and my family that we had a full and clear understanding of what had happened to cause this unexpected and sudden death.

The surgeon was not forthcoming and I left in frustration and disappointment, wondering if he had the faintest idea of the added grief his attitude caused. I did talk to the nurses at the hospital, and they alluded to something going wrong, but were reluctant to talk further. I thanked them and decided I could gain nothing further going down this path and nothing that I found out would bring my father back.

The service and cremation were attended by a large crowd. I knew most of them, especially a lot of the students` parents from the school where my father was the headmaster, as well as many ex-students. While it was good to see so many friends, I could only feel overwhelming sadness. I wore my Air Force Number one dress uniform to honor my father and managed to hold things together pretty well until I stood in front of my father`s casket at the end of the service, before cremation, saluted to honor his memory and his life and to thank him for all he had done for me and our family. My mother and brother and I stayed and mingled after the service, but I was poor company.

My mother was stoic and my brother was able to stay a few days and help my mother sort out the necessary affairs. Amongst everything else, my mother arranged a headstone for my father to be placed on his farm at Inyanga, with the simple and appropriate inscription 'He Loved the Land". That headstone lasted many years until some vandals or terrorists smashed it into pieces. I will replace it if I am ever able to visit what is now Zimbabwe, but more of that later in my story.

Life in the SAAF

Since I could do little else at the time, and I was already overdue for the flying course in South Africa, I left my mother and brother and flew to Cape Town to link up with my fellow officer, a very experienced and capable pilot and instructor from 6 Squadron, Flt. Lt. Tony Oakley, for the flying course at SAAF Langebaan. I was delighted to have Tony with me as we went through the first instructor conversion course on the Impala aircraft.

I knew that the only difficulty we would face would be that of language, especially since the South African Air Force used English and Afrikaans on alternate months! I knew that Tony's background was English and I suspected that he knew little or no Afrikaans. I was slightly better off, having spent the better part of a year on the Air Staff Course in Pretoria, where Afrikaans was frequently spoken.

The conversion to the new aircraft type was straightforward. The South African Air Force instructors were knowledgeable, professional and friendly, and we soon developed a solid relationship, as pilots around the world seem to do. Tony and I were living in the Officers' Club, along with all the other single officers, and we had ample opportunity to share stories and practice our Afrikaans in the bar during the evenings!

We adapted quickly to the instructional techniques required for the different aircraft and were soon ready to move to Air Force Base Pietersburg, in the Northern Transvaal, where we were to conduct training for six instructors from our Air Force on the Impala aircraft. We would utilize the six new Impalas that we had been using at Langebaan and we would have our own crew of engineers and technicians from our Air Force, thus operating as a separate flight on one of the South African Air Force squadrons.

Happily, this meant that my family would be able to join me again and I would be able to spend some time with my two sons; now three and five years old respectively, along with my lovely wife, Jayne. While I knew that they were always safe and content living in the married quarters at Thornhill while I was away on duty, it was never ideal for families to be apart for protracted periods of time. Pietersburg was close to the northern border of South Africa, not far from our southern border and only a few hundred miles from Thornhill, making logistics easier but still classified as a Top-Secret operation.

The Air Force base outside Pietersburg was like most other bases that I knew, with single quarters, married quarters, sports facilities and clubs. I was allocated a small house within the married quarters, awaiting the arrival of my wife and sons. I started to realize the significance of the network of contacts built during my Air Staff Course days. Some of my fellow course members were now senior officers on the base, commanding squadrons and holding senior positions on the base. We were, of course, delighted to be working together again, and the success of the operation was assured by the friendly and respectful cooperation.

I remember very well the day that my wife and sons arrived. Our Air Force Director General of Operations had scheduled a visit to inspect our progress and had kindly allowed my wife and sons to fly on the same aircraft; an old but reliable DC-3, the Dakota, as we knew it. We were well prepared for the visit, with everyone briefed and our flying continuing per the normal program, since we determined this is what the DG of Operations would want to see. Since I would be accompanying the Director General of Operations and any other staff, I had decided not to do any flying myself on that day, and instead wore a normal Air Force uniform to meet his aircraft.

I positioned myself at the door of the aircraft as it stopped, expecting the DG Ops to exit the aircraft first, and as the door opened, I stood smartly to attention, ready to salute. Before the steps could be brought to the door, a little bundle with blonde hair leaped into my arms, shouting, "Daddy, Daddy!" and almost knocking me over. So surprised was I to not see DG Ops first! Luckily, I was able to stay upright and behind Lee came Mark, and as the steps arrived, then came Jayne. DG Ops had decided my family should see me first! Another lesson for me from our senior officers and the thoughtfulness and courtesy offered. I shall never forget it. Air Commodore 'Dickie' Bradshaw is no longer with us, but thank you, Sir.

A few weeks after the arrival of my family, Jayne and I were invited to a formal dinner at the Officers' Club. Jayne and I were very familiar with the procedure for formal dinner nights in our Air Force, but never having attended such an event with the South African Air Force, we faced the evening with some trepidation. We dressed correctly for the event; I in my formal mess dress, Jayne in a formal gown. We arrived at the Club to find that we were to be seated next to our very good friends from the Air Staff Course; Joan and 'Blondie' Cilliers. We felt reassured and allowed ourselves to relax, knowing that Joan and 'Blondie' would guide us through any unfamiliar procedures.

I should mention that 'Blondie' was well known for his unique and persistently wicked sense of humor, which was one of the characteristics that I enjoyed so much about him and was key to a large part of our friendship. With hindsight, perhaps I should have been more mindful of this, but there was too much else on my mind already.

As all the officers and their wives arrived, resplendent in formal uniforms and ball gowns and were greeted by the President of the Club and the Commander of the base, we could mingle, chat and be introduced, and soon it was time for us to take our seats.

Seating at such formal events was usually at large, long tables arranged in a U-shape, and such was the case on this evening, with the President of the Club, the Commanding Officer and other senior officers at the head table, with the other officers in order of descending rank further away from the head table. 'Blondie', as a Commandant, and I as a Squadron Leader/Major, found ourselves only a few seats away from the head table.

Shortly after the President had made his opening remarks and the wine was being poured, I started to feel a little more relaxed. The procedures appeared very similar to our own and I was delighted to have been invited to join the event. However, a few minutes later, Jayne whispered in my ear that she needed to use the restroom. This was an absolute no-no in our Air Force. One was expected to have taken care of this before being seated, so I turned to 'Blondie' to apprise him of the situation and to seek his advice. To my surprise, he said this was no big deal at such an event and Jayne could just quietly slip away, return and no one would be any the wiser.

At this point, alarm bells should have rung in my head, but I told Jayne what 'Blondie' had said, she quietly slipped away and I was relieved that no one seemed to pay any attention. However, this was not my tormentor`s plan. He promptly tapped his fork on his glass in order to get everyone's attention and when the room became silent, he announced "Mr. President. Mrs Slatter has gone to use the Ladies toilet." There was a stunned silence for a few moments while the President looked in our direction, acknowledged 'Blondie's' comment and then the hubbub of conversation resumed.

I did not know what to do but my indecision was interrupted by Jayne's return, blissfully unaware of what had happened. As she tried to quietly seat herself, 'Blondie' made a great fuss of standing up, holding Jayne's chair for her, solicitously adjusting the position of the chair until everyone became aware of Jayne's return, including the President, and a smattering of applause ensued! Although Jane was feeling self-conscious, she was able to thank 'Blondie' and general conversation resumed.

Most people in our Air Force understood 'Blondie's' sense of humor and the prank was taken in the spirit it was intended. The remainder of the evening was uneventful and we returned home without further ado. When I told Jayne what had happened, she laughed, but I'm pleased to say that at subsequent formal dinners, she has never forgotten to use the ladies room before being seated!

The flying conversions for more instructors went smoothly, and supported by our very capable engineering staff, our aircraft performed flawlessly. Soon it was year's end but instead of positioning with our new aircraft to start a new advanced training course for our 'Wings' students, as expected, we received orders to return to our own Air Force Base at Thornhill, without our aircraft! While such matters were beyond my pay-grade, it was apparent that the political compromises necessary on all sides of our conflict were not succeeding to a point where we could openly purchase these new aircraft from South Africa and use them in our own country. I and the others were to complete another AFS on Vampires and another BFS on Provosts at Thornhill during 1975, and wait until the next page was turned.

While the political situation between Rhodesia and the UK was fluid, and there was steady engagement at the highest levels, there was not much demonstrable progress. On the Air Force side, there was considerable work behind the scenes, between our Air

Force and the South African Air Force, to find a solution to our lack of suitable training aircraft. It was late in the year, I was ordered to Air Force HQ and received instructions to position myself and our instructors and ground crews at SAAF Base Langebaan and prepare to receive and train our first 'Wings' course at the start of the next year (1976).

This was exciting news and there was little time to act. 'Operation Virgo' was back on the front burner, but still Top Secret. Officially, in our Rhodesian Air Force Headquarters, I would command 'Op Virgo', as Squadron Leader Slatter, Commander of Number 6 Squadron in the Rhodesian Air Force. Officially, within the South African Air Force, I would be Major Slatter, Commanding 'C Flight' AFS Langebaan! Hello Walter Mitty!

Langebaan Air Force Base

The road trip to Langebaan in the Cape, a distance of some 1,500 miles, took us the better part of a week, stopping with friends in Pretoria and further stops along the Cape Coast. Living on a pilot's pay, Jayne, Mark, Lee and I crammed ourselves and our suitcases into our trusty old Volvo station-wagon, a 1960 vintage with some 100,000 miles on the clock!

The journey was reasonably uneventful, but upon arriving at the Air Force base on a Sunday afternoon, we found out that the operation was so Top Secret that nobody on the base knew anything about us! I determined that I would call the Base Commander on Monday morning, certain that he would be in the picture about our arrival, and we set off to find a small hotel in a tiny village called Paternoster, some 25 miles away.

We had already driven several hundred miles that day and it was late afternoon when we pulled up in front of the village hotel, a very old and rather dilapidated looking single-story building on a dusty street with not much else in sight, save for a few tiny fishermen's cottages. Jayne promptly announced that she and the boys would not stay there and we should look for somewhere else. I must tell you that Jayne was never a fussy person (which should tell you a bit about the appearance of the hotel) but we were all tired and I decided to at least inspect the inside of the hotel.

There was no one behind the tiny reception counter but the place looked clean, and after I rang the bell a few times, a very helpful gentleman appeared and agreed to my request to have a look at the bedroom. The bedrooms were small, with very old furniture, but everything was clean and I was satisfied that we could spend at least one night there. Jayne reluctantly agreed and the family dragged themselves unwillingly into the hotel and stood next to me as I signed the register. While I was doing this, Jayne tugged on my sleeve and pointed at a sign behind the front desk. I looked at the sign which read,

"BATHS – CLEAN WATER 50c / DIRTY WATER 25c"

We burst out laughing, the gentleman explaining that even though 50c might have been a fair price in those times, this was indeed a joke and only a joke! We unpacked and went to the small dining room for supper, which turned out to be delicious, in the old-fashioned way; no a la carte but a simple home cooked meal of soup followed by a main course and dessert and coffee.

Our sons were worn out so we put them to bed and I suggested to Jayne that we visit the bar for an after-dinner drink. Jayne was still a little uneasy about the hotel, so I said good night and went to find the bar. Although it was a Sunday evening, there were half a dozen local farmers having a drink, and they looked at me, with some surprise, as an unknown in this off-the-track place. They were all speaking Afrikaans, but I was able to buy them a drink, start a conversation and before too long, we were on friendly terms, as they too bought drinks for me. Sometime around midnight, I bid them farewell and stumbled to my room, having immensely enjoyed my first evening at the hotel with my new South African friends. Welcome to Paternoster!

The next day, I met with the Officer Commanding of the Base at Langebaan, Colonel Roux, whom I respected instantly and who turned out to be a great supporter of our operation. He too was unaware of our requirement for accommodations, but vowed to jump on the problem right away, this after ascertaining that we indeed had a place to stay for the next few days at Paternoster. This problem could only escalate in the next few weeks, as our ground crews and other instructors arrived. Since there had obviously been a communication problem between our Rhodesian Air Force headquarters and the South African Air Force headquarters, I was grateful for the Colonel`s help.

The good Colonel was as good as his word, providing a three–bedroom house within a couple of days. We moved out of the little hotel in Paternoster, which we had come to really enjoy, especially the dining room and our new friends in the bar, while our sons loved the beach nearby.

The next problem was a complete lack of furniture in the house, but Colonel Roux gladly accepted that challenge as well and some hospital beds and ammunition boxes arrived. Since I could not imagine our Headquarters authorizing the move of our furniture for an indeterminate period, this would have to do.

Within a couple of days, Flight Lieutenant Tony Oakley arrived and we were both able to complete a quick re-familiarization course on the aircraft. This would allow us to take over the brief familiarization courses for our instructors as they arrived. It was a good feeling to be back at Langebaan, amongst many friends from our previous assignments there and reasonably settled with a house and a school for our sons. It was not long before Tony's wife, Gay, arrived and they both moved into the house with us. This worked very well until two more instructors with their wives and children arrived and moved into our one house! It was a very good thing that the house had two bath rooms!

This did not last for long, fortunately, since the Colonel was able to find two more houses and an apartment on the Base to spread the load! Our ground crews were accommodated in the single quarters, since only the senior NCO decided to bring his family with him, and he too was placed in a house nearby. The re-familiarization flying courses were completed quickly and without incident, while our ground crews did their technical re-familiarizations on the aircraft, to keep us flying daily. We were ready to accept our first course of Advanced Flying School student pilots as 'C Flight' at Langebaan and as 29 PTC in the Rhodesian Air Force, the first such external training course in South Africa.

Our student pilots arrived; a great bunch of fine young men. I say that not as a platitude, but because I, and the other instructors, already knew them. We had instructed them for six months on their Basic Flying School and had found them to be at least as determined and capable as other pilot courses that went through very rigorous and extensive selection processes to have the chance to fly for their Air Force. This would be somewhat different, though, because although we had our families with us, the student pilots would be far from home, family and girlfriends for a relatively long period of time, and with little opportunity for communication. They were accommodated in the student pilot's wing of the Officers Club and subject to all the disciplinary procedures of the South African Air Force, as well as our own.

It is to their credit that I never had to appear before the Commanding Officer of the Base to answer to any disciplinary complaints. They quickly assimilated themselves with their South African counterparts, both in their flying training and their extra-curricular activities, including participation in the Base sports program and even representing the Base in some key sports, particularly rugby. Pilot selection in our country placed some weight on sports participation, for good reason, and it was not unusual to have provincial or even national representatives amongst our members.

There was always some concern about our `cover` being blown, the highest risk being the language situation. South Africa required bilingualism – Afrikaans and English – among its Service members, including trainees. The Cape Province was a province where Afrikaans was especially popular, and my concern focused on social and sporting events, where others may wonder how some members of the South African Air Force were not fluent in Afrikaans. We all made special efforts in this regard and at the end of the day, this turned out to be essentially a non-issue, although it did lead to some very funny incidents!

One such incident occurred during an 'Afrikaans only' month and involved a student who was very English but had tried hard to learn the Afrikaans basics necessary for conducting a solo flight. This particular incident was caused by the similarity between the Afrikaans words for 'general' (algemene) and the word for 'pleasant' (angenaame).

Student: "Langebaan, ses nil een, ryklaring, een uur angenaame vlieg, asseblief." (Langebaan, 601 taxi clearance for one-hour pleasant flying, please)

Tower: (pause) and then "Beteken jy algemene vlieg?" (Do you mean general flying?)

Student (not understanding) "Ses nil een, een uur angenaame vlieg asseblief." (601, one hour pleasant flying, please)

Tower: (confused now) "Is jy seker – angenaame vlieg?" (Are you sure – pleasant flying?)

Student: (getting desperate) "Een uur angenaame vlieg, asseblief." (One hour pleasant flying, please)

Tower: (in best humor) "Ry maar - en geniet dit!" (Just go – and enjoy it!)

Who says Air Traffic Controllers don't have a sense of humor!?

Communication with home, whether with family, friends or Air Force, was not easy, due to the Top-Secret classification of the operation. However, we did receive visits and inspections from Air Force Headquarters officers and staff, from time to time, and we were able to catch up on 'home' news, as well as the state of our country. News with regard to any political progress was not encouraging. Britain, in particular, was adopting a very inflexible line, and in some respects, almost seemed to favor the extreme nationalist movements who were strongly supported with training, arms and equipment by Russia and China.

The numbers of terrorists under training outside Rhodesia was growing daily and large camps were being set up in Zambia, for Joshua Nkomo (ZIPRA) and in Mozambique, for Robert Mugabe (ZANLA).

Our resources were being stretched, especially in regard to fuel, and even with South Africa's help, this was a concern. Britain had set up a blockade at the port of Beira, in Mozambique, to prevent fuel supplies from the east reaching their destinations. There was no chance of any supply from the east or the north, those countries being hostile to Rhodesia and emboldened by the United Nations sanctions on our country. Our Forces, already the best anti-terrorist forces in the world at the time, were heavily committed and the drain on the country's reserve forces was starting to be felt and would become more of a burden as the war progressed.

In some ways, flying training missions in South Africa made us feel left out and as outsiders, away from the war and our colleagues who were bearing the brunt of the operations and the inevitable injuries and fatalities. We had some seasoned operational pilots with us on 'Op Virgo', and I know they would rather have been at home, contributing to the war effort in a more direct and tangible manner than training new pilots. We consoled ourselves by agreeing that our contribution would be to turn out the very best qualified pilots at their 'Wings' tests, so that they could hit the ground running when they reported for their Operation Conversion Unit training at the squadrons, to which they might be assigned, and bolster our war effort accordingly.

One of the most pleasing yet serious aspects of my responsibilities as Squadron Commander was to conduct the final handling test for 'Wings' for each of the students. This test was a big deal, not just for the students, obviously, but also for the instructors and ultimately for the Air Force. I was entirely confident in our instructors, had already flown with all the students at various times and was confident there would be no nasty surprises. And indeed, there were none. I was immensely proud of all the students and their instructors in being able to recommend all of them for the award of Rhodesian Air Force 'Wings', especially under the very different training situation.

One of the Final Handling Tests particularly sticks in my mind. Officer Cadet Nigel Lamb was a very promising young student pilot with an experienced and capable instructor, Flight Lieutenant Tony Oakley. Tony and Nigel had spent considerable effort on the aerobatics phase of advanced flight training and were justifiably proud of their prowess. It seems that Nigel had spent a part of his youth studying aerobatics in depth, and this was his opportunity to put his knowledge into practice. Final Handling Tests usually need about an hour and a quarter to an hour and a half to cover all the required areas of handling, and we started the test and moved quickly through all the required phases.

Aerobatics would usually take up about 10 minutes, depending on the sequence and maneuvers that the student had chosen, and would be planned toward the end of the test. When we got to that stage of the test and I asked Nigel if he had some aerobatics to show me, he could barely contain his excitement. He then proceeded to dazzle me with a demonstration of advanced aerobatics that went far beyond the standard required, even for a Final Handling Test. While I was proficient at aerobatics, I had not seen such creativity and continuity in a sequence before. It was a longer than usual sequence but it ended too soon for me.

We then completed the final phases of the test and returned to base using an instrument flown recovery. I told Nigel and Tony that we would debrief the test in about an hour, and I went into my office to add to my notes taken during the test and to collect my thoughts. The debriefing was pretty standard until I got to the aerobatics phase, when I did something I had never done in any previous debriefing.

"Lamb," I said, "your aerobatics were very advanced and to be honest, I`m not sure how to assess them. I`d like you to debrief me and your instructor and give us your own assessment."

Nigel was unfazed and went through a thorough debrief, including criticism of some aspects. Tony, of course was familiar with the sequence and standard of his student, so this was not news to him. I congratulated them both and then prepared the report on his FHT and recommendation for the award of Air Force 'Wings'. It came as no surprise to me some years later to learn that Nigel had been the Aerobatic Champion of Great Britain for 7 years running and more recently had become the World Red Bull Air Races Champion for 2014 as well. I`m proud to have this association and friendship with Nigel and to have seen him recently at a 29 PTC pilot reunion where we shared some happy memories of this event.

The Advanced Flying School for 29 Pilot Training Course was now complete and I believe it`s fair to say it was an unqualified success. Our ground crews, students and instructors operated flawlessly, next to our South African Air Force colleagues and friends, and we made many friends at the Squadrons and on the playing fields. I was and remain immensely proud of our team. Our SAAF friends were always there to support and help us, as needed, and Colonel Roux and his team deserve our thanks and respect.

Durban Air Force Base

It was now back home to Thornhill for the 'Wings Parade' and some leave before the students went off to their operational squadrons. We instructors returned to South Africa, but this time to Air Force Base Durban, to receive our next course of students. It seems that this move was necessitated by the ongoing difficulties in the political world, to reach an agreed settlement that would allow South Africa to complete the sale of the Impala aircraft to Rhodesia, and it was deemed preferable to continue our advanced flight training in South Africa.

Our return to Rhodesia was indeed sobering, as we realized the increasing extent of the war and its toll on the country, especially on our civilian reserve forces who were facing increasingly regular and extended tours of duty in the operational areas. Especially frustrating were the many dedicated efforts to resolve the political stalemate with Britain and the United Nations, only to have our political proposals rejected, time and time again.

Britain was determined not to lose face over the Rhodesian stand for true independence and continued to drum up support for their position at the United Nations, only emboldening the extreme nationalist movements to increase their demands and to make resolution impossible. Rhodesia could hold its own militarily for years to come, but the threat of the loss of our only fuel supply from South Africa was looming larger.

Against this backdrop, we arrived in Durban, a beautiful city on the east coast of the province of Natal, in South Africa, in early January and started to set up the next Advanced Flying School for No. 30 Pilot Training Course. We had spent some time modifying the flying syllabus, because of the increasing demand on the operational squadrons fighting the war back home. We placed increased emphasis on tried, tested and pure handling techniques and reducing the time spent on procedural flying, which was a lesser requirement when conducting close support operations, and we were keen to see how this worked out.

The climate in Durban was very different to the Cape. It was now mid-summer and the temperatures in the day would routinely be 30 deg C to 35 deg C, with very high humidity. By the time you`d be dressed in your flying suit, lower 'g-suit', upper life vest, flying helmet, strapped into the cockpit and taxied to the runway, you might as well have been standing in a shower for five minutes! However, as soon as possible and no later than immediately after getting airborne, one could select cold air from the cabin conditioning unit and dry off!

Flying procedures were different because we were operating from a major civilian airport. All voice communications were in the language of International Air Traffic Control, English, which was a relief to the new student pilots. Durban and the South African province of Natal were traditionally more English-leaning than the Cape Province, and I found myself missing our bouts of Afrikaans and our nights in the pub with our South African Air Force counterparts.

We were attached to a South African Reserve Squadron on the airfield, away from civilian activities and accommodated in flats (apartments) in the nearby town of Amanzimtoti, a short 15-minute drive from the airport. Our families were with us and we were able to put our children into nearby schools, so all was well. Since the operation was still classified 'Top Secret', there was no possibility for our wives to get work permits, but there was plenty to do with the children and, of course, there were beautiful beaches at our doorsteps. The flying program ran like clockwork, due in large part to the excellent engineering support from our own ground crews and co-operation with our South African colleagues, but the lifestyle was very different to Air Force life on an all-Air Force Base, as we knew it.

Promotion and My Return to Operational Flying

It was in April 1977 that I received word that I was to be promoted to Wing Commander (Lt- Col) and to take charge of our Air Force operational activities on our eastern border, back in Rhodesia. I was delighted, as was my family, and while I found instructional flying very satisfying, I missed the operational activity back in our own country. I had got a taste of it when we were back for a short while over the period of the 'Wings Parade' for our previous course of student pilots.

My replacement, a fine, experienced training and operational pilot by the name of George Wrigley, would take over in a few short weeks. Squadron Leader George Wrigley duly arrived and after completing a short conversion course for him, he took over 'Op Virgo' and I left with my family to return to Rhodesia. We had spent the best part of the last two years in South Africa, at different Air Force bases, and I was proud of what the team had accomplished and grateful to our South African counterparts for their help, advice and friendships. These relationships would prove vital over the next few years, as the fighting within and without our borders intensified.

Back in Rhodesia, Jayne, the boys and I spent a few days in Salisbury, getting our furniture out of storage and making arrangements to move to Umtali, the location of the Joint Operations Center for the Eastern districts. We were also able to see Jayne`s parents and my mother for the first time in almost two years, and the emotion of being back in Rhodesia, but without my father, finally caught up with me. I made a silent vow

My Father Roland Slatter. 1960

Hugh left. Bamba the dog. Brother Don right. 1944.

Don 6 Grandpa Clarke aged 97. Hugh 2.

My Mother Eve Slatter 1949. Hugh 7 on left. Don 11 on right.

Jayne's parents' first house on the farm circa 1948. Typical of early farming in Rhodesia.

Air Marshal Norman Walsh,
Air Force Commander
OLM. BCR. ESM.

Group Captain 'Tol'
Janeke DMM..

16 PTC Survival Training Exercise. Matusadonna Wildlife Area.
Author, rear, 2nd from right.

FB 9 and 'Gang'. L-R Pilot Officers Slatter, Cronshaw, Bruce, McRoberts, Bond

Vampire FB9

Air Force Station Thornhill 1963

Percival Provost T1

Vampire T11

Training on the peak of the Chimanimani mountains 1968

Hawker Hunter FGA9

Impala at Durban airport

Slatter mountain flying training in the Chimanimani Range -1968

French Dassault Alpha Jet

Ian Smith, Prime Minister of Rhodesia (center) Air Marshal Mick McLaren (left center) and Squadron Leader Hugh Slatter (right center) with fly past pilots and Warrant Officer Spike Owens (standing behind Ian Smith) and technicians; 29 PTC Wings Fly-Past Crew – Dec. 1976
Interestingly, our engineers and technicians would not usually be bothered with pictures, but with Ian Smith in attendance, everyone wanted to share the moment.

29 PTC Wings Award and Fly Past pilots. 1976.

Staff Course 12; 1972
South African Air Force College

Top row L-R: Major Fred Frayne, Commandant Dries van der Lith, Major Martin van der Linde, Commandant Pierre Gouws, Squadron Leader Hugh Slatter, Major Daan Retief, Major Martin Jooste.

Middle row L-R: Major Daan Haarhoff, Major Francois Oosthuizen, Major Len Facius, Major Daan Fourie, Major Julius Kriel, Major Mick Du Toit, Squadron Leader Geoff Proudfoot, Major Blondie Cilliers.

Front row: Directing Staff: L-R: Major Pidsley, Major Van Den Berg, Commandant Crafford, Colonel Eccles, Commandant De Munnick, Major Guyt, Commandant Dan Zeeman (Course Leader).

Of interest is that many students went on to become Generals in the South African Air Force. Geoff Proudfoot left the Rhodesian Air Force and I became Chief of Staff of the Air Force of Zimbabwe (post Rhodesia). This course was a prerequisite for promotion to General rank.

to my father that I would honor his memory by looking after my mother and serving the Air Force and our country to my very best ability. My Dad had served in North Africa for the Allied Forces during World War II and would understand my feelings.

Our road trip to Umtali was uneventful. I was fairly familiar with the town because it was not too far from Inyanga, where many years ago my father had fulfilled his dream of starting a fruit farm. It was also close to one of the largest farming areas in the country, with several of our farming friends living nearby. We would visit them frequently as well as going to the town for supplies that Inyanga was too small to provide.

Umtali was picturesque, with many deciduous trees, wide avenues and mostly two-story shops and offices. We were happy to have this assignment and I was looking forward to becoming engaged with the 'sharp end' of operations again; representing our Air Force with the Joint Operations Center (JOC) comprised of our Army, Air Force and Police, a system that had proved to be successful as the war developed.

We arrived and unpacked at the house we had rented for the purpose of this assignment. It was a pleasant, typical Rhodesian house, built of bricks with a tiled roof and sitting on about an acre of land, complete with the now necessary anti-rocket/mortar shelter on the grounds. This caused much excitement for the boys, who insisted on inspecting it immediately. It was nothing fancy; simply a large hole in the ground lined with sandbags and heavy timbers across the top, with more sandbags to provide a roof. I went with them to inspect for snakes and scorpions, which were plentiful and loved to hide in such structures.

These shelters had become necessary since the terrorists had started a pattern of sitting on the hills surrounding Umtali and shooting rockets and mortars indiscriminately into the town. Although there was an obvious danger, their aim was terrible and I`m not aware of anyone actually being killed while we were there, although they did some limited damage to property.

Interestingly, I was to meet one of those responsible for those attacks later, after the enforced independence and the birth of Zimbabwe. It happened that both of us and a few others were on a visit to the United States to study military training methods, and we found ourselves speaking together after dinner. He was suffering from a bad back and when I questioned him about the cause, he said he had suffered a fall when he was carrying mortars and setting them up in the hills around Umtali, to attack the town! When I told him I was in the town on some of those occasions, but that luckily his aim was so terrible that I could be with him that day, he smiled and we shared the memory. What strange circumstances wars can create!

Jayne arranged for the boys, now six and eight, to attend a local school, and I checked out the JOC offices, including our own Air Force offices and Communications Center. The JOC offices and operations room were located in the old Cecil Hotel, a wonderful, old, two-story building on the Main Street, built in colonial style with a broad veranda on the front, shaded by large trees. In better times, this veranda was the place where farmers and visitors would sit and enjoy a sundowner. Now, it was usually deserted and any paying guests would be accommodated in the new, modern, five-story building adjoining the old hotel; now HQ 3 Brigade.

While the new hotel was obviously more comfortable, it lacked the history, charm and sense of early Rhodesia that swept over the old hotel. I was happy to work out of the old building, not that I spent much time there. This eastern operational sector had several airfields at its disposal, of which the main airfield was about 15 miles out of town and was called 'Grand Reef', or in military terms, Forward Air Field 8 (FAF 8).

Several days a week, I would drive out to the airfield where our Air Force had a permanent 'Fire Force' capability. This 'Fire Force' would usually comprise four helicopters, of which three would be in a configuration that would carry four fully armed and professional soldiers from any one of Rhodesia's regiments, along with a gunship armed with 20mm cannon or twin .50 caliber machine guns, for close support. To precede and to supplement any 'Fire Force' action, a fully armed Lynx (militarized Cessna 337) was always available for recce (reconnaissance), target marking and additional close support. The 'Fire Force' concept had been finely honed until it provided a very rapid and potent pre-planned or responsive action against the terrorist forces that were continually increasing their numbers and attacks in the eastern and northern border areas of Rhodesia.

I enjoyed my visits to FAF 8, notwithstanding the hairy ride over the last five miles of dirt roads that were subject to land mines and possible ambushes, so I could visit the aircrews and army soldiers who were giving their all, every day, in the defense of our country. I felt a special kinship with the young pilots on the 'Fire Force' and I marveled at how the use of the helicopters had advanced since my tour of duty, almost 10 years earlier. It was especially heart-warming to find some of my student pilots in these roles, including some who had been my students at Langebaan, not even one year ago!

Rob Griffiths

It was one of my ex-students who suffered an extremely serious crash, while flying his Lynx aircraft in a recce and ground support role late one afternoon. While completing a mission attached to our 'Fire Force', and in support of our ground forces, Rob Griffiths had found himself trapped against the side of a large hill, with insufficient power to turn and climb over the sharply-rising ground ahead. His aircraft struck the large, rocky outcrop, a few meters from the crest, and disintegrated into a fireball, bits and pieces falling back down the hill.

Rob had been caught directly in the explosion and suffered severe burns over his body and especially his face. Unable to communicate with anyone, Rob started a long and perilous descent down the hill in a superhuman effort to find someone who could help. Darkness had fallen, adding to his difficulties, and we were now all aware that Rob had not returned to the airfield. We started the process of trying to contact him and to determine where he might be. We knew that he was limited on fuel and it became apparent very quickly that he had either force landed somewhere, had crashed, or had been shot down without being able to communicate his position.

Being on one`s own, as a member of the Rhodesian Forces, at night and without any weapon was a dangerous situation. Terrorists mingled with the locals at night in the villages and were known to be increasing their numbers in the area. Being badly injured made matters worse for Rob. If I remember correctly, weather conditions that night were not suitable for any search mission, and even if Rob was found, a rescue mission with a chopper at night in bad weather would be perilous. Plans were readied for an all-out effort at first light, with Air Force and Police Reserve Air Wing aircraft available to start a search pattern.

There was still no news of Rob, but very early in the morning, I got a couple of calls; one from our Ops Officer at the FAF and one from the local Police. Rob was safe but badly injured and was being transported to the local hospital for immediate attention. Rob`s tale was a harrowing one. Drifting in and out of consciousness he had half stumbled and half fallen down the rocky hill for an unknown distance and had come across a dirt road, where, as good fortune would have it, a local African was riding his bicycle. Shocked at Rob`s appearance, he helped Rob onto his bicycle, somehow, and started the difficult journey to the closest police presence.

This, in and of itself was a remarkably brave act, since the cyclist would have been shot alongside Rob, if they had encountered any terrorists or sympathizers. This plucky cyclist, with Rob hanging on as best as he could and in excruciating pain, found their way to the nearest police presence. With radio access and vehicles available, the police were able to notify the FAF and the hospital and move Rob as urgently as possible to the hospital. To this day, I don`t know what happened to the brave cyclist, but I suspect he was happy to remain incognito and therefore safe from terrorist recriminations.

Terrorist tactics with the locals were to use intimidation, rather than encouragement, and they did this frequently by cutting off ears, noses and lips of suspected collaborators, and even carrying out executions. Whoever you are, Sir, and wherever you are today, you are a very brave and good man and you have our silent and enduring appreciation for your selfless act of courage.

I had dressed and made my way to the hospital, after getting the calls, and was shown to a private room. It was difficult to recognize Rob, due to the serious burns to his body, but especially to his face. Although he was sedated, I believe he could hear and recognize my voice; he should, I thought, since I had spoken to him enough in the cockpit in his training days, and I offered some words of encouragement while trying to deal with the shocking situation myself. It`s difficult when one has worked so long and hard to help a student achieve his life goal of 'Wings', to suddenly realize that he may not even live, let alone fly again.

Rob's parents arrived later that day and I was able to talk with them before they went in to see him. I told them that, like me, they would not recognize Rob, facially, but how important it was to register no shock in speech or behavior that might adversely impact the recovery that we all so wished for. This they did and proved a wonderful and solid support for Rob as he started the long and painful recovery, with many months of skin grafts and therapy. Throughout this lengthy period, Rob had many supporters, but none better than his fellow pilot course members who, although posted to different squadrons, always kept the bond and the faith.

In due course, Rob returned to full flying duties and still flies today, as an outstanding example of perseverance and courage that has his fellow pilot course members, instructors and Air Force colleagues are in awe of. We`re all proud of you, Rob, and I'm particularly proud to have you as a friend, after so many years. The Air Force motto is, '*Per Ardua ad Astra*' (Through hardship to the Stars), and you certainly exemplify that motto, Rob. Well done indeed.

Nick Price

On a lighter note, Umtali boasted a particularly picturesque golf course, close to the center of town, and occasionally, when operations permitted, it was possible to have a game of golf at the Hillside Golf Club in the afternoon. There were several keen golfers within the Army personnel at the JOC headquarters, and a couple of Colonels from the staff loved to challenge the local Blue Job, namely me, to a game, from time to time. I was always up to the challenge, but usually had to scramble to find a playing partner, since our Air Force staff was so small at the JOC (usually only three of us). Since these two Colonels were decent golfers, with handicaps around 10 or 12, as I remember, and my golf game was erratic, at best, I would always end up paying them the $5 wager and buying them a beer, as a gracious loser!

The small staff that assisted me in our role at the JOC was comprised of reservists; civilians who had undergone Air Force training in various support roles, including running our Communications Center next to my office; a vital role. These reservists were subject to frequent call-ups to serve two to four weeks at a time at different operational locations. By pure chance, at one of the changeovers of staff, I recognized the new Communications Center Specialist; one Nick Price. This fine young man was known to most of Rhodesia (and indeed to a lot of the world) since he had won the World Junior Golf Championship, when he was just 15 years old; a remarkable feat. He was now perhaps 19 and could win any golf competition that he entered. He was destined to become the world`s number one player in the 90's, winning many PGA events, including several Majors.

So here he was, assigned to my staff for several weeks, and I could not believe my luck and could scarcely contain my excitement when I suggested casually to my Army Colonel friends that, as things were fairly quiet, perhaps it was time for a game of golf. They agreed readily, always happy to take a 'Blue Job`s' (Blue-Job – Air Force, Brown-Job – Army) money and asked if I had a partner, to which I replied that I would find someone, somehow.

The day arrived and Nick and I walked onto the number one tee-box to greet our opposition. The look on my Army friends` faces was priceless! They knew who Nick was, of course, but they didn`t know he was an Air Force reservist, especially one who was serving at the JOC!

"Slatter, you bastard!" I recall them saying in good humor as they handed over their $5 apiece, fully aware that they were in for a proverbial thrashing! Nick was playing off scratch and I seem to remember him shooting 67, good enough for the Blue Jobs to indeed win the match quite handily. I was only able to take advantage of Nick`s call-up on that one occasion, but the memory lingers! Thank you, Nick!

Tactical Changes

Our engineers had constructed a *'Cordon Sanitaire'* (a protective barrier against a potentially aggressive nation) along selected stretches of our eastern border. This consisted of a double row of heavy, tall fencing, separated by minefields. These stretches were positioned at key terrorist entry points and areas that required special protection, such as vulnerable routes into the city itself. However, the terrorists soon learned to skirt these areas, and although this made entry more onerous, it did not stop it. The fences also stopped the natural movement of most of the wildlife in the area. However, they were no match for elephants and the sound of mines being detonated at night would often result in finding a dead elephant in the minefield, having simply pushed over one side of the fence. It was a sad and unintended consequence of the conduct of war.

'Fire Force' call-outs were becoming a daily occurrence, as more and more terrorists infiltrated across our eastern and northern borders. There were certain heavily used routes in the 'Operation Thrasher' region, one being along the Honde Valley, some 30 miles north of Umtali. This offered a relatively easy entry path, terrain-wise, for those terrorists leaving their bases in Mozambique to make their way into the Rhodesian Tribal Trust lands and the farming communities.

These call-outs were often initiated by pre-positioned observation teams or by airborne reconnaissance (recce), resulting in very rapid response and often, successful ground contact and pitched battles with the terrorists. Their tactics and weapons skills were becoming better, and although our kill ratio remained high, we were experiencing the sad task of retrieving our wounded and dead more frequently. I tried to meet our CASEVAC pilots and techs, who would chopper those seriously wounded soldiers into the hospital landing zone, and thank them for their service as they continued day after day to fly in support of our ground troops, under dangerous and often difficult flying conditions.

Our tactics, too, were improving and the use of armed helicopters, integrated into the 'Fire Force', gave us a powerful weapon to add needed firepower when attacking heavily armed terrorist groups. When even this was not enough, we could call upon heavy strike aircraft from our main bases, in the form of jet ground attack or even bomber aircraft, usually only an hour or so away. With similar challenges on our northern border as well, it became apparent that we would need to do more to eliminate the terrorists who were becoming increasingly emboldened by their safe bases in Mozambique and in Zambia. These bases were growing rapidly and reports of thousands of terrorists inhabiting these bases were confirmed by our recce groups and photo intelligence.

While external operations were not new to us, plans were now developed for several major external operations, designed to eliminate as many terrorists in their bases as possible, to destroy their heavy weaponry and disrupt their supply lines before they could enter our country.

Derry MacIntyre

My Army counterpart at the JOC was Brigadier Derry MacIntyre. I had worked with Derry in 1972, when we were both assigned to the Joint Planning Staff in Salisbury. Derry was a man of action; he had served with the British Paras, was badged in the RLI and had a reputation for getting things done. He was a total team player and to his credit, would never agree to a meeting without me attending as well, whether it was a meeting for operational planning, a meeting with local officials and residents or a meeting with local farmers.

Our local farmers were having a torrid time. A lot of these farmers had bought land in the 1940's and 1950's, after WWII, and had steadily developed their farms like so many Rhodesian farmers; producing beef, dairy, maize (corn) and tobacco in significant export quantities, as well as fully supplying all local demand. They, along with their trusted local workforces, were justifiably proud of driving our country to become fully self-sufficient in daily needs. In most cases, they had nurtured their workforce over the years, providing schools, hospitals and accommodations, right on their farm. Workers and farmers grew to become teams who understood the values of productivity and mutual respect.

The terrorists recognized this stable group as a threat to their plans to disrupt the country, by attacking the infrastructure of the economy, particularly where the targets were soft targets. Farmers were always going to be soft targets; mostly isolated in unpopulated areas, along miles of dirt roads and with little defensive capability to withstand attacks from terrorist gangs armed with rockets and mortars against their undefended homes. Murders of farmers and their families became fairly commonplace. Too many of these remarkable people were murdered in their homes. These attacks were also directed at the workforces on the farms, whom the terrorists recognized as crucial to the workings of the farm. Their brutal punishments meted out to these loyal workforces were designed to intimidate the workers to the extent that they would be forced to abandon their homes and leave the area for safety. It is to their credit that so many workers defied these terrorists until finally, the farms could no longer operate.

As time went by, the remaining farms became better defended, with improved communication networks and perimeter fencing, lighting and better weapons, but they were always extremely vulnerable to attacks, usually at night from even small groups of well-armed terrorists. Even with well-organized deployments of reservists to protect these farms, their defensive firepower was inadequate against well-armed terrorist groups. Gradually, the farmers were forced off their once productive farms and the agricultural machine of Rhodesia, with its huge impact on the economy of the country, started to decline. Herds of beef were slaughtered, crops were burned, dairies were destroyed and labor forces were left with no jobs.

Farms in the outlying areas were the easiest targets and were the first to go, but the ripple effect was spreading and farmers were forced to move their families into the relative safety of the towns. They farmed as best as they could, from fortified farmhouses, approachable only along dirt roads, which were often mined. It was a precarious existence.

My family was friendly with several farmers in this area and other areas that were similarly affected. Many of them had boarded their children at schools in the cities, including those at my father`s school, Highlands, and it was tragic to see their farms deteriorate under such dire conditions. Some brave souls decided they would rather die than give up on their farms, and some were indeed attacked with overwhelming odds against them and paid the ultimate sacrifice. Many of the old farms of Rhodesia have horrific tales to tell, buried under the rubble of burnt homes, barns, cottages and offices.

Derry and I, and the local senior Police representative, would meet frequently with the local farmers, trying to optimize our limited manpower resources aimed at carrying out immediate response actions to any reported sightings, frequently resulting in contacts with those terrorist groups and often eliminating them completely. But it was not enough and the dangerous situation that the farmers faced daily became more and more desperate. Recommendations to our respective headquarters and our central command became more focused on external operations against the large holding and training camps in Mozambique and in Zambia.

Back to Thornhill. August 1977- December 1978

It seemed that my family and I had only just arrived in Umtali (actually, it was a mere four months) when I was posted back to Thornhill; this time as Officer Commanding

Flying Wing. This was certainly one of the best jobs in the Air Force, overseeing all of the squadron's flying activities, both operational and training.

One more time, Jayne and the boys and I packed our furniture and we set off for Thornhill. I was especially mindful that I was leaving this operational area where I had many connections, and I knew I would miss the close contact with the locals and activities at the FAF, but I was delighted that I would be able to contribute on a wider scale from a major Air Force base. Thornhill had been home to us before and we hoped for a longer stay this time.

Other than the Eight Forward Airfields that served as temporary staging airfields for operations throughout Rhodesia, the Air Force had two major bases; Air Force Station New Sarum (Salisbury) and Air Force Station Thornhill (Gwelo). New Sarum was home to the Transport (3), Bomber (5) and Helicopter Squadrons (7 & 8), while the Fighter/Ground Attack (1 & 2), Recce and Light Close Support (4) and the Training (6) squadrons were stationed at Thornhill.

I had served on Number 2, Number 4 and Number 6 Squadrons and I was comfortable returning to Thornhill. I had always hoped for a tour of duty on Number 1 Squadron, but this had not happened and was unlikely to happen at this stage of my flying career. However, since I oversaw all flying at the Station, I felt I should fix this gap in my knowledge and accordingly, with the co-operation of the Squadron, I was able to get a flying conversion onto this beautiful aircraft that Number 1 Squadron pilots were fortunate to fly. There were many western Air Forces around the world that were operating Hunters of various models and any Hunter pilot will tell you it was the most beautiful aircraft of its time and a true classic.

Flown by the likes of Hawker chief test pilot, Bill Bedford, it was sleek and powerful and carried a substantial weapons load, giving it a formidable capability, especially in close support ground attack operations. Interestingly, our Air Force only had FGA 9s, a single seat version, so one`s first flight in the aircraft was on your own! Prior to that, one would cover all aspects of the conversion in a simulator.

Accordingly, it was accepted policy that new pilots to this squadron were required to have significant flying experience and ability. First flight for a new pilot was always a source of entertainment, as the whole squadron would take up good vantage points to witness the customary wing wobble on take-off as the new pilot realized for the first time how sensitive the aileron controls were, compared to other aircraft.

I clearly remember my own excitement, sitting at the end of the runway, doing my power and brake checks prior to rushing down the runway and swiftly into the air, unused to quite as much power delivered from the trusty Avon engine. New solo pilots were traditionally transported to the nearby station swimming pool and unceremoniously dumped into the deep end to celebrate.

On top of its wonderful flying qualities, the Hunter was a very solid, durable aircraft, as we were to discover, on occasion, limping back to base with significant battle damage and allowing its relieved pilot to fight another day! Most pilots whom I knew said it was the happiest day of their lives when they learned they were posted to the Hunter Squadron, and the saddest day when they were posted off the Squadron to their next assignment.

Having just returned from almost two years of flying training assignments in South Africa, I had started to get some feel for the increasing operational activities in my country, from my short stint in Umtali on 'Operation Thrasher'. Those particular activities were limited to the eastern side of the country, busy enough, to say the least! However, now back at Thornhill and with responsibility to provide air support for operations over the entire country, as well as major external operations, the full extent of the accelerating conflict became apparent.

The squadrons were well managed, with excellent Squadron Commanders, Flight Commanders and engineering/technical capabilities; the result of solid, in-depth training and experience. It was always a source of great pride that our ground crews were able to consistently attain serviceability ratings in the 90% range, which was no mean feat, especially considering the difficulties we faced in obtaining spares. When we couldn`t get them, our amazing engineers usually found a way to make a working substitute!

So much for the wild claims from the British Government that our country would collapse in a matter of weeks after UDI (Unilateral Declaration of Independence). It was now 12 years since we had declared our own independence and we were pretty well self-sufficient in everything except oil! Such was the creativity and determination of the Rhodesians of that time that confounded the so-called pundits in the western world, who went about predicting the demise of the country on a daily basis. I suspect this ability to survive and prosper also infuriated the enemy terrorist organizations, given their unlimited material support from Russia and China, along with the hypocritical moral and political support from the United Nations and other world bodies.

Number 4 Squadron was fully involved on a 24/7 basis in its recce and light close support role, with aircraft on continuous deployment to the Forward Airfields, as well as other air tasks directed from Air Force Headquarters. The Squadron Commander and Flight Commanders were experienced pilots and leaders with years of operational flying under their belts. The squadron pilots were young and enthusiastic, most barely into their early twenties and keen to contribute to the defense of their country. I had the utmost respect for these young men, whose contribution to the war effort was borne out by the number of awards and decorations earned by the Squadron during the peak of the war years, up to the end of 1979.

Numbers 1 and 2 Squadrons were on a daily call-out basis, responding to air tasks from Headquarters, usually for heavy close air support with cannon, rockets and bombs.

The squadron commanders, as well as the pilots, were well versed in heavy weapons delivery and could respond to requests for support and strikes, usually in less than an hour. Suffice to say that these three Operational Squadrons at Thornhill, along with Number 5 Bomber Squadron and Numbers 7 and 8 Helicopter Close Support Squadrons at New Sarum, packed a powerful punch for our 'pocket' Air Force.

New Sarum also provided Number 3 Transport Squadron, as well as the Parachute Training School. It`s accurate to say that the operational capabilities of the Air Force were respected by friends and feared by enemies. Although Russian fighter aircraft were based in Zambia, on our northern border, and were seen from time to time, none ever dared poke their noses over our border. We always enjoyed complete air superiority, a huge advantage for our ground forces.

While we always had sufficient firepower for our internal operations, our external operations were becoming more frequent and the targets were becoming larger. These were against well-defended camps in Zambia and in Mozambique, housing anywhere between hundreds to thousands of trained and in-training terrorists. The larger camps were defended against ground attack, in conventional manner, with trenches, bunkers, heavy machine guns and rockets, and they were becoming increasingly more aware of attacks from the air.

Their Soviet and Chinese sponsors had equipped them with defensive weapons, like Strela (SAM 7) ground to air missiles and anti-aircraft (AA) guns, usually with basic visual tracking sights, although rumors had emerged of the arrival of radar laid AA weaponry, which would have caused a major problem for us. However, and to my knowledge, no evidence to confirm this was ever provided.

For external operations against large enemy camps, we augmented our strike capability from Number 2 Squadron, using their extra Vampire T11 and FB9 aircraft with any available pilots. In most cases, this was the perfect excuse for the Base Commander and the Officer Commanding Flying Wing to refresh their operational skills!

The Station Commander at Thornhill, at that time, was Group Captain F. D. (Tol) Janeke, a highly experienced officer and skilled operational pilot, having served in various operational roles from the beginning of the war. Tol had made it his duty to keep current on the Vampires, for demands just like this, and it was always encouraging, especially to the younger pilots, to see his excitement and enthusiasm as he prepared to fly on one of these missions.

Additionally, his experience was, of course, invaluable, both in the planning and execution of the attacks. I was privileged to serve as Tol`s number two at Thornhill and I learned a great deal about officer qualities, as well as flying from this dedicated senior officer. In addition to Tol`s officer qualities, he was a highly talented sportsman and I was able to enjoy practices and matches with him, as we represented our Station at various sports.

Tol's lovely wife, Anne, would join my wife to make a social tennis foursome from time to time, and we are all firm friends to this day, undeterred by a separation of 7,000 miles of continents and oceans! I was always mindful of the privilege of working alongside my direct senior officer and took care never to abuse his friendship, to the extent that after we were both retired, it took me some time to adjust to the more equal status of the relationship, much to Tol`s amusement!

I was weapons current on Vampires and I eagerly anticipated the squadron commander`s invitation to join any external operation when needed. Since it was always the squadron commander`s responsibility to plan the operation, he would decide the number of aircraft needed for the mission, fill the cockpits with his regular pilots and then offer any extra aircraft to me and the Station Commander.

While the single-seat FB9 was not popular with all pilots, because of its lack of an ejection seat, I preferred it to the T11 for its better visibility and extra firepower (4 versus 2 x 20mm cannons), as well as the more spacious cockpit. It was what I elected to fly on these missions.

Strike on Zambia

One interesting and somewhat risky mission comes to mind. We were to operate out of Fylde, a somewhat remote airfield in the northern part of the country, built with the intention of possibly positioning fighter interceptor aircraft and radar for early warning of enemy attack, and also allowing for greater operating range for targets to the north of our border. We positioned late in the afternoon, on the day before the strike, so we could take off at 7 am the next morning and strike the target, a large enemy camp in Zambia, at 7:40 am.

The Hunters had sufficient range for this target to operate from their usual base at Thornhill, and the Canberra bombers would operate out of New Sarum, for the same reason. The Hunters and Canberra would carry out a combined heavy attack, just seconds apart, and we would follow up with our attack immediately. That was the plan, anyway! I had flown enough close support operations and was always aware of the adrenaline and excitement of the mission, but for some reason, I had a strange gut feeling about this mission that I could not shake off while lying in my sleeping bag in the control tower, trying to get some sleep before our early take-off.

We were up early; our aircraft armed and fueled already by our eager and dependable ground crews. We started our engines and taxied on the orders of our squadron commander and our local Air Force Air Traffic Control. We had planned for a take-off at 7 am precisely, in order to meet our target time, and were in position at the end of the runway with two minutes to spare when we received orders to delay our take-off. With precision attacks, this throws a spanner in the works and can cause the excitement level to rise! After some 20 minutes waiting, our squadron commander decided we would need to refuel, since we had no extra reserves to allow us to complete this mission.

Our ground crews worked feverishly and within about 25 minutes, all four aircraft were refueled and we started our taxi again to the end of the runway. In the middle of the re-fueling, we had received word that the delay was cancelled and we were required on target as soon as we could make it. With no time to waste, we swung onto the runway in a 'loose formation 4' and started the roll for take-off.

Two important changes had happened. First, the ground temperature had increased by a couple of degrees, adding to our take-off roll. Since we had taxied quickly with no holding period at the end of the runway, we had more fuel than planned, which also added to our take off roll. I was in the number four slot position behind the other three aircraft, in loose formation, and was focused on maintaining my position, with eyes locked firmly on my leader but aware of the position on the others.

The take-off roll seemed interminable but I attributed this to excitement and the speed with which the mind can work when challenged. As we hit the runway overshoot area, the front three aircraft got airborne, causing a cloud of dust to be blown up by their jet exhausts, and I too lumbered off the runway, keeping low to build up some airspeed. We were on our way!

Although there was limited radio talk, I heard a terse 'Sorry' from our leader, but there was nothing else he could have done. We would now be attacking some minutes after the Canberras and Hunters, instead of immediately after their strikes, for maximum effect, and every second was vital. The rest of our route to target was uneventful and our leader was able to readily identify the main area of attack from the Hunter and Canberra strikes that had just gone in some minutes beforehand, leaving us to identify our individual targets from our photo and Special Forces ground intelligence.

We were attacking east, to west to take advantage of the early sun position, and my target was some small buildings and huts at the far perimeter of the camp. It`s never much fun being number-four on ground attack runs, because if the earlier attacks hadn`t dispersed the enemy, they would now have a pretty good idea of where you`re going to be coming from and where their weaponry should be directed. The camp was situated in a fairly narrow valley, making different attack directions difficult, although we could vary our attack directions by a small amount.

I stayed as close to the number-three aircraft as I could, allowing time for him to clear his target and avoid any ricochets from the four 20 mm cannon that I was using. Flying along the valley at high speed and low level with four cannons firing is as exhilarating as it gets. The FB9 is a small, single-seat aircraft and with the recoil from all cannons firing, it feels a bit like a bucking bronco, making gun sight control a bit more difficult. And then I was through the target, staying low to avoid giving the enemy a clean shot at me with Strela missiles or any form of anti-aircraft weapons, and looking to pick up the rest of the formation, who had already safely exited the target area.

Safely away from the camp, I turned onto the pre-determined heading for Fylde and started a gentle climb, quickly picking up the rest of the formation just ahead of me. So far, so good, but when our formation called for a fuel check, I was surprised to discover that I was not as well off for fuel as the others. Following normal practice, the number two aircraft slid under the formation and came to check my aircraft.

Sure enough, there was some damage to the fuselage and fuel drop tank from ground fire. Not too significant but enough to decide to return at a higher altitude in case the fuel situation got serious enough to necessitate a glide to reach the airfield. In any event, we all made it back safely, no one had much fuel left and my tank was practically empty.

All the Canberras and Hunters had made it home safely and the ground operation proceeded successfully, destroying what was left of the camp. As a bonus, our ground forces rescued some shell-shocked but delighted prisoners from the underground tunnels where they had been kept by ZIPRA. Despite my apprehension about this mission, it seems that someone was looking after me that day!

Safe return of all our aircraft was never a given, and in these latter stages of the war, we were to lose some of our dedicated and brave crews and precious aircraft as we came up against better trained and equipped enemies. These events saddened us, of course, but also made us even more determined to win this war and avenge our comrades.

Social Life

The yearly presentation of 'Wings Parade' and the 'Wings Ball' was always the happy highlight of the year, in times that were becoming increasingly intense as the war continued to escalate. While the full time Service men and women, such as myself, expected to operate 365 days a year, it was becoming increasingly difficult for the civilian population, who were subject to call-up for military service for periods totaling up to six months. For small farmers and small business owners, this was becoming an unbearable burden. Exemptions or deferrals were rare and farmers especially would have to move their families into towns, while they were away, for protection.

Some small businesses and farms eventually had to shut down, and as owners recognized that the situation was unlikely to improve in the foreseeable future, some even made the previously unthinkable decision to leave the country. Most of those who did leave, moved to South Africa, although others left for various corners of the world; the UK, Australia and New Zealand being the most sought after for those who had the means. For the rest, the indirect impact of the war was significant, although obviously not as drastic as for those who lost loved ones in the conflict.

The 'Wings Parade' and 'Ball' were always held at Thornhill, the home to pilot training. The Parade typified the traditions of the military, with men and women in dress uniforms, military bands, fly-pasts, and of course, the new pilots and their instructors. The weather was usually clear and I cannot remember ever having to revert to a bad weather plan. Families and friends were able to sit and enjoy the spectacle at close range and even hear the words of the reviewing dignitary; sometimes the Prime Minister, sometimes the President or some lesser dignitary, but always a much-admired figure in our country.

The most popular was undoubtedly our Prime Minister, Ian Smith, who enjoyed the respect of most Rhodesians and who loved nothing better than to mingle with Air Force pilots and technicians, given his World War II flying history. After the parade, he would visit the various Clubs (Messes) and delight everyone with his presence. Even in those days he would, on occasion, ride his bicycle a few miles from his home to his office in town with nothing more than a security officer, also on a bicycle, next to him; a far cry from the siren-screaming, gun-toting, traffic-clearing motorcades demanded by the present government.

The 'Wings Ball' was held in the Officer's Mess in the evening and was a grand and happy event, with the new pilots and their girlfriends in the limelight. The ladies wore ball gowns and the men wore full Air Force Mess dress. It was fitting that included in the list of invitees to the Ball were our senior Army and Police counterparts; signs of the respect and camaraderie that our Forces held for each other.

My rule was that the student pilots were required to introduce their lady partners to me, so that I could tell them how proud I was of these new pilots on that day. I especially wanted to meet these delightful young ladies because many of them would go on to become the wives of these young pilots and would help to provide the love and stability that was so needed during the stress of war. There is no doubt in my mind that the wives played a huge role in the emotional health of all of us, as we learned to deal with the too-frequent tragedies of combat.

It was not unusual for these balls to go on into the early hours of the morning, long after the band had stopped playing, and move to one of the nearby bars, put on some music and continue dancing until the sun came up. Some of us would head over to the nearby tennis courts where the ladies would tuck their gowns into their pants, the men would discard their mess jackets, tennis rackets would appear and the games would begin! At about this stage, those instructors who were left would call it a day, while the new young pilots, who had disappeared earlier to perform the required duties of an attentive partner, would head out for two weeks of well-earned leave.

It would be wrong not to mention the important role played by the wives at Thornhill. While some of the wives worked full-time or part-time in the nearby town of Gwelo, a lot of them were homemakers who bore the brunt of their husband being deployed, away from home frequently and for weeks at a time. As a result, firm friendships and support networks among the families grew and flourished. The children were in a stable environment, except for the occasional overflow of emotions caused by accidents or war casualties. Fortunately, and in most cases, these were relatively short-lived. For those wives and children directly affected by the loss of their husbands and fathers, there was a strong bond of continuing support and love; no substitute for a lost loved one, but comforting and reassuring nonetheless.

Like many others, I had the difficult task of visiting and notifying families and parents of the loss of our Air Force members resulting from flying accidents or war losses. I cursed the war and the enemy who were probably saying the same thing about me! The daily demands of the war were certainly made a bit easier by the strength of the community of wives and girlfriends, and I trust they know how much that helped all of us and how much we valued them all.

Flying operations continued apace on a daily basis from Thornhill, with both internal and external strikes in support of ground operations. Resources had been added in the form of Internal Affairs and Guard Force troops, freeing up our regular Army fighting troops to focus on offensive and external operations in the main. Our country suffered a lot of criticism for these external raids on the terrorist camps, but the international principle of `Hot Pursuit` was well known and widely accepted.

The criticism was hypocritical and largely for propaganda purposes by the international and liberal media. The demands on these regular professionals, including the Rhodesian Light Infantry, the Rhodesian African Rifles, the Selous Scouts, the Special Air Service, the Greys Scouts and others, grew by the day and it became obvious that our strategy had to shift from containment and eradication of the terrorists within our borders to a more aggressive strategy; to find and destroy the main holding and training camps outside our borders.

External operations were planned and conducted on an increasing basis, but with mixed success. In some notable cases, the targets had been emptied just hours before the actual strikes, leading to a great deal of suspicion about possible leaks of planning information at a high level. Internal air strikes in response to terrorist sightings and ground force requests were carried out on a daily basis, while external strikes were planned and executed more frequently than ever before. For those interested in historical detail, there is an excellent record titled 'Rhodesian Air Force Operations with Air Strike Log,' written by an extremely experienced ex-Air Force officer and my fellow 16 Pilot Training Course member – 'Prop' Geldenhuys.

Promotion and Transfer to New Sarum.

January 1979 - January 1980

It was late in 1978 that I was summoned to Air Force Headquarters and told I was to be promoted to Group Captain and would take over as Commanding Officer of Air Force Station, New Sarum, just outside Salisbury. I was happy that I would be on another operational station but realized that my flying opportunities would be limited, since I had only served on a single squadron at New Sarum during my entire Air Force career; Number 7 Squadron (Helicopters).

There would be little chance of flying helicopter operations again for me and none whatsoever on Number 5 Squadron (Bombers) or Number 3 Squadron (Transport), since I had never served on either. Sadly, it dawned on me that I had seen the last of my operational flying, but I would be on an operational Station and I was delighted.

We had decided to rent a house for six months on our move to New Sarum. Jayne found a suitable house in Chisipite, a pleasant suburb in the north of Salisbury, which was close enough for the boys to get to their school at Highlands and for Jayne to get to her work with a nearby dentist. It was a longish drive for me to get to New Sarum, but there was no traffic on the back roads, especially at the early hour that I left the house.

New Sarum was a different Air Force Station, compared to Thornhill. Whereas Thornhill provided married quarters on Station for almost all personnel, New Sarum did not, which meant that most of the married personnel lived in the suburbs in their own homes or in rented properties. The changed atmosphere struck me almost immediately. Since one lived and worked on station at Thornhill and spent most of one`s day together, there was a feeling of belonging to a large family. The various clubs were on station too, making for an easy way to socialize in the evenings if one so wished. It was new for me to see Air Force buses arriving in the morning and departing in the afternoon, carrying many of the station personnel.

Although I had served almost four years on Number 7 Squadron at New Sarum, earlier in my flying career, station life for me and others on helicopters was limited by frequent deployments away from Base, and so the change was not as on my return. Also, the duties of a Station Commander were very different to those of an Officer Commanding Flying Wing.

While my impulse was to spend time with the flying Squadrons, I had to be mindful that I had an Officer Commanding the Flying Wing already and he certainly didn`t want the Station Commander in his business all day! Consequently, it was an adjustment for me. I visited and inspected sections of our Air Force that I had never seen before, previously being focused on operational flying. There were many lessons to be learned about the excellent work carried out by these support sections, in difficult times, occasioned by years of universal sanctions.

I remember one section and, particularly, the Warrant Officer in charge. His name was Les Grace and he was a dedicated serviceman with many years of service and experience. When I asked him what he was working on at the time, he showed me an altimeter from a Hunter aircraft that was being refurbished. As I recall, Les was painting the details on the face of the instrument, by hand, and he proudly showed me a picture of the instrument from the RAF manual that he was using. I stared and stared at the instrument against the picture, and could see absolutely no difference – absolutely none

– so professional was the work that Les and his team were performing.

It was only then that I began to realize the real extent of the behind-the-scenes work that was going into the machines that I simply flew and then returned to our engineering staffs, after completing a mission. I remember feeling humbled and proud at the same time that our Air Force could continue to operate so effectively, in spite of the brash predictions from the UK Government that it would be a matter of a few weeks before we collapsed! I thanked Les and his team, just one of our many support functions that had refused to be shut down, because of sanctions, and had found ways to 'keep 'em flying!'

The squadrons on Station were heavily involved in the war, as the controversial election, sponsored by Britain and supported by the West and the U.N., drew near. The Canberras were kept busy with major external attacks on large terrorist camps, in conjunction with the Hunters and Vampires from Thornhill. One of my fellow pilot training course members and close friend, Squadron Leader Chris Dixon, led the external bombing raid into Zambia, to destroy a large terrorist camp in a much publicized raid, characterized by his `discussion` with the very surprised but capable Zambian Air Traffic Controller who had the unenviable task of keeping the airspace clear until the raid was completed!

Number 7 Squadron, along with the newly formed Number 8 Squadron, operating the newly acquired Augusta-Bell 205 helicopters, were deployed internally in close support operations on a daily basis and on external operations frequently. Number 3 Transport Squadron faced increasing demands for troop and supply movement, often into precarious and highly risky locations with little protection.

On one such external operation into Mozambique, another of my fellow pilot training course members, Flt Lt Bruce Collocott, was hit by a rocket while taking off from an enemy airfield and perished on the runway. While this was obviously not an isolated incident, it always seemed especially devastating when it was a pilot with whom I had spent years of my life together, training to protect our country. I`m sure that other pilot courses who lost some of their course members feel exactly the same, and there is no distinction when I say 'thank you' to all for your dedicated and selfless service to our Air Force and our country.

As the pace of military operations increased, so did the political activity, as efforts to resolve the Rhodesian situation ramped up. Meetings at all levels, between the British Government and our government, were an everyday matter. At one stage, in April 1979 and after successful elections in the country, the moderate Bishop Abel Muzorewa was appointed Prime Minister of a multi-racial parliament. This was unacceptable to Mugabe (ZANU) and Nkomo (ZAPU-PF) who demanded total control of the country. The British Government quickly reneged on their verbal agreement to support the result of the`79 election, the talks re-opened and the war intensified daily.

Two civilian passenger aircraft had been shot down inside the country with sophisticated ground to air missiles, causing extreme concern throughout the country but little condemnation internationally, reinforcing the belief that the propaganda machines of the extreme elements of the Mugabe and Nkomo factions were winning the day.

External raids were becoming increasingly dangerous, as the enemy numbers grew at a high rate and their equipment became increasingly sophisticated. Even with considerable help from the South African Defense Forces, in the form of manpower, aircraft and artillery, it was proving impossible to eliminate the large foreign enemy bases and our own Forces` losses were mounting at an unsustainable rate.

Ceasefire and Mugabe Victorious

More talks between the parties finally resulted in an agreement to allow a British Governor (Lord Soames) to take up residence, in late 1979, and oversee the affairs of the country with the intent of arranging a ceasefire and developing the process leading to an early general election in 1980.

Interestingly, I was directed by the Commander of the Air Force to represent the Rhodesian Forces (along with my Army counterpart) at the joint military planning talks chaired by Lord Soames and including two leaders from ZIPRA (Dumiso Dabengwa and General Lookout Masuku) and ZANLA (Generals Nhongo and Tungamirai). These talks focused mainly on planning an urgent ceasefire and the accommodation and use of the returning (now officially called 'guerilla') forces.

This was my first exposure to 'the enemy' and the atmosphere was tense, although the relationships improved over time. Although Mugabe and Nkomo had made much in public about the solid relationship between the two parties, I was struck by the distinct lack of unity between their two military arms. Dabengwa was highly intelligent and articulate and Masuku was clearly a competent military man. Little did I know that we would be imprisoned in the same prison, just a few years later, all three of us considered `enemies of the State!`

The months preceding the general election were marred by severe intimidation in the countryside, particularly where the locals were without protection and were subject to much physical abuse, especially from ZANU. Although the international monitoring force finally declared the elections `free and fair`, they certainly could not have made such a judgment if they had they been in place for several months, rather than just days. Ian Smith`s approach to sensible, shared government was crushed by the huge global propaganda machine extolling the benefits of immediate unqualified majority rule and driven by the misguided interests and power of the western world, led by Thatcher and Carter and supported by the UN.

Thanks, in no small way to the bias of the West, ZANU, under Mugabe, won the election in a landslide. Many Rhodesians, who had seen the handwriting on the wall, had already left the country to settle elsewhere; mostly to South Africa but also to the

UK, Australia and New Zealand. Those who stayed faced an uncertain future. Mugabe had been painted in a very poor light (by western world standards) and started with an extremely bad reputation amongst Rhodesians. Jayne and I had discussed our options and we had decided to stay and serve, since we reasoned that one couldn`t fix a problem by leaving, and this was, after all, the land of our birth. Personally, I believed I could play a key role in the future of the Air Force and help to provide some much-needed stability in the Defense Forces.

New Era

Almost immediately after the election and the granting of Independence to the new Zimbabwe, we were suddenly no longer a pariah! Sanctions had been lifted just before the election, offers of aid and support were pouring in and hopes for the new country were high. Two positive developments that affected my opinion directly come to mind.

First, I was put in charge of a small team of officers from all the different factions to visit the USA and study what training assistance might be useful. The trip was interesting and useful and our hosts were gracious and eager to help in any way useful. I felt we could make use of this introduction to our new country`s benefit, sooner rather than later. Disappointingly, I realized quickly that Mugabe would not be seen to align himself in any way with the super powers of America and Russia, preferring instead to work with his wartime supporters, China and North Korea.

Second, and within a couple of months, I lead a small team of purely Air Force specialists to conduct an evaluation of four different aircraft types that could be suitable to replace our aged jet trainers. This was an intense, month-long evaluation of the latest jet trainer/ground attack aircraft on offer from Britain, France, Italy and Spain. Our team comprised two experienced technical officers; Dave Haynes and Les Authers, along with two pilots; Steve Kesby and I.

We had spent a good deal of time putting together a detailed evaluation checklist, covering everything from aircraft handling and performance to engine and airframe durability and maintainability. This disciplined approach stood us in good stead, as it allowed us to make clear and substantiated distinctions between the aircraft types, based on solid data.

The British team demonstrating their Hawk aircraft was thoroughly professional and extremely capable, as expected, and the aircraft met or exceeded our evaluation requirements; both in essential as well as desirable criteria. Their test pilot team of Andy Jones and Chris Roberts were superb and were backed by one of the all-time famous test pilots, Bill Bedford. Finally, their sales and marketing support, led by Mike Mendoza, left no stone unturned, answering our endless questions and demands.

The French offering was the Dassault Alpha Jet. This may have been the most enjoyable and interesting test flying, largely because of the wonderful Dassault Chief

Test Pilot, Jean-Marie Sergay. Jean-Marie was an avid aviator and was current on all of the Dassault military aircraft line-up; a remarkable feat in itself. On the first day of our test flying, we went through some briefings that took longer than expected and Jean-Marie suggested we have lunch first.

I noticed that Jean-Marie was drinking some wine with his lunch and I assumed he had decided to postpone the flying until the next day. When I commented on this, he laughed and told me that he had been drinking wine since he was six years old and always had a glass of wine with his lunch. It`s the French way, he explained!

We did fly, putting the airplane through its paces, including a series of inverted spins! What the hell for, I wondered! Jean-Marie`s handling was superb and he included his famous air show maneuver; an outside, rolling turn through 360 degrees, which is not comfortable if you are not the one doing the flying! We did several test sorties in this aircraft and were generally impressed, but the aircraft failed to meet one of our essential criteria; 450 knots through the target with external stores.

The other two aircraft, the Spanish 101 and the Italian 339, while proving decent, pure trainers, could also not meet some of the essential close support requirements, and after a month of dedicated flight and technical testing, the Hawk emerged as the clear winner.

This exercise proved much more rewarding because the Commander of our Air Force, Air Marshal Frank Mussell, agreed with our report`s recommendations and submitted it to the government with his support and recommendation, resulting finally in the initial purchase of eight Hawk advanced trainer/ground attack aircraft, an excellent addition to start the rebuilding of our Air Force.

The early years of Zimbabwe were difficult, from the military side, as we tried to integrate the guerilla forces. The Army was the first to have to deal with thousands of new faces, from privates to Generals and with the attendant issues of training, culture and discipline, among others. It's fair to say that the Rhodesian Army was held in high regard by friends and foes alike, with experienced and capable officers and excellent training. While some of the senior guerilla officers were capable leaders with decent training, the bulk of the thousands of returning guerillas had only minimal training and seemed to lack real military discipline.

Integration into the Air Force was slower, because of the specialist flying and technical requirements. This became a particularly thorny issue as proud young aspiring pilots and technicians returned from eastern bloc countries with certificates of competence that did not meet our own most basic requirements.

Having taken up the post of Director of Operations, with the flying training branch reporting to me as well, I was concerned when I started to receive reports from our basic flying training school that the first batch of returning `pilots` were nowhere near the 'Wings' standard that their log books purported. There were 15 or so of these young men, as I remember, who had been trained to fly in Bulgaria. They all had about 200 hours flying time in their logbooks and our training staff had wisely decided to evaluate them according to our basic flying, 30-hr flight test to enable a decision as to how to proceed to integrate them into the squadrons. When it became apparent from some of our most experienced and capable instructors that they were not even at this standard, I elected to fly with them myself; not to override our instructors but because I would be better equipped to brief the Minister of Defense on the situation.

Of the 15 or so students that I flew with, only one would have passed a 30-hr test, while the rest would require a full basic flying school program. This news, of course, did not sit well with Minister Mnangagwa, who implied that I was being racist. I explained to him that some of these students would be flying him around the country one day, and I was concerned for his safety. When I offered him the opportunity to visit the training establishment and see for himself, he responded by telling me that was my job. I agreed and thanked him. Against my advice, these students were awarded their 'Wings' without sufficient further training. To this day, I have no idea what has become of these young men because not long after these events, I was arrested on false charges of treason and was unable to follow any Air Force developments from the inside of a cell.

There are many excellent books detailing the political process and events of this time, culminating in the creation of the new state of Zimbabwe, in 1980. It is not the intent of my story to accurately document or elaborate on those events, since the transition to Zimbabwe is only one aspect, albeit an important once, of this book and my story. I am not a history scholar and my story is from memory.

Air Force HQ. 1980-1982

When I was moved from New Sarum to become Director of Operations at HQ and later, Director-General of Operations and then Chief of Air Staff, one of the interesting aspects of my work was the occasional requirement to brief Robert Mugabe, who was the Prime Minister at that time. Mugabe was always interested and involved in the briefings and I developed a favorable impression of him. He was a good listener, he asked thoughtful questions and I was happy to get the chance to explain our operations and issues. He was polite, he always thanked me and I was hopeful that his interest and support would continue and allow us to further develop our capabilities. When I told my wife about my impressions, she said simply that she did not feel she could trust him (female intuition?).

Although the heavy load of daily flying operations had obviously diminished with the amalgamation of the warring factions, the antagonism between ex-ZIPRA and ex-ZANLA forces continued and the Air Force was required to intervene on occasion to support the government of the day. Whether ZIPRA's grievances were real or imagined, or whether the government was provoking such actions, is unclear. What is clear and undisputed is the genocide committed by the 5th Brigade in the Province of Matabeleland; traditional ZIPRA territory.

Estimates of those killed by the North Korean manned and trained Brigade run into the tens of thousands of civilians, including women and children. These atrocities were hushed up by the government, but rumors had been circulating about the mistreatment of the Matabele people since shortly after the election. I had received word of some of this from our young helicopter pilots who had operated in the area, and while I was Chief of Staff and Acting Air Force Commander (while the Commander was away), I decided to look more closely into the matter.

The Army Commander agreed to my request and we made a tour of some camps in Matabeleland. However, my impression was that our visit was staged and I left with no evidence to support any of the reports. It was many months later that evidence of some of these reports became generally known, but the government would take no action and effectively squashed the matter. With hindsight, this was the start of the iron fist of the ZANU Government; to crush absolutely any opposition, real or imagined. The classic one-party, police state was emerging.

As Chief of Staff, my flying opportunities were curtailed but I could still make the occasional flying visit to some of the outlying stations and airfields, although there was little activity compared to the hive-like business during the peak years of the war. The Director of Operations at this time was a very capable and experienced officer by name of Gordon Wright. Gordon was current on a light reconnaissance aircraft and he and I would lurch off to various Forward Airfields to spend time with our deployed pilots and crews, as well as our Army and Police counterparts. It was always refreshing to get away from Headquarters and its administrative load!

Due to the new Zimbabwe government`s close relationship with North Korea, it was necessary, from time to time, to attend functions with high level officials of that country. Although I was never invited to social functions, I can remember spending some hours on parades at Heroes Acre, a cemetery outside Harare for ZANLA war heroes, listening to lengthy speeches. On one occasion, I even participated in a lengthy parade there, hosted by Mugabe in honor of Kim Il-sung, then President of North Korea.

The speeches seemed to go on for hours. It was a very hot day and there were several soldiers fainting and collapsing on their weapons. Being in heavy, ceremonial uniform, I can remember at one stage the point of my sword getting stuck in the melting tar surface. Panicked, I jerked it out and vowed to not lean on my sword anymore and stuck it out until the dignitaries departed and the parade dismissed. I hoped to be out of town next time, but this never happened. Unknown to me at the time, some radical elements of the government had different plans for me.

As Chief of Staff, one of my tasks was to interview our young pilots who wished to break their contracts and leave our Air Force. Normally, pilots signed 10-year contracts to cover the cost of their training, but given the exceptional circumstances and the radical changes resulting from the election, this was not strictly enforced. This was an important task for me, because I knew we needed these new pilots to create a building block for our new Air Force, and I did my best to explain to them that they were facing a great opportunity, as well as a duty to their country.

I told them of my briefings with the Prime Minister and my hope for his continued support and fair-mindedness. I told them it was my intention to remain, hopefully to lead the Air Force in the future and to retain our Air Force as the efficient and respected force it had always been. At the same time, I did not skirt the challenges we faced, especially the sensitive one of integration, but I felt this was manageable. I am not sure how many of these young men heeded my advice or even delayed their departure, but I learned after my arrest and forced eviction from the country that most had left the country to start anew. After my treatment at the hands of government, I could not blame them!

Sometime around July 1982, the first of our new Hawk aircraft arrived; lead on the ferry flight from the UK by our Air Force Commander, Air Marshal Norman Walsh. While Norman had been out of the country, converting to the aircraft and preparing the ferry flight, I had been acting Commander of the Air Force, and I met Norman and the other pilots when they landed at New Sarum.

Our Prime Minister, Minister of Defense and others were there to welcome the arrival, with congratulations and smiles all round. It was a happy day and the culmination of the work that I and my evaluation team had started over a year ago. The remaining four Hawks on order would be ferried in a similar manner, some months later. This was just the morale building boost that our Air Force and country needed to signal that we were indeed on a sensible growth path and could look forward to similar acquisitions in the future.

Shocking News

In August, still with the euphoria of the new Hawks so evident and with the Air Force Commander back in office, I took a vacation to spend time in Malawi with my father-in-law, and then some time at Inyanga, in the eastern mountains, where my father had developed a small fruit farm while he was still alive. Trout fishing was always fun in this beautiful region and we enjoyed a few days with friends from the American Embassy; Peter and Siobhan Shields. Early one evening, I received a call from our Air Force HQ and was told by our Director of Operations that a serious incident had occurred at Thornhill and that I should contact the Air Force Commander. I did this but was not able to get much detail, except that some of our aircraft had been damaged or destroyed in what appeared to have been a military attack on the airfield.

I was shocked! We were not at war with anyone and we posed no threat to anyone while we rebuilt our country`s forces. I cancelled the rest of my vacation and headed back to Salisbury, where I met the Commander. Norman was grim-faced and the seriousness of the situation started to dawn on me. An unknown enemy had slipped past the Station defenses in the dark of night and had gained access to the aircraft hangars. They had planted explosives in selected aircraft (Hunters and Hawks) and then made good their escape. The explosives had been detonated by timing devices, some time later, and had damaged and/or destroyed 6 Hunters and the 4 new Hawks; a devastating blow to our Air Force and country.

A Board of Inquiry had been formed immediately, staffed by experienced and capable officers, and was already on site at Thornhill. The Commander himself had made a visit to the Station immediately and was aghast at the damage. He readily agreed that I should visit the Station urgently, to see the damage for myself, but particularly to talk to all the airmen who had tried so bravely to rescue the aircraft, under very dangerous conditions, and to help restore their morale, which was under severe stress from ZANU political elements, who were already blaming Air Force members for sabotage.

It seemed that elements of the Army had been ordered onto the Station, ostensibly to defend against any further attack, but were using their presence to harass Air Force members and their families in the married quarters. By all accounts, the situation was unpleasant and tense, with tempers at the boiling point.

When I arrived at Thornhill, I was met by the Station Commander, Group Captain Dag Jones, an exceptional pilot and solid officer. He explained to me that most of the airmen and women who were not on essential duties were assembled in one of the undamaged hangars, ready for me to say a few words. I was unprepared for such an audience but I spoke from my heart, sharing their shock and grief at the damage and loss. I spoke for some 10 or 15 minutes only and ended by saying we had been through tough times before and would likely do so again, but that we always overcame the odds and we would do so this time too. I thanked them and asked them to return to their duties and continue their good work.

I did not spend much time looking at the damaged and destroyed aircraft, other than to get a feel for the damage inflicted. It is difficult to explain how an airman, who has spent most of his adult life flying and loving aircraft, feels over such carnage, but I got into the CO`s car with a heavy heart.

Dag had invited me to have lunch at his home on married quarters. As we drove the mile or so to his home, I was struck by the situation and the atmosphere on the base. Everywhere I looked it seemed there were ZANLA troops, reportedly some from the infamous 5th brigade. They did not look like professional soldiers to me and when we stopped at the guard gate to enter the married quarters, I was soon to find out.

Two scruffy soldiers toting AK rifles stood in front of the official Air Force car and leveled their weapons at us through the windshield.

"Get out!" they ordered Dag. "We will inspect the car."

This was ridiculous, I thought! Here we were, in the Station Commander`s official car, still on our Air Force base, and we were being harassed by some unidentifiable troops. When they opened the trunk and discovered Dag`s parachute, things heated up. I got out of the car, planning to settle things down, but the sight of me in my Air Vice Marshal (Major General) uniform seemed to infuriate them more. As I looked into their wild eyes, the thought struck me that they were perhaps on drugs, so irrational and undisciplined was their behavior, and I became alarmed.

Were the rifles that they waved about so carelessly actually loaded? There were no Air Force guards in sight and it became apparent that the ZANU troops were occupying the base in numbers. I tried to explain to them that the Station Commander carried a parachute in his car at all times to facilitate any urgent flight he might have to make. They sneered and then, still waving their rifles in our direction, told us to get back in the car and leave.

I was shaking with anger but glad that we had both kept cool enough to avoid getting shot. As we drove, Dag said that this behavior had been going on for a couple of days, especially harassing the wives and families entering and leaving the base, and that these troops had arrived within hours of the attack on the base. I decided to call the Air Force Commander at HQ and briefed him on the ugly situation. I requested he call the Army Commander right away and the Minister of Defense, if necessary, to remove these troops from the base before a serious altercation ensued. The Commander listened carefully and told me he would do that immediately.

I was somewhat relieved but saw no change in the situation when the Commanding Officer drove me back to the Flying Wing. Here I was to discover that all flights from the base had been forbidden, by order of the Minister of Home Affairs, of all people! This minister, by the name of Herbert Ushewokunze, was known as a volatile hothead and what we were witnessing seemed to be an internal power grab over the much more predictable, sensible and level-headed Minister of Defense.

As the afternoon wore on, there was word that a helicopter was needed to position at New Sarum and I decided to fly back in this manner. Flying back alongside the young pilot, a previous student of mine I seemed to remember, I felt some sanity returning to my mind, but I was still seething about the overreach of the Army, the Minister of Home Affairs and the intolerable situation for all Air Force people on their own base.

I got home and called the Air Force Commander and briefed him on the deteriorating situation at Thornhill. He explained that he had spent most of the rest of the day, after my earlier call, trying to resolve the situation with his counterpart, but could get no assurance that anything concrete would be done. The interference by the Minister of Home Affairs and the deployment of ZANU troops to the base signaled an ominous development at high levels of government. Since my earliest pilot training days in our Air Force, I had always held Norman Walsh in the highest regard, and now that he was our Air Force Commander, I thought to myself that if Norman can`t fix this, then I`m afraid our Air Force, as we knew it, was doomed.

The next few days at Air Force HQ were tumultuous. The situation at Thornhill was out of control, with the Central Intelligence Office (CIO) sending their agents onto the base, arresting Air Force members and taking them away for interrogation, with no notification to anyone, including their families. Sometimes these airmen were released in hours, sometimes in days and sometimes not at all, and they all had harrowing tales to tell of their treatment.

Dag Jones himself was arrested but was released in a short timeframe. The Air Force Commander worked tirelessly at his level to inject some sensibility to the whole mess and to get some understanding of the reasons that all fingers of government were now directed at the very Air Force that had protected them through the early years of independence.

White airmen and officers were the only targets of the CIO, it seemed, and the plot thickened when all white agents of the CIO and CID were removed from the interrogations, arrests and investigations and replaced by an all-black team of junior and inexperienced agents.

The official Board of Inquiry, headed by Air Commodore Phil Pile, found its work more and more difficult as the disruption on station increased, with no one knowing what the Army would do next or whom the CIO would arrest. Those Air Force members who had decided to stay and give the new government a chance, now had their minds firmly made up for them and an exodus of talent and experience started.

PART THREE

The Nightmare Years

Arrests Begin

THE SITUATION WORSENED *when the CIO started to arrest some of the members from the Security Section, whom the Board had questioned and then, astonishingly, some of the Board themselves. Among the many arrests made by the CIO and their agents were the Officer Commanding the Security Section on the Station, an excellent man by the name of Johnson Ncube. He was one of the first black African Squadron Leaders in our Air Force and he headed up a large unit that included security and fire-fighting staff. He was badly beaten up by the CIO interrogation team and released, totally intimidated by the ex-enemy faction within the CIO, and threatened with similar treatment if he refused to appear as a State witness, against whomever the CIO decided to accuse of being responsible for the attack.*

Also arrested were the Station Security Officer, Air Lt Barry Lloyd and Air Lt Nigel Lewis–Walker, a station defense specialist. Lewis-Walker was detained for some 18 months at a detention camp north of Thornhill and was never charged with an offence. Lloyd was arrested, beaten up, released, then rearrested and vanished from sight for some days while the interrogation team worked on him. He then `disappeared` again. It soon became apparent that the interrogation pattern of torturing a victim into incriminating others never produced the truth, but did produce some opportunity targets for the CIO to pursue in their desperate efforts to produce culprits for their new political masters.

Within a few days, the CIO picked up Wing Commander John Cox and `disappeared' him too. John was the senior Security officer at Air Force Headquarters, with overall responsibility for all security, including the large General Service Unit. He was a career officer who had also decided to work with the new government. Almost immediately after that, the CIO picked up Wing Commander Peter Briscoe, the senior Staff Officer Training at Air Force Headquarters and a senior member of the Board of Inquiry investigating the Thornhill attack.

All efforts by the Commander to establish the grounds for their arrests and their whereabouts lead to nothing. The Police Commander and the head of the CIO refused to respond to any questions about the whereabouts of these officers, and the Commander of the Air Force could get no support whatsoever from the Minister of Defense or the Prime Minister. It was becoming clear that this witch hunt was supported or even driven by the highest levels of government.

While one reads of citizens of lawless nations having simply `disappeared,` it is almost beyond belief that senior serving officers in a supposedly civilized country could simply `disappear` with no trace with no normal channels to locate them. Lawyers were hired, but they too were given confusing and erroneous information until finally, they insisted that the Court issue writs of *habeas corpus*, but by then, it was too late. Lloyd and Cox had been tortured into submitting false statements, incriminating themselves and others, and were imprisoned. The pattern of interrogation to produce more alleged culprits continued.

Next on the list to be picked up by the CIO and immediately `disappeared` was Wing Commander Peter Briscoe, the Staff Officer Training at Air Force HQ and a member of the official Board of Inquiry into the Thornhill attack. Peter was a close friend of mine, we had flown many missions together and I would have trusted him with my life. He too had elected to stay and serve our country under the new government, and I was grateful for his decision. Our country needed more good people like him if we were to succeed in retaining a viable and efficient Air Force.

As with the others arrested, the Commander could ascertain nothing from the CIO or high-level government officials as to Peter's whereabouts or any reasons for his arrest. I knew Peter`s family well and I was particularly angry and frustrated that we could do nothing to bring any clarity to the situation.

Some days later, I was asked to meet with some CIO agents at Air Force HQ and answer some questions. It seemed they had already spoken with Air Commodore Phil Pile and searched his office too. Normally, I would have had no reason to be concerned, but given the recent behavior of the CIO, I wondered exactly what they wanted. I came in civilian clothes from home, since I was finishing the last couple of days of my vacation, and met them in my office.

They asked if they could search my office and started a cursory look around. When I asked what they were looking for, they did not answer but said they would like to come home with me and search the property. Somewhat irritated now, I suggested that if they told me what they were looking for, I could probably help save time. This suggestion fell on deaf ears and for the next hour or so, they searched my home and garden but found nothing that they considered useful in their quest. I became even more irritated and now a bit concerned when they said I should come with them to CIO headquarters in town.

Fortunately, Jayne was just turning into our drive on her return from work and I could tell her as confidently as I could that I was going for some questioning and would be back soon. Little did I know that in fact, I would never see my home again and I would not see my sons for another 13 months! The Chief of Air Staff was about to go from a respected Operational General to a 'treasonous criminal' in less than an hour! The situation was farcical, but this was no farce. The nightmare was just beginning.

My Arrest: August 1982

"You will talk!" he shouted. "If you don`t talk to me now, I will give you to some people who are not nice. And they will do things to you that are not nice. And you will talk! I promise you, you will talk!"

The man was almost maniacal. He was an agent of the CIO, or as he preferred to be called 'Secret Police,' sitting alongside two other agents behind a desk. I was the subject of his anger, shackled in front of him. I was exhausted after days of questioning, with little sleep, food or even water. I had explained my position so many times to so many unknown people; that I was Chief of Staff of the Air Force, that I had no previous knowledge of the attack on Thornhill, that I was not authorized to confer with the Board of Inquiry because I would be required to review the Board on its completion and pass it on to the Commander and Minister of Defense for subsequent action.

"Lies, lies – all bullshit," he went on. "Take him away and give him to 5 Brigade."

I was removed from the brightly-lit room, pushed into a dark cell and the door slammed behind me. I tried to gather what strength I had left and clear my thoughts about what had happened to me since my arrest in Harare (previously Salisbury) at the end of the month. The sequence of events slowly came to mind.

After taking me from my home late that afternoon to CIO headquarters, I found myself sitting in the car with one of the agents, while the others went inside. After waiting some time, another agent arrived and announced we were going somewhere else. This did nothing to make me feel more comfortable, and we drove off, through town and headed south to a small police station, where we got out and went inside.

When I asked what was happening, they told me I was to be checked in for the night and they would fetch me in the morning. This was obviously not what I was expecting and I said so, but to no avail. I had my details taken, my belt and shoes removed, as well as my watch and wallet. I was still dressed in a thin cotton, short-sleeved shirt, with lightweight slacks and no jacket, which I had left at home. I found myself in a concrete cell with some others. I had no means of communication and decided that I could only try to resolve this in the morning, and was left wishing there was some way to let Jayne know what was happening.

I watched as the others settled in for the night, some propping themselves against the walls, and others lying flat on the concrete floor. I soon became uncomfortable and although it was chilly, I opted to remove my thin shirt and make a pillow, as I tried to stretch out. It was an uncomfortable and long night and when the light dawned, and some hours later, the police opened the cell and beckoned me, I was relieved. Now, let's get on with whatever questions you have and take me home, I thought. But it was not to be. I was bundled into a car with the same CIO agents and we drove off, in a southerly direction, away from the city.

As we drove further and further south from the city, I recognized some landmarks, including the little town of Enkeldoorn, about 90 miles from Harare. If one kept driving further south, one would end up in Gwelo and Thornhill. I assumed this was our destination, but since no one would respond to my questions, I had no option but to wait and see. It was becoming increasingly evident that this was not going to be a co-operative or friendly investigation.

Later in the afternoon, we arrived at the little village of Umvuma, which I recognized by the tall chimney stack from an old mine. This village was about 30 miles from Gwelo, and I assumed we were still headed to Thornhill. Eventually we arrived in Gwelo and stopped in front of the Police station where I was told to get out. The CIO agents took me into the main office and proceeded to have me checked into a cell; removal of shoes, belt, watch, wallet, leaving me in my same shirt and slacks as before.

None of this made any sense to me, but my protests were to no avail. I thought at least I could make a call to my wife to let her know I was alive, but my request was denied and I found myself alone in a cell, this time with a plank on the floor as a bed. This was to be my home for the next ten days or so.

My repeated requests to speak to a senior officer got no acknowledgement, and I then started asking to call a lawyer, since it seemed everything was loaded against me. This too proved futile. I had not been allowed to wash or change clothes since I was picked up and there was little useful food. I discovered much later that there was much activity from Jayne and the Air Force Commander about my complete disappearance, with Jayne even taking clothes and washing items to the CIO in Harare, who said they would make sure I got them right away!

Thankfully, on the second day of my disappearance, Jayne saw through this charade, and arranged a lawyer in Harare, an excellent man by name of Mike Hartmann, who immediately started the process of trying to establish my whereabouts and the reason for my apparent arrest. He was soon to learn that this was no normal legal process, and he was bounced from the CIO to the Police and back almost daily as the government agencies continued their interrogation tactics of torturing their chosen culprits into incriminating themselves and others, as they wove their absurd trail of blaming the white elements of the Air Force for the attack at Thornhill.

Each day my pants got looser, my beard got longer and I had started looking for old matchsticks in the courtyard, with which to attempt to clean my teeth. There was a shower, of sorts, in the one corner of the courtyard and while I was allowed out of my cell, I would vainly stand in the cold water and try to clean myself; difficult without soap of any kind.

My daily requests fell on deaf ears and at some stage, I was handed a detention order and asked for a statement about my alleged involvement in the Thornhill attack and my activities in the sabotage.

I was stunned. Why would any sane person believe that the Chief of Staff would blow up his own Air Force? But I did write a statement outlining my duties as Chief of Staff of the Air Force, along with my ideas as to how to keep our Air Force running as an effective fighting force for our country. I handed it to the police for collection by the

CIO and was naïve enough to think that would clear matters up and I would be released.

I had no idea of what was going on outside of my cell and the courtyard. I was the sole prisoner, with no papers, no radio and no visitors. It was only later that I found out no one knew where I was and no one could find me. The days and nights dragged and many thoughts ran through my mind. How was my family? Were they safe? What was happening in the Air Force? Had the Board of Inquiry been allowed to complete its investigation? I knew that I was getting physically weaker from a lack of food and a surplus of anxiety, and I kept wondering why the CIO did not release me, or at least question me.

I seem to remember that on the night of my 10th or 11th day in this cell, I was suddenly woken by a policeman in a state of great agitation and taken to the main office, where three obvious agents of the CIO (Secret Police) had the Police check me out and hand me my belt, watch, wallet and shoes. It was always interesting to me that the regular police were so fearful of the CIO, indicative of the absolute authority and lack of accountability that this agency enjoyed. I had no sooner got dressed than one of the agents got behind me and pulled a heavy hood over my head, while the others held my arms. I resisted the natural impulse to panic and forced myself to breathe slowly. That helped and I realized that I was not going to suffocate. I was put into a car and we drove off.

One of the agents in the car spent most of the drive shouting, threatening and cursing at me for not cooperating with the secret police. My attempts to talk through the hood and explain that I had already written a detailed statement, denying any knowledge or involvement in the sabotage, infuriated him even more, so I gave up and could only listen to his rants and threats that he would hand me over to 5 Brigade to loosen me up.

I could scarcely believe my ears; 5 Brigade had a ghastly reputation for atrocities and were known for their tactics of intimidation and violence with no apparent accountability. After perhaps an hour, the car stopped and the chief interrogator got out. Almost immediately, I heard him shouting again. "Is this Briscoe?" Then I thought I heard Pete`s voice, which I knew well. I could not see anything, but I guessed they could not have been more than a few yards from me. I heard another car door open and the shouting started again.

"Get in that car! I`m taking you to 5 Brigade! They will make you talk, you will see!"

I was shaken. It had certainly sounded like Pete, but what was he doing here? And where were we? And where were they taking him? These and many other questions raced through my mind, and my unease grew. Soon I was removed from the car and taken inside, but my hood was not removed. My shoes, belt, watch and wallet were taken and I was lead outside and pushed into a cell, while simultaneously the hood was tugged off my head and the door slammed shut before I could see anyone.

The cell was dark but there was enough light from a high window to see a plank bed on the floor. As I sat down, I saw some sweets on the bed and it struck me that indeed Pete had been here, just now and in this very same cell. It was becoming clearer to me now that this was a deliberate attempt by the government and the CIO to frame the white senior officers of the Air Force, but to what end?

Since no one had been able to find me in the last ten days, and having just been moved again, I had less and less confidence that I would be released any time soon. I sat on the bed, increasingly aware of my baggy pants, filthy shirt and beard and feeling more and more concerned for the safety of my family. Unbeknown to me, Jayne was in full action mode, as was the Air Force Commander and the lawyer that Jayne had engaged, Mike Hartmann.

The police and the CIO had made it impossible for Mike to find me and even the lower courts had deliberately delayed matters. It was only when Mike decided to submit an urgent writ of *habeas corpus* that the court agreed to hear the motion within days. As it turns out, this further delay was what effectively sealed my fate.

The next morning, I was taken into the office of the police station to be confronted by more agents of the secret police, who demanded that I give them a statement. I asked them what had become of my previous statement and was told I was wasting their time, that I needed to co-operate or things would get very difficult for me. I decided to ask at this police station for a lawyer, but this was brushed aside with the remark that I did not need a lawyer and besides, they were very expensive!

After more threats, I was given a notepad and pen and taken to my cell to write another statement. I spent the rest of the day writing a similar statement to my previous one, but added some detail about my Air Force career, my service to the country and my decision to work with the new government and keep the Air Force as the efficient fighting force it had always been. Later that afternoon, a policeman came and collected my statement and I felt surely they must realize when they read this that they are wrong to accuse me and would realize that I was in no way involved.

It was difficult to sleep. I was cold and suffering from spells of shivering caused by something unknown. Anxiety? Fear? Sickness? The night passed very slowly until I was fetched from my cell the next morning to be confronted by the usual team of CIO agents.

The shouting started immediately; "Your statement is bullshit. All lies. Why don`t you tell us the truth? Why don`t you co-operate?"

I held my ground. "My statement is absolutely true and I will not change anything just to suit you."

"We have statements, written by your own Air Force officers, who state that you were involved in the attack. You will see!" he continued ominously. I was flabbergasted by this last shot. What on earth could they be talking about? I had never thought there was any Air Force involvement at all.

"I don't believe you," I said. "I'm sure that there is no Air Force involvement in the attack."

One of the agents pulled some papers out of his case, scanned over them and then passed two pages of typed notes and told me to read them. My blood started to boil as I did so. Here in writing was an incriminating statement from Wing Commander John Cox, where he gave some details of the attack, including his (alleged) role and naming others, including myself as the mastermind of the attack, and even threatening his family if he did not co-operate!

I looked at the signature at the bottom of the statement. It certainly read 'J. Cox' but was this real? Or forged? Or fake? Or even forced somehow? I had not done a lot of direct work with John, but I knew him as a solid and dependable officer of high standards. I could not begin to imagine his involvement in the attack.

"Well?" sneered the agent. "Now we want the truth from you."

"I don't believe that is a genuine statement." I said, "Cox would not be involved in such an action."

"Cox's statement has been confirmed by a magistrate already. Show him!"

Sure enough, I was handed an official-looking document, signed by some local magistrate that the statement was true, and freely and voluntarily given.

"We have other statements too!" he yelled, "They all say it was you! Show him!" he directed.

I did not know what to expect at that stage, but what they showed me was the biggest shock that I could ever imagine. Here was a statement, very similar to John Cox's statement, incriminating the author and naming me and others as being directly involved, but this time, it was signed by Peter Briscoe! I looked at the signature closely. I knew Peter's signature from flight authorizations and administrative matters over the years and I could tell that it was his signature.

I was floored completely. Peter and I had served on many operations together over some 12 or 13 years, and I had the highest respect for his service. He was one of the most loyal and dependable officers I had known and I would trust him with my life. What had caused Pete to write such utter lies? My mind went back to the other evening when I heard Pete being put into a car to be taken to 5 Brigade. Is that what had happened? Had Pete and the others been tortured so badly that false statements were the only way to get the torture to stop and to have a fighting chance to appear in a proper court to tell their stories?

Shocked to the core, I still held my ground. "I was not involved and I knew nothing of this attack. Why would I be involved in destroying my own aircraft?"

The senior agent told the police to put me back in my cell and he told me, "We are fetching a very senior man to talk to you. You had better tell him the truth."

'Good!' I thought. 'Perhaps I`ll get someone with some common sense who will understand what a charade this all is!'

I was taken out of my cell in the afternoon and back into the police office where the senior officer awaited. I attempted to be professional, and asked his name. He ignored my question and immediately began the same line of questioning and threats. I told him that I had already written two truthful and comprehensive statements about my Air Force activities, but that I knew nothing about the Thornhill attack and was not involved, and never would have been involved. I told him that I didn`t believe the statements that I had been shown. I said that they were not truthful and that they must have been coerced.

This drew a very angry reaction. He glowered at me and left the room abruptly with one of the others. There was an immediate hardening of the atmosphere in the room, with the CIO agents strangely silent. After a while, the senior officer drove off and the agent returned telling the Police to fetch my possessions.

"Hurry up!" he directed. "We have a long way to go."

We were soon on the road. I was put in the back of the car between two agents and shackled, but not hooded. The atmosphere was tense as the driver sped along, with constant references to time. All of a sudden, things were happening.

We headed north – much easier to figure out when you don`t have a hood over your head! There was no conversation, no more questions directed at me and I had time to reflect on my situation. I had not shaved or really washed in some 12 days. I had eaten very little, the odd mouthful of *sadza* (maize-porridge) and had not much water to drink. I was aware that my clothes were filthy and my slacks even baggier than the day before. I know I was weakened by the lack of sleep and the stress, but I was determined not to give them the satisfaction of thinking they had won this absurd charade of trumped up charges against me and the others.

We passed through Enkeldoorn and pressed on to Harare and refueled. Where the hell were we headed? We drove north out of Harare, straight past the turn off to my mother`s home and I was glad that they seemed unaware of this, although they had told me earlier in a veiled threat that they knew where my family lived.

After driving for some more time, and just as it was getting dark, they pulled over to the side of the road and suddenly grabbed me and again, pulled a heavy hood over my head and face. And then they pulled another one over the top of the one which was already covering my head. Resisting the urge to panic and suffocate, I forced myself to calm down and to breathe in very shallow breaths. I wondered to myself how long this could go on.

As we started to drive, the threats started again.

"We are going to disappear you – do you remember what happened to Sithole? You will never be found, unless you write a fully cooperative statement soon."

The reference to Sithole was chilling. He was a well-known black nationalist who simply disappeared while in custody, never to be seen again.

"God," I thought, "don't they ever stop?"

I decided not to respond, not wanting further outbursts and threats. My situation was tenuous, at best, handcuffed and hooded in a car with secret police agents, not knowing where we were going and pretty sure that neither my family nor my lawyer or the Air Force Commander knew my whereabouts.

After an hour or so, we stopped and I was taken from the car and put inside some sort of building. My shoes and wallet and watch were removed, but not the hoods, and I was unshackled. I was led by my arm outside and pushed through a doorway and at the same time, had the hoods yanked off my head as the cell door slammed behind me before I could see who had lead me there. I was in a dark cell but after a while, when my eyes adjusted, I could make out that it was a standard police cell. I sat on the floor, shivering and wondering what had made the other Air Force officers write their false statements and why things were moving so quickly now.

Unbeknown to me at this time, my lawyer `s application for *habeas corpus* had been granted by the Court. But it was all too late. Lloyd`s and Cox`s statements had already been confirmed by magistrates in different parts of the country and their lawyers were only now becoming aware of their harrowing stories. My lawyer got word of this and went so far as to notify the Court that if any magistrate at any court confirmed any statement that I might make without my lawyer`s presence, the statement would be considered invalid. But, try as he might, he was unable to break through the deliberately unlawful actions of the CIO and their agents who had continued to move us around the country separately, while continuing the process of torturing junior officers to incriminate themselves and other officers, and then moving up the command chain until they had their prize. I was the last in this chain, since by this time the others had already been tortured until they had given their statements of guilt.

So, here I was at some unknown location in the African bush at the complete mercy of these CIO agents, and neither my lawyer, my family nor the Commander of the Air Force could even get close to discovering my whereabouts and the CIO was running out of time to get their `prize` to sign a false and incriminating statement.

Torture in the night

I did not have to wait much longer. The cell door was flung open and two unknown men took me into a nearby building where we waited in a brightly lit office. It was not long before a couple of CIO agents arrived. They sat across a table from me and the bigger of the two started very gently by asking if I could perhaps help them with their investigations into the Thornhill attack. My spirits lifted. Could it be that there was a sensible agent among them who was actually interested in the truth? I said that I had been trying to help by giving truthful statements already to the CIO, whereupon the short and heavy-set agent launched into his tirade.

"All bullshit! We know you did it. Just admit it - tell the truth!" he shouted.

I got angry again, angry at the stupidity of it all and the refusal to believe anything except what they wanted to believe. I asked if they had read my statements and got the reply,

"We don't read bullshit like that! Now tell us the truth."

The session became more and more heated and the agent became more furious.

"I will give you one last chance or I will hand you over to 5 Brigade. They will make you talk. They will do things to you that are not nice and they will make you talk!"

But I was not prepared to cave to their demands and I said so, still wondering what had happened to the others to make them write their so-called statements. The highly agitated and vociferous agent began shouting again, and it suddenly dawned on me that this was the same voice I had heard yelling at Pete outside the cell in Umvuma, the same voice that said they were taking Pete to the 5th Brigade.

"We are leaving now," he shouted. "Take him to 5 Brigade. When you have had enough, tell them you will give a statement, and they may stop."

With that, I was put back in my cell. Things were getting bleaker for me, but I still wondered if this was some elaborate hoax to get me to confess to acts I had not committed. After a short while, I was led from my cell, a heavy hood was dragged over my head, my wrists were shackled and I was bustled into a vehicle.

"Take him to Inyanga now - to 5 Brigade!" I heard.

It was well known that the 5th Brigade was headquartered near Inyanga, a small village in the eastern area of the country. If that's where we were going, it would be a long drive. After a while, we turned off the main road and onto a bumpy dirt road for some more time. Finally, the vehicle came to a stop. I was pulled from the vehicle, my handcuffs were removed while someone bound my wrists with layers of soft cloth and the handcuffs were replaced with my hands now behind my back. Then I was forced face down onto the seat of the vehicle and someone sat on my back so I could not move.

"Bring my pistol and the axe. You will find that 5 Brigade knows how to make people talk!"

Now I was getting really alarmed. My bare feet were hanging out of the vehicle. What if they were simply to chop them off? What if I was to be shot while trying to escape? Next, I felt my shirt being lifted and a couple of sharp pricks as if needles were being inserted at the top and bottom of my spine.

"Now tell us what you know about the Thornhill attack - tell us everything, or we will kill you right now."

"I was not involved in the Thornhill attack," I started, but could get no further as my back arched in sudden spasms. The feeling was as if hot fish hooks were tearing my back muscles apart and it was all I could do to stay conscious. After a while, the electric current was reduced, and I could hear the questions again.

"Why don`t you talk? We can disappear you. No one will ever know what became of you. We can disappear your family."

I now realized this was no elaborate hoax. Their threats were quite credible and I found it especially chilling that they had introduced my family into the situation. I lay still, trying not to suffocate under the heavy hoods and wondering how long I could last this treatment. Suddenly and without warning, the current was reapplied, and again the spasms started. Again and again, my back arched until it felt it would snap, saved only by the heavy body already on top of my legs. The shouting started again: "Come on, you white bastard! Tell us now! Tell us all you know!"

My breathing was becoming more and more difficult and I felt sweat running over my face. Each time it seemed I would be at the point of passing out, the current was reduced for some seconds, and then as I got control of my breathing, it would start again.

"Just answer some questions and we will let you go. We will take you to your family."

So the questions started again. Initially, simple questions that had already been answered in the others statements. I was not sure of some of the previous answers and so every time that I gave the 'wrong' answer, the current would be increased for a while until I could guess what they wanted. It was now obvious to me that when I had decided to call their bluff, it was not a bluff and they were making good on their threats.

Amongst the brief pauses, I rationalized that if I were to survive this treatment, I should concoct a statement that would mimic what the others had said and it might get me a chance to challenge the untruths in a proper court of law. But some of the questions, even if the answers were in the other statements, escaped me, and the whole process would start again.

Utterly bewildered, awaiting another session, I told them I would give them a statement, thinking this would end matters, and if I was fortunate, I could appear in a court of law and hopefully my family would be safe. But they wanted more, and every time I skipped a point that they wanted me to make, the current and the spasms would start again. Sometimes, it would take several guesses to find out what they wanted me to say, and each time I would be prompted by the current and spasms. Finally, after what seemed a very long time, but was probably only an hour or two, they seemed satisfied.

"Now you will write a good statement. Do not change anything. Do you understand?"

I felt drained and could barely bring myself to speak.

"Do you understand? Say 'yes'!" he shouted.

"Yes," I said as best as I could, still under the heavy hoods, and sweating and breathing with much difficulty at this stage.

"Good," he said, "now we can go."

I felt the person who had been sitting on my legs get off and my legs were swung back into the vehicle. The engine was started and we began to drive away. Suddenly, I was cold and shivering uncontrollably. Then something happened that I will never forget. The person sitting next to me held my arm and gave a gentle squeeze of reassurance and perhaps sympathy. I`ve sometimes wondered about that person and have concluded that it was probably a local police officer who still had some sense of decency, and did not like the brutal and counter-productive behavior of the special agents. Whoever you are, and wherever you may be, thank you.

But I was far from out of the woods and my situation was no better than when we had started. Not only had I falsely incriminated myself and confirmed the others` lies, I still had no idea where I was and certainly had no guarantee that I would be allowed to live after writing their precious statement.

The journey back seemed to pass quickly and after the vehicle stopped, I was lead into a room and my hood removed. Inside the room were the same two men whom I had seen a couple of hours before, and in particular, the heavy set one who had been so agitated.

"Now they tell me that you are ready to write a good statement. Here, write on this."

His tone was less belligerent, but far from pleasant.

I hesitated for only a minute. While I could possibly endure more torture, if it would change their minds, that now seemed a forlorn hope. I had taken what I had hoped, in my own way, was a test to see whether they were bluffing. They were not. They had cleverly tortured the others, one by one, and then used those false statements to incriminate the rest, and especially me.

Unbeknown to me at this time, was the fact that Barry Lloyd, under torture, had never mentioned my name at all. Instead and when he could stand no more, he had concocted a story that Air Vice Marshal Len Pink, the previous Chief of Staff of the Air Force, had been the chief organizer of the attack. Barry knew that Len had recently retired and had left the country and would therefore be safe. So, when the CIO agents discovered that Len Pink was no longer in the country, they simply decided, in their best Sherlock Holmes manner, that they would move on to the next Chief of Staff; me!

What was of most concern to me was their reference to my family. By this time, I had begun to realize that they would stop at nothing to get the statements they wanted, and I was not prepared to put my family in this danger. So, I started writing, trying to remember what the others had said and what they had tortured me to say. After I had finished and handed them the so-called statement, they seemed pleased and demanded that I sign it.

At this stage, the only thing I could think of doing to negate the statement was to somehow change my signature. I would have to do this subtly so as not to draw attention to it, but in a way that I hoped I could show in court that it was not my usual signature. So, I put a small cross over the two `t`s in my signature, hoping that no one would question it while hoping I would get a chance to show an honest court the difference.

As it happened, no one questioned the difference and they departed in a happy mood.

I, on the other hand was devastated. The enormity of the statement I had just signed was enough to have me executed, if they even allowed me to get that far in a court. The Air Force life that I loved was gone. I was not even sure that my life was safe any longer and perhaps now that they had the statement they wanted, they would simply shoot me and claim I was trying to escape. I was, however, hopeful that my family would be safe and left alone.

I was lead back to my cell and left alone with my thoughts and all the implications of the last few hours to haunt me. If I`d had a way to end my life, I might well have done it there and then. As the night wore on, a degree of rationality returned to my thinking.

"Fuck them and their lies and torture!" I thought. "I`m not about to be falsely accused by a bunch of thugs, and I must hang on! I must wait it out and try and make sure that I get to a proper court of law where I can tell my side of the story!"

When they opened my cell the next morning, this time with an egg and bread and tea, I felt an inner strength and ready to go on again, but at the right time. I had no appetite, although I had barely eaten a mouthful in two weeks. I was physically a wreck but now I was mentally strong again. I was allowed to stay outside my cell, behind a fence from where I could see a railroad on the other side, until the Police called me and gave me my belongings.

The same CIO agents arrived soon and took me to a small country court where they told me that I was to confirm my statement to a local magistrate. They pointed out that they would wait outside the court and that if I tried to change anything, they would hand me over to 5 Brigade again. I stood in front of a local magistrate who asked if my statement had been given freely and voluntarily! Under normal circumstances, this might have even been funny. But this was not funny. My very life depended on it.

I could see the CIO agents just outside an open window in the court room and wondered if they could hear me. I hesitated for long enough for the magistrate to ask me if I had heard him the first time. I hesitated again, hoping that by showing my reluctance to answer, he would record my apparent concern. I wondered if any suspicion of ill-treatment was passing through his mind as he saw in front of him a gaunt man with filthy and smelly clothes, a two-week beard and trembling uncontrollably, but if this caused any question in his mind, he did not comment. Finally, he said, "You don't seem very happy."

I hoped this meant that he understood my reluctance to have the statement approved, and I felt this was the best I could hope for under the circumstances. And so, when he asked me for the third time, I agreed that he could confirm the statement.

My now friendly CIO agents welcomed me outside with a smile, which I did not return. They put me in their vehicle and we drove off. I was tempted to ask them why I was not hooded, but thought better of it and sat in silence. After driving some distance, we arrived at another Police station where I was signed in and then put in the courtyard with other prisoners. I was told that one of the other Air Force officers would join me shortly. I expected that this might be Air Commodore Phil Pile, who had been arrested at the same time that I had, when to my surprise, a Police truck arrived and offloaded a very bedraggled and thin Wing Commander Peter Briscoe.

The CIO had also kept Peter hidden from any contact with anyone else for almost three weeks, by moving him around the countryside and refusing his lawyer`s constant requests to see him. They had made absolutely sure that up until now, we had no contact or knowledge of each other`s whereabouts. Now that we had all been tortured into giving false statements that suited them, they were not interested in us any longer, and Peter and I ended up together in a remote police station somewhere in the countryside at this point in time.

Peter was distraught, and I was not much better.

"I`m so sorry, Sir," was all Peter could say. I seem to remember putting my arm on his shoulder and saying, in a voice that I hoped sounded braver than I felt, "It`s alright, Pete. We've done nothing wrong and we'll be okay."

Although our situation was dire, it was comforting to see a friendly, familiar face again. There had been times in the last two weeks that I wondered if I would ever see anyone known to me again!

We were still concerned that the CIO might have their agents embedded amongst the other prisoners, or even amongst the police, and so we spoke in whispers, sharing a few of our experiences and our hope that we could get our stories told in an open court.

After a while, we were called, given our belongings and taken to a vehicle outside. It was an open truck, we were put in the back and we drove off. We were shackled together and there was a guard in the back with us. So, once again, we spoke quietly and tersely about our plans, if we could finally see someone who would listen to our story. After some time, it became apparent that we were headed for Harare (Salisbury), and after a while we pulled up outside the main prison, where we were offloaded. This was to be our next home for some weeks and the beginning of some very difficult and emotional meetings.

PART FOUR

Life in an African Prison

HARARE. SEPTEMBER 1982

STILL SHACKLED IN LEG IRONS *and handcuffs, we arrived at the main holding prison in Harare, were offloaded from the truck and led into the office area to be checked into the system. Amongst the trauma of these recent events, a heartwarming incident of reality suddenly occurred. One of the prison inmates who was performing duty at the check in area came running over excitedly and spoke to Pete.*

"Hello Baas (Boss)", he said excitedly.

Pete looked a bit nonplussed. We were still not thinking straight and it took a few seconds before Pete recognized whom he was and shook his hand.

"Lovemore", Pete exclaimed. "What are you doing here?"

"Aaah, I've been a bad boy", said Lovemore, sheepishly. "I will be here a long time."

We were hustled away but the incident stays with me because it was typical of the Rhodesian/Zimbabwean relationship between employees and employers. Lovemore had been one of our Air Force friend`s housekeeper and/or gardener when we all lived at Thornhill, in Married Quarters, and there were years of friendship between the two of them. It was a touching moment of the decency of real life, as opposed to the horrors we had been subjected to in the last few weeks.

We were stripped of our filthy, smelly clothes that we had been wearing for the last several weeks, were each given a pair of khaki shorts and a shirt and then taken into the chief warden`s office. It was a change to see a white Prison Officer in the traditional prison uniform, which had not been altered since Rhodesian days. In fact, the Prison Service seemed to be the last government agency to be subjected to the enforced, rapid integration of mostly untrained and politicized ZANLA and ZIPRA combatants.

The Officer in charge said we would be able to see our wives and our lawyers the next day, and we were led away to our separate cells. I was still concerned that the CIO might decide to pay us a visit, but I had to put my faith in the integrity of the Prison Service and the hope that we could tell our story to our lawyers the next day and start the process of proving our innocence.

After a fitful night under the harsh light of the cell, I was taken out of my cell in the morning and met with Pete, also being let out of his cell. I was still shocked at Pete`s appearance, as I`m sure he was equally shocked at mine. We had both lost significant amounts of weight. My normal weight was around 186 lbs, yet when I was weighed at check in to the prison the day before, I weighed only 165 lbs; a loss of over 20 lbs in 13 days. Not a good way to lose weight!

We could ask for a razor and got most of several weeks worth of hair growth consigned to the trash bin, as well as a quick cold shower with a bar of soap, the cleanest I`d felt in a long time! We were much better prepared physically now, to meet our lawyers and wives, but we were ill-prepared mentally and emotionally for the meetings. My lawyer, Mike Hartmann, arrived first. The emotional relief in seeing someone who was known and could be trusted was overwhelming and it took an hour or two to tell Mike all that had transpired.

Mike, of course, had spent the best part of the previous 14 days trying to find me, but being given the runaround by the Police and the CIO, he had had been forced to apply to the courts by filing a writ of *habeas corpus.* While the Prison staff had not been infiltrated yet by radical elements of the new government, we felt it was highly likely that there were plants in the prison, and we were careful to keep our meeting as private as possible, by holding our discussions in a quiet corner of a small courtyard.

At some stage in the meeting, Pete had suggested that the electric torture marks might still be visible on his back, and when Mike checked visually, he was able to identify the needle marks associated with a specific type of torture. Mike then checked my back and found the same telltale evidence. This was to be a crucial element of our defense, and our lawyers were astute enough to call in a local medical expert, Mr. George Patrikios, under the guise of being part of our legal advisors team. Patrikios was very thorough and made notes and diagrams, took pictures and confirmed that the marks were indeed consistent with needles being inserted under the skin to allow maximum flow of current, for the purpose of torture.

Pete's lawyer, Rhett Gardener, also arrived and was just as shocked as Mike Hartmann by our condition. I had known Rhett for many years, since his family and mine had lived in the same neighborhood and we were well known to each other. He was, like Mike, a well-known, experienced and trusted lawyer with a good reputation in the country.

After a long and emotional morning, our lawyers left to meet at their offices to discuss the next steps. I was concerned that they would be targeted by the CIO and the Police as soon as it became known that they would be representing us. And it did not take long for my concerns to be tested.

Finally, I was allowed to see Jayne, who had been trying for every minute of every day to find me, but who was also deliberately thwarted at every step of the way. It was a very emotional meeting. I was extremely concerned for the safety of my wife and family. I now knew these ruthless and cunning agents of the government would stop at nothing to achieve their goal, which was to rid the Air Force of its command element and to replace us with some of its highly politicized military comrades. Jayne was able to tell me that our boys were fine, but missing their Dad! I kept reiterating to Jayne that she must take the boys, that all of them must leave the country immediately and start a new life elsewhere.

I pointed out that the agents of government had cunningly set me and the others up as the fall guys for the Thornhill attack and we would face the death penalty for treason in a government-controlled court case, which was likely to be a political sham trial. I implored her to take what she could, leave me and this life behind and start anew. Jayne's reply (in less polite terms) was to the effect that she had already made plans for the boys to be out of the country, with relatives in South Africa, for as long as necessary, but that she was not going anywhere until I was a free man again.

We had been married for 15 years by this time and I knew what a strong person Jayne was, especially having lived all those years of war as an Air Force wife. But this really drove the point home to me. I had some misgivings about this, but since I was helpless in prison and Jayne was in control outside, there was not much else I could do or say, except to ask her to be especially watchful and careful. We hugged each other for a long time and then she left to go and tell the boys that Dad was alright. I was still emotional but for the first time, I was starting to feel that we had a path forward. Little did I know how long and steep that path would be.

Later that afternoon we had a visit from a wonderful Catholic father named Mel Hill, who had performed Pete's wedding ceremony. Mel had been a Catholic priest in the Bronx for 12 years and had seen pretty much everything there was to see about human life, so it came as little surprise to him to be confronted with the challenge of counseling two disturbed and despondent officers. It was remarkable to me and Pete that when the Prison Service decided that Father Mel would not be allowed to see us on a daily basis, he promptly joined the Air Force as a Chaplain and instantly became eligible to see us on a routine basis. We were also to receive a very welcome visit from the Services Chaplain-General, Val Rajah. These two extraordinary men, along with our Air Force Chaplain, 'Boet' van Schalkwyk, were to play a major role in our lives over the next year, as they counseled, nourished us and helped our families.

The next day, we were visited by our lawyers, who wanted to discuss with us the possibility of holding a press conference to get all the details of our horrific treatment out before the government slapped a gag order on them. They felt it was vital to let the world know the methods and tactics the Zimbabwe government was using to torture innocent prisoners into making false statements, against all tenets of international law, and prevent any access to the victims.

This was a brave move and would certainly have serious repercussions for our lawyers, but they felt strongly that this was the best course, under the circumstances. We had no objection to this approach and agreed that this would certainly get attention, probably more attention than they themselves needed! The senior partners in the law firm were opposed to the plan, believing that it would only provoke the government. But the Air Force Commander, Air Marshal Norman Walsh, who had become more and more disgusted with the treatment meted out by the government agents, agreed that it would be a risky but key part of any plan to prove the innocence of his trusted officers.

Mike and Rhett set up the Press conference with some trepidation and called both local and international press officers to attend. The press conference was well attended by all the major news outlets, the local press and it certainly produced the desired effect. The international outlets were soon humming with the details of our treatment, torture and deliberate actions of government to prevent access to us. As predicted, the government was furious.

The local, government-controlled media went out of their way to slant the details against the lawyers and Pete and I, claiming this was a plot to paint the government in a bad light. Seemingly uninterested in justice and fair play, the state promptly charged our lawyers with contempt of court. On top of the charge, our lawyers were subject to continuous intimidation and harassment, for days on end, by various elements of the Police. They were even threatened with indefinite detention, a nasty hangover from the war years, and still on the books. Finally, Mike and Rhett appeared in court, were found guilty of contempt of court and were each fined. On appeal, these convictions were overturned, but their situation was perilous.

The agents of government continued to make life so threatening and unpleasant for them that they left the country permanently after the trial. I still feel overwhelmed by their bravery in the face of a paranoid and dangerous set of government agencies, which lined up against them and were backed by the highest levels of an increasingly dictatorial government that seemed out of control and whose arbitrary actions could have ranged from prison terms to indefinite detention.

I was able to see Jayne on the next two days, but sadly, had no chance of seeing my boys. It was on the third day after the press conference that we received some bad news. We were told to get our meager belongings and be ready to move to prison in the town of Gweru, close to Thornhill. This was a shock and unsettling at this stage. We would be far away from our wives and lawyers, making things that much more difficult. In spite of our objections, we were moved that day. On reflection, I believe this was just another way for the government to show that they were in charge and simple vindictiveness against our lawyers. Once again, we were shackled in leg irons and handcuffs, put into a covered truck and set off for the 160-mile drive to Gweru.

Gweru Prison

While Pete and I were emotionally better prepared, this time for another check in process at another prison, we were ill-prepared for the conditions of the prison. We were handed filthy, unwashed clothing to wear, the dirty toilets and cells making us realize that this was probably the new norm in a Zimbabwe prison. We were finally able to see our other colleagues, Phil Pile, John Cox and Barry Lloyd, who were already imprisoned there, but we had no chance to discuss the brutal chain of events that had led to all of us being incarcerated here in Gweru.

There was worse to come. We were then put into solitary confinement, which continued for almost 4 months. Since our official status was `detainee`, this was clearly illegal but such niceties were wasted on the government. Solitary confinement meant that you spent 23 hours a day on your own in a brightly lit cell, with one hour a day in a small courtyard to wash and walk. Any other toilet needs were supplied by a bucket in your cell. There was no waterborne sanitation and the only other furniture was a metal bed with an old coil mattress.

Other than the electric light, there was a small opening high in the wall, and if you pulled your bed to the wall and stood on it, you could see parts of an enclosed courtyard. Each cell was enclosed by solid brick and mortar walls with a solid, heavy, wooden door and a peephole for the guards to observe you. There were markings on the walls from previous prisoners, a calendar scratched into the wall behind the door and some expressions of lost hope.

It is commonly known that one`s mind can start to play tricks when in solitary confinement for protracted periods of time, if one allows it. Father Mel Hill had given me a bible when we met in Harare prison, and I had flipped through a few pages and refreshed some boyhood memories of a few famous scriptures and had found comfort in the words. Now was the perfect time to read, so I started at page one of the Old Testament. I read carefully, slowly and had to admit that I found many parts heavy going and difficult to grasp. Since I was obviously not going anywhere, I had time to ponder the meaning and even to draw pictures in my mind of the prophets of those times.

We were visited by our lawyers and by our Air Force Commander, who was still madder than hell at our treatment. These were brave acts because the government considered anyone who had contact with us (other than approved officials) to be an 'enemy of the state' and subject to further investigation with predictable consequences. It soon became obvious that any court case which the government might approve was a long way off, and our hopes of a rapid trial and our early release were overly optimistic.

We settled in for a long wait while our lawyers, and indeed most of the western world, pressed for an early trial in an open court. We now realized the full value of the press conference that our lawyers had bravely conducted. As a direct result, most of the free world was aware of our treatment and it would be difficult, although not impossible, for the government to hold a closed trial. If they did, it would reek of political skullduggery.

Time dragged onward, made more difficult by the solitary confinement, and occasionally we would enjoy our daily hour out of our cells with the others, and slowly we began to realize the horrors that all of us had suffered, in one way or another. As time passed, we became less concerned that agents from government would take us out of the prison, for whatever reason they wished, but we devised a system which we hoped would at least let us know if any of us were taken out of our cells, without the others knowing about it.

Since we were all housed along the same corridor, in adjacent cells, if any of us was taken out for any reason, the person being taken out would shout out to all of us remaining and then let us know when he was brought back. If his absence seemed more than a half hour or so, we would start shouting until a guard would appear and attempt to discover what was going on. We used this system often, and it worked.

One day, and for no apparent reason, we were all lead into the courtyard together and then lead back into a communal cell for all five of us. There were three double bunks along the walls and the inevitable bucket! We were delighted and that night we sat on our bunks like excited schoolboys and talked and talked, sharing our feelings and emotions for the first time in the months since our arrest. Using the bucket in front of your colleagues was uncomfortable, but soon became the norm and was a small price to pay for the camaraderie of being together.

The next day we were taken out of the cell at 8 am, lead into the courtyard and told we would be there until 4 pm! We could scarcely believe the change in our lives and wondered if world pressure had finally had some effect. I know that our military chaplains had been pressing for improved conditions for a long time, as had our lawyers. Val Rajah and 'Boet' van Schalkwyk, in particular, had worked hard with the head of the Prison Services. Whatever the reason, we were grateful.

Our lives changed significantly for the better. Our wives were allowed to visit us on a weekly basis and for an hour each time. We could talk together in an office and were supervised by Prison staff, a big improvement from having to sit and talk on a phone, separated by a wall of glass. It was a long drive for them, but they travelled together and brought some rations and foodstuffs that the Prison permitted.

Pete, bless him, would always give a bit of a pep talk before these visits to ensure we did not disappoint our wives with tales of woe! When the wives would have to leave, we would head back into the courtyard with our packets of rations, which would last us until the next visit. We made a point of sharing some of these rations with the one or two other prisoners who shared the courtyard, and even with our guards on occasion. We showed respect to the guards and they reciprocated, with one even addressing me as `Sir` and asking me to keep an eye on the other prisoners while he went for a smoke! I believe the guards knew we were innocent, but they had a job to do and they did it well, all things considered.

We now had ample time for discussions amongst ourselves, and a key topic was 'Who did sabotage our aircraft?' Phil, who had been leading the official Board of Inquiry, along with Pete, believed they were firmly on the path of securing enough evidence to implicate the South African Defense Forces. Since Phil and Pete had been collecting evidence and interviewing many people for more than a month, including our own Air Force people, about the state of airfield security and events on the night in question, they clearly had some data to support their position.

I was not privy at that time to the Board`s data, and since I would be required to review it upon completion and make recommendations to the Commander, I had different opinions. Having worked so closely with the South Africans on my Staff Course and having studied the same strategic thinking for the country and the continent, we all knew that it made sense to do everything possible to promote stability in the neighboring countries, especially in Zimbabwe, with its infrastructure already at some risk from a new and inexperienced government. Since many of my Staff Course members were now Generals in positions of influence, I could not see any of them planning and authorizing such a destabilizing event.

Zimbabwe was no threat to South Africa and I believed that only a madman would plan and execute an operation that would throw the Air Force and the country into complete disarray. And yet, it seems that this is what indeed did happen. Like most countries, external operations by South African forces required government approval at the highest level. Again, I did not believe that the South African government would approve such a hare-brained plan and I persisted in my arguments.

Since the time of our release, there have been reports, including the famous Truth and Reconciliation Commission, which all corroborate South African Defense Force involvement by a Reconnaissance Group on an unapproved, yes unapproved, external operation. I can only say that I was stunned by these revelations. I would add that if the Officer involved in planning and executing this mission had passed the Staff Course and understood strategy in a broad sense, his thinking would not have been so short-sighted and the damage to individuals and families, and indeed, Zimbabwe, would never have occurred. Added to this officer`s lack of understanding of strategy was his apparently willful disobedience to seek timely government review. Perhaps he knew in his mind that government would never approve such a wild and damaging plot. The fact is that the raid happened and the real culprits have never been held accountable.

The time passed slowly and we devised methods to keep ourselves occupied. We were allowed playing cards and soon we had a thriving bridge school. One of my Air Force friends, remembering that I liked to paint, was able to get permission for me to have some art materials, and soon I was painting again, sitting on the tarred surface of the courtyard and holding the canvas on my knees!

One afternoon, I was working on a wildlife painting that I wanted to give to my son, when another prisoner approached me. He admired the painting and asked if I would do one for him. I told him I`d be delighted but when he asked me to have it ready by the next day (his departure date), I had to explain that it would take a while to paint a similar picture and sadly, it would not be possible!

My son still has the painting to this day; an African elephant that has given us many happy memories. I was able to paint another picture for my other son too. This time a lion. It hangs from my son's fireplace today and brings back memories. On seeing the enjoyment that I got from painting, Pete and John started to paint too and we were able to spend many hours, helping and critiquing each other's works.

The prison routine required that we appear in front of a local magistrate, on a weekly basis, to have our charges re-read and to re-enter our pleas. The magistrate was a dour, older man who followed the routine meticulously. Finally, John could stand it no longer and when the magistrate asked John if he was the accused, this after some dozen or more appearances, John replied,

"No, your Honor. I am the victim."

This humor was too much for the magistrate, who demanded that the proceedings start again, with the proper answers!

Mail was always a bright spot for us. Once every few days, we would be given an ever-increasing pile of censored and edited mail. Again, the benefits of the press conference were paying off in unexpected ways. We were receiving mail not only from far-flung friends but from complete strangers who had read of our plight and were offering their support in the cause of justice. It was heartwarming and made us realize what a good place the world could be.

We were allowed to send one censored and edited letter a week from prison. I would usually write to Jayne and include messages for Mark and Lee, which Jayne would relay to them via our relatives in South Africa. This was emotionally difficult for me because it forced me to focus on my young sons, whom I had not seen in months, and I was not sure when or even if I would ever see them again. These letters took a long time to compose because I wanted to portray a very positive outlook and a bright future, while inside I was cursing the government agents for their incompetence and unmasked racism. Not only had they not caught the real culprits, they now seemed content to sit back and let innocent men face the most serious charges and, possibly, execution.

At other times, I would use the opportunity to write to my mother. I was glad that my father was not around to witness the farce of my arrest and imprisonment. My mother was an unusually determined woman and it was typical of her character that she hounded the Prime Minister's office until she got a personal meeting with Mugabe; almost unheard of in those days. My mother told me later that she had explained to Mugabe my love of the country and the Air Force and that it was inconceivable that I would have been involved in the attack. For his part, Mugabe assured her that there would be an open trial and that the law would take its course.

This was a step in the right direction and it is a credit to Mugabe that he held his ground against some hothead ministers in his government who, it appeared, would have preferred to simply string us up from the nearest scaffold. Later, and after the trial, when we were declared innocent and the hothead Minister of Home Affairs immediately detained us again, my mother contacted Mugabe's office and reminded him clearly of his earlier assurance.

Just before Christmas, our wives were allowed to visit us, and although the visits were always too short and always with staff present, they lifted our spirits considerably. It was reassuring to get news of home and our families and to know everyone was at least safe and healthy. For our part, we made sure that we were upbeat about everything and made sure our wives appreciated their long trip to visit us for an hour. When our wives left, we collected some bags of food that they had left and which the Prison staff had searched to ensure there were no weapons or tools for escape!

On opening the bags one time, we found some Christmas cake and, somewhat unusually, some bottles of Coke or Pepsi. We decided we would save these treats for Christmas day and when we were allowed out of our cell, we gathered in the courtyard and shared our treats. I thought at the time that the soda tasted a bit strange, but I attributed the taste to the fact that it had been so long since I had tasted a soda that I was probably imagining things. However, and after drinking a half bottle, I realized that I was starting to feel slightly drunk! The others were finding the same effect and it dawned on us what our wives had done! The soda bottles were plastic with screw off lids and our wives had mixed some vodka into the dark-colored sodas and then recapped them. Luckily, the guards had not test tasted the sodas! Not having any alcohol for many months, the effect had been almost instantaneous!

Harry Ognall QC

One of the biggest practical problems facing us was the question of paying our lawyers. As the days, weeks and months dragged on, it became apparent that our legal fees would overwhelm us. While our lawyers were magnificent and wrote off substantial costs, we needed a concerted effort to raise funds. Jayne sold my beloved car, and then our home and my mother sold our farm. Our Air Force Commander's wife, Merilyn Walsh, dedicated herself to a concerted fund-raising drive and achieved considerable success when the requirement was known.

When the government harassment of our lawyers became untenable, and it became apparent that we would have to engage a lawyer, probably an international lawyer whom the government could not intimidate, our financial needs rocketed. The well-recognized civil rights lawyer, Sydney Kentridge, was fully committed in South Africa, but recommended a QC (Queen's Counsel) from England; one Harry Ognall. Harry Ognall had become a top QC and was the lead lawyer who had successfully prosecuted the infamous 'Yorkshire Ripper', Peter Sutcliffe. After our trial, Harry went on to become a High Court judge in the UK and was later knighted for his contributions to justice.

So, we started on our journey in pursuit of justice. The stakes were very high, with the hangman's noose dangling in front of us, if we were convicted of treason. While many people were active through various stages of our arrest, imprisonment and trial, including Air Marshal Norman Walsh and Senator Tom Eagleton, of Missouri, it is fair to say that none contributed more directly at this stage than Harry Ognall. When it finally was known that our trial would indeed start in May, in the High Court of Zimbabwe, it was arranged for Harry Ognall to visit us in Gweru prison and to start the process of collecting the evidence he would need to defend us.

We were to be moved to Chikurubi, a maximum-security prison on the outskirts of Harare, in early May, just a few weeks before the trial was to begin. Harry visited each one of us, separately, for an hour in a private office in Gweru prison, and I was immediately struck by his focus. He listened intently as I recounted my story, including names, places and times where I could remember them. Harry listened quietly, making notes and asking a question here and there. After a half hour or so, he thanked me and said he would see me in court in a few weeks time! I was stunned! I asked if he needed more time with me, to which he replied that he felt he had what he needed and if he needed more, he would get in touch (from the UK)! The same process took place with Phil, Pete, John and Barry. I must admit that I was a bit worried about the extent of preparation for our upcoming trial; the charge of treason carried the death penalty.

We were duly moved to Chikurubi, and after being checked in thoroughly and after passing through four or five separate stages of security, we were put into our individual cells. Chikurubi was three or four floors of concrete, and very cold. Our individual cells were quite small, but they did have a toilet and a very high observation window for the guards, as well as the standard heavy door with a peephole. There were also showers, although only with cold water, but they were clean. We were all along the same corridor and we could shout to each other, if need be.

We were also joined by Neville Weir; the sixth man accused who, for reasons unknown to us, was detained at a detention center on the other side of Gweru while the rest of us accused were in the Gweru prison. The only plausible reason for this was the fact that the government agents had offered Neville the opportunity of turning State witness, with the opportunity to leave the country after the trial. All credit to Neville that he told them to 'pound salt', but it didn't stop them trying until the last minute.

Shortly after arriving in Chikurubi, I was visited out of hours by Val Rajah, the Chaplain-General, with some very bad news. Jayne had been severely injured in a car accident, was in hospital and amongst other injuries, it seemed likely she would lose her leg. I was aghast and powerless but at least I knew Jayne would be looked after. Again, the Air Force Commander came to the fore, jumped into the situation, insisting that the surgeon make every effort to save the leg and even refusing to allow any other course of action. I have much to thank Norman for, but that decision may be one of the most important for me. Thank you, Sir.

The prison officials still had their humane side and I was granted permission to see her in hospital. When I went to see Jayne, an officer by the name of Mike Mays was in charge. I was deeply touched when he unshackled me outside the ward and allowed me to see her alone. This was contrary to the procedures he was bound to follow and he did so at risk of disciplinary action being taken against him. I was filled with gratitude and to this day have a very special memory of the event and his extraordinary kindness, courage and compassion.

The Trial

The day to start our trial dawned on the 23rd of May, 1982. Interestingly, it was the very day that I was due to take overall command of the Air Force. I had learned that my appointment had been approved by the Minister of Defense, as well as the President, but had come to a halt after my arrest. I had checked with Harry and told him that we were planning to wear our Air Force number one uniforms to our court hearing, to make the point that we were serving Air Force officers and not criminals. Harry Ognall, our attorney, was fine with the idea and there was much excitement as we dressed in our uniforms, which our wives had brought to the prison earlier. The prison guards and escort were impressed and we were offloaded from the prison transport under heavy security and lead into the basement waiting area under the main high court.

Harry came down to see us, to wish us well and to give us a confidence boost. After some delay, we were summoned to appear in court. Our appearance in full uniform infuriated the prosecutor, who looked as if he might have a heart attack and tried to insist that we appear in prison garb. After a private ruling from the Judge, we were allowed to continue and to change into suits at the lunch break. But, we had made our point.

My first sight of the Judge, Enoch Dumbutshena, who would determine our fate, gave me a much needed boost of confidence in the system. Here was a dignified, well-spoken and experienced man who filled me instantly with a sense of his inherent honesty. I had feared some political figure, operating in cahoots with government to ensure our demise, but that was obviously not the case. The system in Zimbabwe is comprised of a Judge and two Assessors, instead of a jury, and the system, at that time, still allowed the independence of the judicial branch of government. To say I was relieved would be an understatement.

As 'Accused Number One', I was first to give evidence in my defense. With Harry's advice ringing in my ears to 'tell only what you remember and absolutely truthfully,' I spent the next three days on the witness stand while the prosecutor did his utmost to rattle me with government witnesses who lied and denied any mistreatment or torture. Occasionally, my temper flared when I could not tolerate the prosecutor's patently false accusations, and the Judge, sensing my indignation, stepped in and calmed things down.

This was when Harry showed his true worth. He had told us that the last thing he wanted to do was to create the picture of a 'big shot' lawyer coming into an African city and belittling the process, but he quietly and meticulously dismantled the prosecution. I was amazed that Harry could remember all the African names, the places and times pertaining to my arrest and torture and not once in the three days, while I was on the stand, did he hesitate.

Armed with this knowledge, his intellect and memory, he destroyed the government witnesses, one by one, as they fell into their trap of lies and more lies to cover up the first lies! It was also interesting to watch the Judge, who was listening intently and making the occasional note. I was physically and mentally drained after every session for those three days, and during breaks, Pete and the others would massage the knots in my neck that developed from the stress!

Then it was the turn of the others, and the pattern was very similar. One by one, over a period of days and weeks, the prosecution would bring witness after witness who would all attempt to continue their lies through the proceedings, but to no avail. Harry had the complete knowledge for each of our experiences and was able to catch the government agents in their lies, time and time again. This became a familiar pattern and even the Prosecutor advised the Judge, finally, that he was withdrawing his chief witness whose evidence he considered unreliable!

Harry's respect for Judge Dumbutshena was obvious, and his remarkable attention to every tiny detail did not go unnoticed by the Judge. It was fascinating to watch Harry's demolition of certain government agents, who were obviously used to bulldozing their lies past lesser lawyers and who now had to deal with someone who not only called their bluff, but would not let it go until the lie was clearly and unequivocally proven.

On top of the compelling arguments and observations by Harry Ognall, expert medical proof of torture was provided by Doctor Patrikios, who had taken a huge risk in travelling from South Africa. He personally delivered his report of the examinations he had conducted on me and Pete, when we were first admitted to the Harare prison. His medical report was corroborated by another expert witness, Dr. James, from the university. Finally, our own original lawyers came forward and gave thorough evidence, backed by contemporaneous notes, of ongoing and continuous government obstruction of justice by preventing the lawyers any access to their clients (us).

Retired Air Vice Marshal Len Pink, the previous Chief of Staff, who had been 'fingered' as one of the original 'culprits', had bravely offered to come and give evidence on our behalf. However, the Zimbabwe government would not consider granting him any form of immunity and he sensibly decided to remain in South Africa. He did, however, write a letter to Mugabe, protesting our treatment, supporting our innocence and outlining our service to Zimbabwe. He got neither a reply nor even an acknowledgement.

The letter probably never got to Mugabe and I suspect it was derailed by some cynical member of his office staff.

Finally, after nine weeks of seemingly endless government witnesses, the prosecution and defense summed up. Amazingly, but not surprisingly, the lead prosecutor ignored the results of the cross-questionings by Harry Ognall and laid out the same case he had tried to make at the very start of the trial. Harry, on the other hand, outlined the actual course of events and produced strong, supporting evidence of the government agent`s lies, mistreatment and torture of innocent airmen and deliberate obstruction of justice by these same government agents.

Judge Dumbutshena listened carefully, took notes and then adjourned the court to allow time for him to formulate his decision. Harry Ognall bid us farewell and left for the UK, with plans to return when the Judge was ready to recall the court and issue his judgment. We were taken back to Chikurubi to wait. I felt fairly confident that the Judge had seen through the government lies, but I could not shake a vague unease about some sort of political interference beyond his control. This concern was to prove well-founded.

The next six weeks waiting for the verdict were spent at Chikurubi. We were well treated and even the warders seemed to recognize that we were innocent men who had been badly treated and should never have been imprisoned in the first instance. We received even more mail than before, since the trial had been headlines on a daily basis throughout a good part of the world and even featured in such popular publications as Time, Newsweek and many others. Mail also poured in from many unknown sympathizers around the world and it was heartwarming to discover how many people cared about our situation.

Wives were allowed to visit weekly, albeit sitting across from a glass partition and speaking on a monitored phone. Jayne was in hospital after her road accident and I would get regular reports from Mel Hill, Val Rajah and 'Boet' van Schalkwyk, as to her condition. Thanks to Norman Walsh, her leg had been saved but she was in traction 24 hours a day, as the surgeon tried to get her shattered femur to knit.

I was able to see my mother on occasion. She had sat through the court proceedings, steadfastly, the strain showed on her face and I noticed the constant fidgeting with her hands. Again, I cursed the government agents who had brought this unnecessary suffering on innocent people and I wished the whole affair would be over soon. For my part, I longed for the time I would be able to see my sons again. Jayne and I could not speak in any detail about them, because of our concerns for their safety, but she was able to let me know that they were fine. It was a great comfort to me to know that they were safe and well looked after by my relatives in South Africa.

Judgment

Finally, some six weeks later, it was judgment day; one year since my arrest! The court was packed to overflowing with friends, families and representatives of the world press. The trial had been followed closely by the international media, and some of the reporters had followed the process every day since the beginning; it was almost as if they had become part of the court. The international press had covered the trial accurately and fully but the local, government-controlled press stayed true to form and reported only what suited the government, painting the prosecutor in glowing terms while belittling our lawyers and distorting our evidence.

The reporting from the local press had become so biased and untruthful that even our prison guards noticed and commented to us, when they would bring us copies of the local newspaper, with all news of the trial censored by the Prison staff. Harry Ognall and our other lawyers were present as Judge Dumbutshena entered the court and delivered his findings and judgment. As expected, he delivered an accurate and meticulous set of findings, covering the entire trial, and it did not take long to understand the direction of his conclusion.

In essence, he quickly found the State had acted illegally in denying access to us until after confirmation of the false statements. He then went on to rule the statements invalid, due to our treatment and torture. He explained that since the statements were the only evidence that the State had produced, it was up to the State to prove their validity. This, he ruled, the State had failed to do, due largely to the dishonesty of the witnesses and the distortion of the facts surrounding our treatment. Accordingly, the statements were inadmissible as evidence. He then pointed out that the evidence of our lawyers was consistent and reliable and that our own evidence on the stand had 'the ring of truth.' Although the findings took some three hours to deliver, his final words were brief but riveting:

"The accused are found not guilty and are acquitted."

There was a momentary pause while this sunk in, and then the courtroom erupted. Friends and family rushed over to celebrate with us. My wife Jayne had discharged herself from the hospital that morning, against her surgeon`s advice. Her father had come from Malawi for the trial and had brought her to the court. She came over to the railing carefully on her crutches and we hugged each other in joy and relief. Then we spoke for a short while with our lawyers and with Harry Ognall, grateful for their efforts and help. The happiness on my mother`s face was a huge relief for me, as we spoke briefly, and I thanked her for her determined perseverance.

Then we left to go downstairs and collect our liberation papers from the prison staff, while families and friends waited outside for our return. Long-awaited family reunions were planned for that evening, in joyful celebration of justice.

We Are Re-arrested

But it was not to be. Downstairs, the prison staff were pushed aside and a special government agent thrust papers into our hands; indefinite detention orders, issued by the infamous hothead Minister of Home Affairs, Herbert Ushewokunze, whose actions were in direct conflict with the judgment just handed down by Judge Dumbutshena, the Chief Justice of the highest court in the land! The Minister's statement that it was the government who made the rules, not the courts, sounded more like something out of North Korea than a sensible reaction to a highly respected government judge.

We looked at the papers in shocked disbelief. The charges were identical, word for word, and the same as the charges to which the top judge in the country had just declared us innocent! Even the prison escorts seemed nonplussed, but there was little we could do and it was back into the prison transport for the trip back to Chikurubi prison. As we got into the truck, we raised our shackled hands to all those who could see us so that they could understand what had just happened. There was booing and some angry shouting as the crowd realized the turn of events, and the police moved in quickly.

Back in Chikurubi, our usual guards were also surprised to see us, having followed the trial on a minute by minute basis. They allowed us time together in the courtyard to discuss things amongst ourselves. Our lawyers arrived shortly thereafter to brief us. Harry Ognall had already made a statement to the world press, condemning the action, and the wires were humming. As evidence of the integrity of the man, Harry elected to stay in Harare until he felt there was sufficient world attention to guarantee our release.

Our lawyers had already started an appeal process, as well as inviting the UK and US Embassies to stand up for justice. We asked them to let our families know that we were in good spirits and looked forward to reuniting with them soon, and I hoped that I looked as confident as I sounded.

Indefinite detention was a very tough executive decree to overcome, and it was obviously going to be a fight between government factions, to try and save face on the one side, against the path of justice promoted by those countries who had so vociferously supported the creation of the new Zimbabwe on the other. It should be noted that at this time, Mugabe was still a hero in the eyes of the world, and Britain enjoyed cordial relations with Zimbabwe.

Much was to happen over the next few weeks. We were visited by our lawyers daily and updated on their progress, if any. My mother, bless her, requested another meeting with Mugabe, to remind him of the commitment he had made to her a year previously; that justice would be carried out. Again, I marveled at her persistence in getting meetings with the Prime Minister when many could not. While I have no proof, I believe that the Minister of Home Affairs had acted without Mugabe's approval and that he now had to set about the delicate balancing act of sorting out the mess, without alienating the hotheads in his government.

After a few days, things started to happen. Phil and I were called to a meeting with our lawyers and officials from the British High Commission. Their news was that the government had reviewed my and Phil's case and they were satisfied that we had nothing to do with the Thornhill attack. They would release us, if we agreed to leave the country immediately and say nothing that would embarrass the government.

Since they had no plans for Pete, John, Barry and Neville, it did not take long for Phil and I to refuse. This caused some consternation among the group, but we were adamant. We returned to our cells, briefed our colleagues and waited for the next shoe to drop. At least things were starting to happen.

The next day we were called to another meeting. The conditions for release were the same, except that Pete was also included this time. The government plan was obvious and despicable; to make sure we kept our mouths shut, they would keep John, Barry and Neville as hostages, until the whole sordid affair had faded from world view, and they would then also be released. I asked if the Prime Minister had agreed to this plan, since without his approval, any of his ministers could renege at any time, and received the assurance that the PM himself had indeed approved the plan. We were advised that this was the government`s final offer, otherwise the law of indefinite detention would take effect.

We discussed this with our colleagues and we all agreed that it was the only way forward. It was now September and I took John aside and we spent some time formulating a contingency plan that would be put into effect if they were not released by year-end. While the plan was only a skeleton at the time, it was a viable plan to secure their release and I hoped it gave some comfort to John, Barry and Neville.

Then the government struck another cruel blow. We were advised that they had changed their minds about Pete and he was not to be released! My immediate reaction was to refuse to leave without Pete, but I was advised this would play into the extreme element's hands and that we could do more, when released, than sitting in prison, incommunicado. Government also dictated that we would not be allowed any time with family, even to sort out our affairs, and we were to be taken directly to the airport and put on an international flight.

I wrote my letter of resignation in disgust at this attitude. The paper guarantee of a normal retirement with full pension and benefits proved to be just that; a useless bit of paper. We spent another night in our cells, disappointed and frustrated, but accepting this was the only solution. At the same time, we recognized and were grateful for all the extremely grueling work that had been done by our lawyers and the British Consulate to prevent our indefinite detention and to secure our release.

It was ironic that it was one of our guards who broke the news to us early the next morning. He had been listening to the BBC and had heard we were to be released that evening. The local media put their usual twist on the news and announced that the government was deporting us as 'undesirables!' I was beyond caring at that stage and we shared out our books and other meager possessions among those who would be left behind.

Jayne and Phil`s wife arrived with Travelers Checks for the princely amount of Zimbabwe $300 (about US $360 at that time) and a suitcase of clothes, which was all we were allowed to take. I was leaving the country of my birth, having devoted the majority of my life to serving the government of the day as an apolitical Air Force officer, with barely the money or clothes to last a week in a foreign land.

I had already outlined a basic contingency plan with the others, if everything went bad, and then we said our goodbyes, with difficulty, to Pete, John, Neville and Barry and were put into our cells at the usual afternoon hour of 4 pm. Immediately afterwards, Phil and I were lead from our cells for the last time and taken to the main administration office in the prison, where we were handed our release papers. We sat in the office as free men, chatting with the helpful and professional main warden, Mike Mays, and waiting for the police to take us to the airport.

The flight to London usually took off at 9 pm, and the Police finally showed up at about 8 pm. They insisted, in spite of our protests, on shackling us as we got into their transport, and we rushed off at great speed. I was furious and when we got to the airport and they told me to get out, I refused point blank.

PART FIVE

Leaving Africa

I Fly to England

"I am a free man! *I will not walk through the airport in shackles! Take them off or you can take me back to the prison!" I said.*

This caused major consternation amongst the guards. However, I had experienced enough of this dictatorial treatment and I was really sick of it. I was very tired of being treated like a criminal and I felt strongly that it was time to take a stand against these political and racist elements of government. When they realized that I really was serious and that I wouldn't get out of their vehicle, the senior member frantically made some calls. Shortly thereafter, our shackles were removed and I got out of the vehicle. Finally, one for the airmen!

We walked inside where we saw our wives, briefly, and my mother. There was also a crowd of friends, and of course, our trusted lawyers to whom we owed so much for their determination to do what was right, without regard for their own safety. However, there was little time left and we were hustled through immigration by scared officials in the way that dictatorships demand.

I was upset that we were given no time with our wives and I barely had time to smile at my mother and reassure her that I was well. Jayne whispered to me that friends would be waiting for me at Gatwick airport in London, but beyond that, I had little idea of what would happen. And then we were escorted by officials onto the plane and took our seats, mere minutes before planned take-off time.

I recognized some of the overseas journalists who had covered our trial and our re-arrest. They had learned of our departure on this flight and had booked seats in an effort to interview us for their papers. I explained to them that we were not in a position to give interviews, in accordance with our undertaking to protect our colleagues. They had seen enough of government abuses over the last year, the last three months in particular, to understand our dilemma, and they did. Then we were airborne and I watched the lights of the city of my birth disappear under the wing.

What bittersweet emotions; glad to be free but sad to think I might never return to the land I loved. What did the future hold? What was to become of the country I loved and its mostly wonderful people? And what of those wretched detainees and prisoners who were not able to be represented by a lawyer who could not be intimidated by a cruel and capricious regime? What of their families? These and many other questions kept coming into my mind, but Phil and I were free!

We now had much work to do to keep the pressure on for the release of our colleagues, locked in their cells and, doubtless, wishing that they too were winging their way out of the country that had started to show its ugliest side. I mused that I had spent much time in police cells, in some half dozen different locations, as well as considerable time in various prisons throughout the country. While this may be a unique experience, I told myself that this would definitely not be my overriding memory of a once wonderful country and life. A chapter had closed.

Captain Tony Thomas

We had been airborne for perhaps half an hour when the Captain of the aircraft came on the intercom. To my surprise, he announced a special welcome to a 'couple of celebrities' who were on the flight; namely, me and Phil! The cabin erupted in applause and shouts of "Good luck to you!" Phil and I were touched and we tried to acknowledge their good wishes and expressions of support. Our situation was well known, and even more so than usual on that day, due to the significant development of our release that morning.

I happened to know the aircraft Captain, Tony Thomas, and while I was delighted with his welcome, I was concerned, for his sake, that this should not be construed by anyone on board as anti-government behavior. Later that night when the main cabin was quiet, I asked the cabin crew if I could speak with Tony, and I went up to the cockpit, shook his hand and thanked him. I told him that while we were grateful for his kind welcome, I did not want him to jeopardize his position, bearing in mind that the airline was, in fact, a government airline.

Tony brushed aside my concerns and said that he was not worried, especially over such a harmless remark. However, my worst fears were realized when it turned out that there was a government minister sitting in the first-class cabin, who had heard the welcome and decided to make it an issue. It typified the paranoia of the government that Tony was instantly grounded on arrival at Gatwick, for alleged anti-government activity, and had to spend the best part of a year in a legal challenge to be reinstated as a Captain! This was just one more example of a paranoid dictatorship showing its ugly side and baring its teeth when challenged.

I had been forewarned, by one of the journalists on board with us, that there would likely be a large press gathering when we landed and that we should at least be prepared to say something. Phil and I conferred and decided it would be best if I alone spoke, saying we were grateful for their interest and support but regretted we were unable to go into more detail. We decided that we would take no questions and hoped our behavior would tip off the press that we were not in a position to speak freely.

On landing, we thanked Captain Thomas, cleared immigration and were lead into a large room full of reporters and journalists from all the major outlets. How I wished we had been free to blow the lid off the whole sordid charade, from our unnecessary arrest, through our torture and imprisonment and our second arrest, on exactly the same charges we had just been acquitted of in the highest court in the land! But that would have put our colleagues at severe risk, so we stuck to our agreed upon plan.

Most of the reporters and journalists were seasoned professionals, and although they would have loved some juicy details, their subsequent reports highlighting Phil`s and my physical appearance and agitated manner proved that they had a good idea for the reasons for our apparent reticence. We owed much of the far-flung public sympathy to the largely accurate reporting of the international press. We were grateful and asked for their continued interest and support.

Leaving the briefing, we went through to a private lounge where our friends were waiting for us. Phil had many friends in the UK, especially from his very recent assignment as military attaché in London, and was soon on his way. For my part, I was overjoyed to see our old ex-Rhodesian friends, Bobby and Roy Neep. Jayne had worked with Bobby in Airways and they had been friends for many years, and Roy was the chief engineer with Autair, a well-known local helicopter company.

Penniless in England

I had been welcomed into their fold when I started to date Jayne and had been friends for some 15 years. They were close and true friends and had offered immediate help when they knew I was to be released. We had not seen each other for many years because they had left Rhodesia and settled in the UK in the early 70's, but it was as though we had never been apart. Bobby was working for a large travel company in the beautiful and historic town of Warwick, while Roy was working near Coventry, for a good-sized helicopter company (Dollar Helicopters) as their chief engineer.

The owner of the Company, David Dollar, had kindly offered his private airplane to fly us out of Gatwick to a small airfield, close to Bobby and Roy. It was a short ride and flying over the wonderful green English countryside was really the start of my feeling that I was no longer in the grey walls of my cell and the unpredictable paranoia of the Zimbabwe government. Looking across at Bobby, Roy and David, I felt an outpouring of love and gratitude, not only to them, at this time, but to all those who had fought so long and hard to cause this to happen.

My thoughts strayed to my family, to our lawyers, to Mel Hill, Val Rajah, Boet van Schalkwyk and to Norman Walsh, the countless friends, known and unknown, around the world whose prayers and kindnesses could never be repaid. They were so vital to seeing that justice would eventually be done for us and I hoped that soon my colleagues would also be free and able to savor their own freedom again.

Bobby and Roy lived in a small (tiny by American standards) townhouse, next to the Avon river, between Warwick and Leamington Spa. Downstairs comprised a combined sitting and dining area and a small kitchen. Upstairs was their bedroom, a small spare room and a bathroom. I`m sure that Bobby and Roy did not realize (or if they did, they never mentioned it) that I would be their non-paying guest for at least the next month and that we would then be joined by Jayne and our sons, Mark and Lee, for the following three months. It was a sign of true friendship that during this entire period, there was never a cross word uttered. To this day, I am so thankful to our great friends for their support and caring through what were still worrying times as I tried, unsuccessfully, to find a way to support my family.

Other than the Z$300 which Jayne had given me, in Travelers Checks, I had no means of support. It was the first time in my life, since I was 19 years old, that I was without a job, and I set to work immediately writing job applications for every opportunity that I could find.

In addition, I had been given a list of the many people who had provided support to help defray our legal costs, and I started writing thank you letters to them all. And, most importantly, I started the process of writing to the UK Government so the plight of our colleagues would not be minimized or quietly and conveniently forgotten. While I was grateful to the UK Government for their assistance, we wanted no stone left unturned in our efforts to get the others released as soon as possible.

I was able to speak to Jayne, to advise her of my safe arrival and to establish that her leg injury would prevent her from traveling to join me for some time yet. This was a huge disappointment, but I cheered up when she told me that our sons would be joining her soon and that they would all come to England together at the earliest opportunity.

Harry Ognall had called me shortly after arriving at Bobby and Roy`s, to invite me to a lunch with him, and he drove to Warwick from his home, some distance away. It was good to see him and to be able to chat freely. I thanked him profusely, on behalf of the others as well, and told him how we all marveled at his grasp of the detail of our treatment and our constant movement around the country by the agents of the government. I`m sure that his skill and professional manner during the trial made the Judge`s task a bit clearer and provided more weight to the Judge`s findings.

I was delighted to see him and I consider it a measure of the man that he took such an extraordinary interest in our welfare, even after the trial.

Mugabe Under Fire

Two other matters of importance were receiving a lot of attention over this period. Mugabe was travelling through the UK and Ireland, to visit the USA, and was under a barrage of questions and criticism from the media, most of which focused on our trial, detention and the future of our colleagues back in Zimbabwe. This was, of course, a double-edged sword. On the one hand, the ongoing pressure made Mugabe realize that he had to address the issue, and promptly. On the other hand, there was a risk that the constant criticism could drive Mugabe to dig in his heels and refuse to budge on the indefinite detention issue. At one memorable press-conference Mugabe grew irritated with the persistent questioning about us and pointed out that the reporters were demonstrating a racial bias. He correctly stated he had hundreds of black Zimbabweans in detention without trial and yet the press seemed uninterested in their plight. Why, he wanted to know, were they only quizzing him about white Air Force officers?

At the same time, the vindictive Minister of Home Affairs, Herbert Ushewokunze, had decided to lodge an appeal against Chief Justice Dumbutshena`s judgment in our trial. The good Judge had been roundly criticized by Ushewokunze, in an attempt to justify his decision to arrest us again, with even more rash statements about the role of the courts in the country. For anyone who knew anything about Ushewokunze, this came as no surprise. He was a well-known extremist, given to anti-white outbursts on a regular basis, and he did Mugabe and the rational elements of the new government considerable harm.

Predictably, the appeal was dismissed by the Court of Appeals, prompting yet further outbursts from him, but to no avail. I had wanted to write to Judge Dumbutshena, thanking him for his understanding of the gravity of the police and government agent actions, re-assuring him of my complete innocence and for getting the verdict right. However, given the highly-politicized nature of the charges and the paranoia of certain, high–level government officials, I decided against it and hoped that he understood my respect for and gratitude to him for not flinching under such adverse conditions.

The international pressure on Mugabe and the Zimbabwe government was relentless, and a few days later, Pete Briscoe was released from Chikurubi, in the same manner as Phil and I, and landed at Gatwick where we met him. Although it had only been a few days since we had left, it seemed longer because of all the activity. We were delighted at this development and hoped this would lead to the early release of the others too.

After giving us news of John, Neville and Barry, Pete was driven away by friends of his from his Staff College course in the UK, the year before. It wasn`t long before Pete was joined by his wife, Paddy, and two young children, Hilary and Drew, who had also been unable to see their father for over a year. A joyous occasion indeed

Phil, Pete and I had several meetings over the next few weeks, as we continued our efforts on behalf of our colleagues, as well as completing the pile of letters of thanks to all those we knew had helped us throughout our ordeal. Those letters were a labor of love, as we tried to voice our gratitude to the many friends that we knew, to many whom we had never known and would probably never meet. It is heartwarming to think of those people, some on the other side of the world, who had felt strongly enough about our plight to get involved and to help, even though the only way we were known to them was through the international media.

I recall being able to visit John's father, who was in poor health, but he was delighted to meet me and get first-hand news of John. He was a delightful gentleman, as I remember, and I tried to give him a solid assurance that John would be released very soon. I hoped that my words sounded more convincing than the nagging doubt in the back of my mind, that the political extremists in Zimbabwe could still block their release. He thanked me for the visit and I left, hoping that he would soon see his son. Again, I cursed those who played callously with others' lives and wondered what had become of justice, so warped by the paranoia of a dictatorial government.

I had requested a meeting with Margaret Thatcher, the British Prime Minister at the time, to express our gratitude for her help, and in a further effort, to keep the focus on John, Neville and Barry. Although this meeting did not happen, I did receive a letter of assurance from her Secretary and I was able to secure a meeting with her Minister of Foreign Affairs, Malcolm Rifkind, where he was kind enough to let me express my views and feelings about the situation. Not only did I have the overriding concern for our colleagues still in detention, but I wanted the UK government to keep the Zimbabwe government`s feet to the fire, about our lawfully earned pensions, without which we were practically penniless.

In terms of the Lancaster House agreement, one could argue that the UK Government had an indirect responsibility to ensure that the new Zimbabwe government would honor the usual financial obligations associated with government pensions. I had little faith that this would be the case and I was proved correct. While the government eventually returned my pension contributions that I had made over my 21–year Air Force career, I never received my due pension.

To say that I was irritated would be an understatement, since not only was it a deliberate failure to honor a sacred trust, I felt the British government was responsible (in part) for insisting on an election that left the country with a predictably shaky future.

Jayne had been wise enough that when she used what little monies were left to book the air tickets to fly overseas, she paid for flights not just to the UK but also to the US. Since the government would only allow her to take Z$300 out of the country, this was one way to add a bit extra and, as we had no idea where we would end up living and working, it was sound insurance that we would be able to fly to the US, if needed.

In my efforts to keep pressuring the Zimbabwe government to release John, Neville and Barry, I decided to get a ticket to Washington DC to visit Senator Eagleton, who had done so much to keep our situation alive while we were in prison. I had already written him a letter of thanks, but this would be an opportunity to look him in the eye, shake his hand and express my gratitude for all his efforts on our behalf. He was gracious enough to take my call, and not only did he agree to meet me, but he invited me to stay with his family for a week and get to know a bit about DC.

Senator Tom had taken a keen interest in our situation, since his visit to South Africa shortly after our arrest. He had accompanied Senators Mark Hatfield, of Oregon, and Paul Laxalt, of Nevada, on a fact-finding mission. My good friend Tol Janeke seized this opportunity and spoke to General Peter Walls, retired Chief of the Defense Forces of Zimbabwe, who was able to secure a meeting with the Senator and Pete Briscoe`s parents. This is the action that started the involvement of Senator Eagleton and was finally the key to securing our release from our re-imprisonment. Thank you, Tol.

I arrived in DC one evening to be met by a tall man carrying a placard reading my name. I assumed that this was probably a driver sent to fetch me from the airport and take me to the Senator`s home. We stuck up a conversation and after a while, I asked where the Senator might be at that time, to which the driver replied, "Hugh, I'm Tom Eagleton!"

Tom Eagleton

I started to learn more about this remarkable gentleman, who happened to be a very highly respected and senior Senator in the US Senate, at that time. We had numerous interesting discussions and over the course of the week, I learned a lot about Tom's work as a US Senator, the Capitol and the city. We would leave Tom's home each morning around 7 am and get to his offices pretty quickly. Tom had arranged several meetings for me, with others in the government and in US industry, including heads of business from McDonnell–Douglas, Lockheed, Boeing, Martin Marietta, General Electric, Northrop and others.

I was overawed by these giants of industry, and even more so when I received invitations from some for further meetings. That was the first time I started to think seriously about starting my new life with my family in America. It started to dawn on me that not only had Tom wanted to help get me and the others out of prison, but that his interest and goodwill extended to helping me to recover and to get back on my feet. There would be many hurdles to overcome, especially the overriding challenges of being allowed to immigrate into the US, but also being offered a real job, whereby I could support my family.

Tom must have indicated that I had a good chance of coming to America because both McDonnell Douglas (MDC) and General Electric (GE) made follow up calls to me while I was still in the US. McDonnell-Douglas' interest in my expertise hinged on my work for our Air Force, when I lead the evaluation team for an advanced trainer/ground attack aircraft. As described earlier and after an extensive evaluation, our selection was the British Aerospace Hawk. Coincidentally, McDonnell-Douglas was the contractor for the US Navy, who was ordering a version of the Hawk as their advanced trainer. I felt that I would indeed be able to make a meaningful contribution to this program and we started a conversation in earnest about my joining their team.

At the same time, GE wanted to interview me for a possible job in their military engine business, so I spent some time in GE's Washington office, discussing possible openings and opportunities. Tom was pretty high on GE, and so was I, although I was more confident that I could hit the ground running on the Navy Hawk program with McDonnell-Douglas, rather than starting in an unknown field with GE.

Author. Pre-flight check.

Defence Minister PK van der Byl on right in flight over the operational area.

Nov. 11, 1973 - Independence Day Fly-Past Pilots. Author seated 3rd from right.

Live hoist training at Martins Falls in the Eastern Highlands. Slatter on the cable. Petter-Bowyer piloting.

A sad sight. One of the sabotaged Hunters at Thornhill Air Force Station. 1982. How can anyone do this to an aircraft?

British Aerospace 'Hawks' Arrive at New Sarum Air Force Base, Harare. Air Vice-Marshal Hugh Slatter welcomes the Air Force Commander, Air Marshal Norman Walsh, who led the British Aerospace team. Prime Minister Robert Mugabe looking on 3rd from right.

Air Marshal Frank Mussell presenting me with the Defence Medal for Meritorious Service at Air Force Station New Sarum 1978.

Foreign Secretary Carrington, Mugabe and Prime Minister Margaret Thatcher.

Lee, Hugh, Jayne and Mark outside townhouse in England. Oct. 1983. First reunion in 14 months.

Bobby and Roy

Comrades in arms, three weeks after release from prison. Phil Pile. Wing Co. Garth Wensley, Wing Co. Pete Briscoe and AVM Hugh Slatter

Captain Hal Bolo (USN retired) and my first GE Boss

Senator Tom Eagleton

'Granny' Frazier

Nick Price (right) after F16 flight.

Citizen Hugh 19 April 1991.

Patty Riley (Bamber) - Hal's wonderful secretary.

Joe Sutter and Jayne.

Hal`s sign at the beach.

Mark and Sean

Ray Wagner and Pete Briscoe

Denise and Sean

Boeing 777

747/GE90 test bed and 777/GE90-115B

Phil Condit

Lee and Kaylee-2017

Hugh and Jayne

Our flag flies with pride on our point.

With much to mull over, I left Tom and DC after a week, which had not only allowed me to fulfill my wish to meet him and thank him for his help to me and my colleagues, but had unexpectedly lead to some very positive opportunities in the USA, in a field in which I was fairly comfortable and felt I could contribute usefully.

I returned to England and to Bobby and Roy, who were delighted with my news. It certainly was exciting stuff, particularly when I considered my opportunities in the UK. Of some fifty job applications that I had submitted, I had only received three acknowledgements and zero interest! Since our initial thinking had been to find work and to settle in the UK, this was disappointing.

However, I was so encouraged after my trip to the US that I became more confident I would be able to find suitable work and be able to support my family again. I had never been without a job or a means of support in my lifetime and the situation was unnerving and deeply distressing. Adding to these difficulties, I now realized that after 21 years of solid work, the Zimbabwe government had made sure that I had nothing to show for it, on top of which I had a wife and two young sons to support.

On the Dole

My days were spent writing job applications in the mornings, walking into town to the Post Office and to say hello to Bobby at her workplace. It was a longish walk of about 3 miles and I used the time to focus my thinking on what might lie ahead and what I needed to do to start this new life.

The walk along the main street into Warwick town took me past some lovely old buildings and historic monuments. Warwick has a long and interesting history, not the least of which belongs to the famous castle which sits on the bank of the picturesque Avon River. The castle had been painstakingly restored and was inhabited by waxwork figures of the times, all exquisitely crafted by Madame Tussaud`s. It is a particularly beautiful castle that attracts many visitors every year, and it became a favorite place for us to take friends who were starting to visit from overseas, including my mother and my brother. It was a relief to see my mother in a more hospitable environment, and much less anguished than when I last saw her at the trial, and then at the airport before my departure from Africa. My mother, bless her, had very little money, but she offered me some if I needed it. I politely refused but she did insist on buying me a warm jacket, which I have to this day and still wear on occasion, in fond memory of her.

She told me that she had made plans to leave Zimbabwe as quickly as possible, driven largely by my poor treatment at the hands of the government and by her lack of confidence in the ability of the government to run the country efficiently. How right she has been proven!

My plans to find employment started looking none too optimistic, and with no money coming in, I sucked up my pride and visited the local unemployment and welfare offices. Since my picture had appeared in most English newspapers, including the local ones, I was easily recognizable and I was asked to step into a back office where I was introduced to the manager.

He started by introducing himself and saying that he recognized me. I explained my plight and it seemed he was already aware of my background from all the media coverage. I filled out some forms, which would allow me to receive a fortnightly (every two weeks) allowance of ninety pounds sterling for me and my family, as long as I agreed to accept whatever job they could find for me.

While this was not a lot of money and would not cover our expenses, I was extremely grateful to him and the British government, and I assured him I hoped I would not be a drag on his office or the British taxpayer for long. It was awkward, not being in a position to contribute to expenses for Bobby and Roy, although they never expected anything, but this would go a small part of the way to help.

Family Reunited

Then some wonderful news! Since her leg seemed to be healing, albeit slowly, Jayne was fit enough to make the flight with the boys to join me in the UK. Her leg was clamped firmly in a caliper that prevented any bending of her knee while the bone was knitting together, but she could walk slowly with the use of crutches. Jayne and the boys boarded the British Airways (BA) flight in Johannesburg late in the evening and bound for London Heathrow.

Of necessity, Jayne had to sit in a first-class seat, because she could not bend her leg to sit in a normal seat, while the boys were seated as close to the first-class cabin as the helpful crew could arrange. This was the start of the trip from hell for Jayne. Before take-off, and as is always the case in a first-class cabin, the cabin crew were serving some canapés and drinks. Since Jayne is highly allergic to any seafood, she carefully questioned the cabin staff as to the contents of the canapés. She was assured there was no seafood content at all and that nothing had been prepared in the same dishes as any seafood.

It was not long after take-off that Jayne became violently ill, causing her to have the cabin staff help her to the toilet. To her horror, she discovered that she was unable to shut the door, because of the caliper on her leg, causing the lower part of her leg to stick out of the half-open toilet door and the flight attendant to stand guard! If this had happened just once, it would have been quite funny, but since Jayne now had severe food poisoning from something in the canapés, this was only the first of many such excursions, with all the attendant problems and embarrassment. The boys were worried but also slightly amused. Jayne was absolutely mortified and the rest of the first-class cabin was irritated, to say the least, at having to use the toilets in the (God forbid!) economy class section of the plane!

I had driven with Bobby and Roy to be at Heathrow in plenty of time for Jayne's and the boy's arrival, and when we entered the airport, we went to the BA desk to make sure that Jayne had a wheelchair at her disposal. The BA ground staff somehow knew our situation and I was taken to a private waiting area, closer to the arrival gate.

Anyone who knows Heathrow airport knows the lengthy corridors one must walk after deplaning, to get to immigration and customs. Jayne`s airplane arrived close to the scheduled hour and the deplaning process started, with Jayne, Mark and Lee having to wait until last, to minimize delays for the other passengers.

At long last, they were able to leave the airplane, get Jayne into the wheelchair and start the walk to my waiting area. I saw them from a distance and broke into a run, as did Mark and Lee, until we met at a gallop! It had been more than a year since we had seen each other, and at their ages (14 and 12), appearances change in a year. They both looked bigger than I remembered (obviously) and they started to chatter eagerly. By this time, Jayne's helper had arrived with Jayne in her wheelchair and we hugged each other, as best as we could.

I was so happy to see my wife and boys in a safe environment, and I marveled at her fortitude over the last 13 months, having to deal not only with my imprisonment and the arrest of our lawyers, but with the absence of our sons, her serious accident and hospitalization for the last few months. What a series of challenges Jayne had faced and come out on top!

I stood there, so proud of her and our sons, while the wheelchair helper stood patiently, probably wondering what on earth was happening. After a time of simply reveling in the moment, and worried that Bobby and Roy were probably wondering what had happened, we made our way carefully to the main arrivals area to find Bobby and Roy. They of course, were delighted to see Jayne and our boys, having last seen them years ago when we were all still living in Rhodesia.

Bobby and Roy were Godparents to Mark, and that had helped to keep us firmly in touch over the years. Now it was over ten years since we had seen each other, but it was as if we had never been apart! We drove home, all chattering at the same time and enjoying the wonder of being together again, even though it was strange circumstances that had brought us together after all those years.

Back at Bobby and Roy's, we had to adjust our living arrangements. Fortunately, the next-door neighbor, a lovely lady by the name of Di, had a spare room and offered to put Mark and Lee in it. We happily accepted and Jayne and I shared Bobby and Roy's spare bedroom. Since Jayne was on crutches and the bedroom was upstairs, this made for an interesting activity. On descending the stairs, Jayne would send her crutches down first and they would come clattering down the stairs and end in a pile on the floor, alerting us all to Jayne`s imminent arrival and prompting Roy to remark,

"Here comes 'Thing'".

Then Jayne would come down the stairs, one by one, on her bottom. Jayne had been nicknamed 'Thing' for years, by Roy, stemming from the TV show 'The Addams Family,' where the mysterious hand named `Thing` would appear and help with chores. Because Jayne often stayed with Bobby and Roy, she often did chores; hence 'Thing.'

With the arrival of Jayne and our sons, there was renewed interest from the media, with interviews and pictures completed on the banks of the Avon and at Bobby and Roy's home. I was more than happy to see this interest because it helped keep the issue alive, at least in Britain, and helped to keep the plight of our colleagues in full view of the British government, who were working as hard as they could to get the Zimbabwe government to release John and the others.

There were some encouraging reports, but it was clearly a face-saving exercise for Ushewokunze and others who had enjoyed the self-aggrandizement of the original charges and the re-arrests. So, in order to show who was in charge, they would act only when they saw fit!

Jayne's leg did not seem to be healing as it should, so she visited an excellent specialist who, after looking at some X-rays, was surprised that the surgeon in Zimbabwe had attempted to set the two parts of the broken femur, with insufficient major contact area to heal together again. Jayne`s knee was jammed solid with muscle, tendon and ligament that had grown into the joint during the lengthy traction of her leg while she was in hospital for months in Zimbabwe. The only course of action was to attempt to manipulate the leg in an effort to get the knee moving and line up the femur properly.

The English surgeon, Dr. Duke, started the procedure. The fact that the leg was not healing properly was immediately exposed, since Jayne`s femur promptly broke again at the same place! This turned out to be a blessing because Dr. Duke decided to perform a full operation, clean out the knee and insert a titanium rod inside Jayne's femur to strengthen it and to keep it straight while it healed. The operation was a success, but of course it put Jayne back on crutches with a lengthy rehab required and more work to be done on the knee. I would visit the hospital twice a day to see Jayne, and would often find Dr. Duke visiting her on his rounds.

He was a godsend for us both and we were very grateful to him and the staff at the hospital. I liked to tease Jayne that Dr. Duke must have had a 'thing' for her because his nurses told me he never spent much time with his patients! I was amazed and surprised that this treatment cost Jayne nothing. Jayne held British citizenship and she was entitled to free treatment through the much-maligned National Health Services. Our experience with this government-run group was superb. Thank you!

America Beckons

With little to no interest in my work experience from British companies, I started to wonder if all the publicity and media attention from the trial had played any part and perhaps caused the usually conservative British culture to keep me at arm's length. Whatever the reason, it was becoming clearer to me and Jayne that our best chances for our future lay across the Atlantic, with one of the interested American business companies who had contacted me. I was in frequent contact with McDonnell-Douglas (MDC) and GE, as well as Senator Eagleton, who was laying the groundwork for my entry to the US as a seeker of political asylum.

This was a painstaking process and I was thankful to have the good Senator in my corner. I learned that having a guaranteed job in the US would expedite the process, and I doubled up on my efforts with MDC, who had told me to expect a formal job offer within days. It was now November, almost two months after my arrival in the UK, and I was becoming concerned that we were overstaying our welcome with Bobby and Roy.

Just as I was advised by my contact at MDC that the job offer was ready for signature, a major strike and a series of layoffs began at MDC! I was told that the hiring freeze would probably last into the New Year and they asked if I was prepared to wait that long. I advised Senator Eagleton of this latest development and told him I was going to start looking more seriously at any GE opportunity that I might be offered. Tom told me that my immigration paperwork was progressing but that he could not put a timeframe on it.

It was a bit of a 'Catch 22' situation; it was difficult to get a job without guaranteed immigration for me and my family and it would be quicker to advance the immigration process if I had a guaranteed job! And then, in December, GE asked me to have an interview with one of their Engine Division General Managers who was visiting the UK. The interview must have satisfied the GM because after a few days, I received an invitation to visit GE`s Engine Division Headquarters in Evendale, Ohio, in the USA, for further interviews. Evendale was a small municipality within the greater Cincinnati area.

Now I felt I was getting somewhere and I advised Senator Eagleton of the encouraging development. He wished me well and said a positive outcome would strengthen his position with the Immigration and Naturalization Services, who were considering my situation. Jayne and our sons were excited, as were Bobby and Roy. I took up Roy's kind offer to wear his smart overcoat for my travels, since it would be winter in Ohio with freezing temperatures and probably snow, being very different to my 40 years of tropical weather in southern Africa!

This started a round of interviews the likes of which I had never experienced. I was not used to interviews, the last one being in front of the selection panel for flight training in the Air Force, some 22 years previous, and I had never been trained in interview technique! I seem to remember some seven interviews with different managers and heads of sections. The first and most important was with the General Manager of the Military Division, and clearly the most important of the interviews. He was an extremely articulate and knowledgeable man, of British descent, who was able to put me at ease and we had a thorough and useful discussion. He went on to lead one of GE's major businesses and contributed much to GE`s successes under the legendary Jack Welch.

From there, it became more difficult for me. The managers I met were solid engineers, interested mostly in detail and acronyms, it seemed, and while I had some technical training from our Air Force, I was no design engineer and barely able to spell 'engine!' As a pilot, I was often accused by our Air Force engineers of breaking our engines, and I was somewhat relieved when I was told that the last of the managers with whom I was due to interview, Hal Balo, an ex-USA Navy Captain, was out of town. There would be no more interviews on that visit. I mention this only because of the remarkable turn of events that revolved around this fortuitous happening, which will become clear in my later dealings with GE.

Finally, I met with the head of Human Resources, a fine man who seemed to take a special interest in my case. After a very positive interview, he surprised me by asking what sort of salary I would expect. I was not expecting this question, having always worked in the Air Force with set wage scales, and I decided my best course would be to tell him my last salary as an Air Vice Marshal (Major General). We did a quick conversion into US dollars and his next statement made me realize what a good and honest Company GE was.

"I believe we can do better than that, Hugh, and I will let you know."

My recollection was that he could easily have settled on a low number, but he did not and I was struck by his integrity, support and by association, his Company. This was one of several instances of unusual fairness that I experienced with GE people and which would cause me to be a proud and willing contributor to this fine Company. Since this was the third set of interviews I had completed with GE, I knew there must be some interest, and I returned to the UK with words from the Human Resource Department that they would contact me in due course.

My Co-Accused Are Released

Time was passing and then John and the others were finally released! As expected, there was no major communication from the Zimbabwe government and not as much publicity from the international media who, it seemed, were caught a bit off guard. As opposed to the situation when Phil, Pete and I were released and driven directly to the airport, John, Neville and Barry were given a few days to sort out their affairs before having to leave. With much joy and happiness, John and Neville arrived in the UK and we celebrated their long-awaited freedom.

As their senior officer, their situation had weighed heavily on me, and I was relieved that I did not have to consider starting the rescue plan that we had discussed, had their situation deteriorated. Barry had opted to go to Australia and we did not see him in the UK. However, we all met at a pub, The Stag, in Warwick, for lunch and drinks along with our wives and children looking like a bunch of refugees, which indeed we practically were. We had a wonderful reunion and made a start to wiping away the long periods of extraordinary stress, anxiety and emotion.

As I recall, it was probably mid-December of 1983 and no one amongst us had a clue what the future held for any of us. After some hours, we broke up our gathering and everyone set off for their temporary homes. Although no one was too far away, travel in England took considerably longer than on the comparatively empty roads of Zimbabwe. As we all climbed into borrowed cars, we waved farewell and I could not help wondering where we would all be in a year, or even five or 10 years. Our lives had changed forever.

Meanwhile, I was in constant communication with Senator Eagleton, who continued to push my case, as well as Peter's. Pete had a brother in the US and he was to find immigration into the USA a bit easier, although he still needed a job as much as I did. Fortunately for Pete, he was able to get a temporary visa, as I recall, and lived with his brother for some months while looking for work. Once again, the good Senator was instrumental in getting Pete introduced to some key business leaders, and things fell into place.

The Senator relayed one piece of an exchange between himself and the Immigration and Naturalization Service (INS), which luckily helped bring things to a head. Apparently, some senior official within the INS had suggested to Tom that it might be better if I returned to Zimbabwe and file my immigration application there! Tom simply exploded over the lack of understanding of the gravity of the situation and decided to go directly to the head of the INS. This certainly got things moving and the next time I spoke to Tom, he was able to tell me that things were progressing quickly!

Christmas came and went and we enjoyed visits from friends whom we had met during the aircraft evaluation process, and who had followed the Zimbabwe fiasco with interest and great sympathy. Their outpouring of support and love was a huge comfort to me and my family and it went a long way to help us on our road to recovery.

Mark and Lee were getting restless. We had decided not to put them into school, for what we had hoped would only be a delay of a couple of months, at best. I wanted to have more time with them, after being apart for so long and before we all had to start our new lives. While we were able to keep them reasonably occupied, they were certainly learning more about England and its people on a daily basis. With an occasional trip to London and the odd days at work with Roy, Jayne and I were mindful that we needed to get this next stage of all of our lives moving! The main hurdles, however, were largely out of our control, at this stage. Immigration to the USA and employment in the USA, always seemed just out of our grasp.

PART SIX

New Life in America

Granted Asylum

In the middle of January 1984, *I heard from Senator Eagleton that my application to immigrate, as a political asylum seeker, along with my family, had been approved with immediate effect! At the same time, I got word from GE that I could start work with their Aircraft Engine Division in Ohio, in effect, from the first of February. We were overjoyed and we now had a path forward, thanks to the tireless and comprehensive efforts of one remarkable Senator. Thank you again, Sir.*

Using Jayne's pre-purchased tickets, we booked our flights to Cincinnati, Ohio, the closest airport to my new work place and our new place of residence, Evendale. We planned to leave on the morning of the 31st of January, which would get us in to Cincinnati that afternoon, with time to check into a hotel and get ready for work the next day; the 1st of February, 1984, an auspicious day for us all!

The remaining two weeks in England seemed to drag. We had no preparations to keep us busy, since we had no affairs to settle and just a suitcase of clothes each, which was all we had when we left Zimbabwe. There were no banking issues either, since we had no bank and no money. Bobby and Roy had offered to lend us US$1,000, an offer which we gladly accepted, since we would have to wait a couple of weeks before the first pay-check from GE.

We were mindful that we would be leaving our very good friends, Bobby and Roy, without whose help and support the previous four months would have made things much more difficult, and we had no idea when we might see them again. It was a strange thought that we would be moving far away, to a country where we hardly knew a soul and almost nobody would know us. It would be a very different world from our Rhodesian and our Air Force days.

The day of departure dawned and Bobby and Roy drove us to Heathrow, early in the morning for our mid-morning flight to Cincinnati, USA. It was a sad farewell to our friends who had looked after us in such an extraordinary way. Their love and special care had meant much to us and had strengthened our resolve to never look back, or even sideways, but simply to focus on the future and reclaim our lives. Roy was an unusually talented joke teller, and although he may not have realized it at the time, our joint washing up sessions after dinner, with Roy telling his jokes, all with the correct accents while I dried the dishes, was a strong dose of rehab for me.

Those moments helped put life back in perspective and made me realize that there is not much that humor cannot cure! Bobby, for her part, had been seriously ill, although she would never dream of mentioning it to me, instead focusing her activity on getting us back on our feet again. And that`s why they were so special. We had other good friends, of course, but none of them had to put up with the four Slatters for almost five months in a tiny townhouse! We hugged each other, fighting back the inclination to start crying, and went inside the airport. I'm sure that Bobby and Roy felt the same as they drove off, back to a quieter and more peaceful home!

As luck would have it, our flight was cancelled just an hour before our scheduled departure time. Obviously, it was very important that I showed up at work the next morning, my first day of work for GE, so I scurried around, finding another flight. Luckily, there were several flights to the USA and even one directly to Cincinnati, although it would only land late that night, leaving me little time to rest and prepare for my first meeting. The airline changed our tickets and then we busied ourselves around the airport for the rest of the day.

Our excitement was palpable as we boarded our airplane and took our seats. While I had been fortunate enough to visit the USA three times in fairly short succession; once in my role as Chief of Air Staff, once to visit Senator Eagleton and finally to the interview with GE, Jayne, Mark and Lee never had that opportunity. This was a new experience for them and a very different experience for me. This time we were travelling to the USA to settle and to start our new lives in a new world.

Growing up in Africa, America had always had a unique attraction for most people. This was the Superpower of the World, the land of opportunity and dreams, the land where anything was possible, if you were prepared to work hard. We read books about America, we watched American TV shows and I had a radio that allowed me to listen to the Voice of America, plus baseball and hockey games. We traded American comics, we coveted American cars and we even tried to buy American clothes. Although our heritage was mostly British, we felt a special kinship with America, especially when we, as Rhodesians, tried to do what America had done so bravely in 1776.

In 1965, we declared our independence from Britain! This led to a bitter 15-year war, with most of the world against us and even, sadly, America. However, we recognized that the Founding Fathers of America were bigger than some of the politicians of the day, and our feelings for the true American spirit never wavered.

Since the flight was in darkness, we were unable to see anything of the topography as we flew over eastern Canada and then south over the northern states of the USA. We were able to see many of the brightly lit cities and towns, *en route*, and wondered aloud at the density of the population in some areas, as compared to Africa! We landed in Cincinnati around 10 pm and collected our bags. Since the Cincinnati airport is actually in Kentucky, we called a taxicab and drove north through downtown Cincinnati towards Evendale, some 25 miles from the airport.

Cincinnati

Cincinnati is an old, industrial city that sits astride the Ohio River, a major waterway that links with the Missouri River, the longest tributary of the Mississippi River, which in turn flows all the way to the Gulf of Mexico. There was snow on the ground and the drive took us some 40 minutes to get to the hotel. I watched the taxi meter anxiously. Although I had $1,000 in Travelers Checks and some loose dollars, that was all the money we had until my first payday.

Traffic was relatively light, since it was almost midnight on a cold Sunday evening, and we quickly took our bags and checked into the hotel which GE had kindly booked for us. GE had also arranged a rental car for me, which was at the hotel and which I would use to get to work the next day. We tumbled into bed, pretty well exhausted from the long day and the anticipation of what lay ahead.

I wanted to be at GE, which seemed to be no more than a five-mile drive, by 7 am and decided to give myself plenty of time to find the office by leaving the hotel at 6:30 am. Jayne had some money for lunch, although she would not be able to walk anywhere because of the weather and the fact that she still could only walk on crutches, while her leg was healing. But Mark and Lee were fit and ready to explore and I promised I would be home soon after 5 pm.

The next 30 minutes proved a challenge! It was still very dark at 6.30 am, with plenty of snow on the ground, although the highways and main streets had been cleared. My rental car was obviously a left-hand drive, since the rule of the road in the USA is to drive on the right side; it was a new experience for me. There was no GPS guidance in those days, so I had prepared the route from some regular maps and attempted to memorize the main features. Suffice to say that I finally ended up in the GE parking lot in a pool of sweat and very frightened, although I`m sure that some of the other drivers on the road must have been just as frightened by my attempts to navigate the highways and the on/off ramps.

Fortunately, most Americans are good drivers, as well as being courteous, and I was given a wide berth on several occasions as I made last minute turns, rather than missing my exit and having to calculate a whole new route! This was an experience that I was to repeat for several days until I became more familiar with the route and the traffic, although it was dark when I drove to work and when I returned! Growing up in Africa, near the tropics, the sun rose around 6 am and set around 6 pm every day, and I went to work in daylight and returned home in daylight! This was a whole new experience for me.

Hal Balo

After completing all the paperwork necessary for new hires with the very helpful Human Resources group, I set off to meet my new boss, Hal Balo, in another building. That meeting proved to be the highlight of my day, and looking back, one of the highlights of my entire life. I liked Hal instantly. He was an ex-US Navy Captain and was still serving in the Naval Reserves. He gave me a warm welcome, showed me my cubicle (no offices for junior staff) and introduced me to his large staff with the words,

"This is Hugh. He talks funny, but he's okay!"

That is how I started my first day in a new life! Hal asked me to jot down my thoughts about aviation in Africa. I collected some paper and pencils from Patty, Hal`s lovely young secretary, and sat down in my cubicle to gather my thoughts. I had not written much before I needed to make some corrections. Back I went to interrupt Patty and the first example of George Bernard Shaw`s famous observation about America and Britain being "two countries divided by a common language" became evident.

"Patty, excuse me for interrupting, but I need a rubber," I said.

Patty hesitated before asking me, with a strange look on her face,

"Hugh, can I ask you what you need a rubber for?"

It seemed an obvious request that I`d made, but I explained patiently that I had made some errors in my written notes for Hal and I wanted to correct them.

Patty`s face lit up,

"Hugh, that`s not a rubber – that`s an eraser!"

"We always called it a rubber", I persisted.

Patty, bless her, kept her poise as she explained,

"Hugh, in America, a rubber is a condom!"

I blushed and apologized. Patty laughed and broke the tension and I learned my first lesson; the English speak English and Americans speak American! It was only the first of many such examples which would reinforce Shaw`s observation several times during my early years living, working and socializing in our new home.

Another episode about Patty concerned a letter that I had composed to Margaret Thatcher, the Prime Minister of Great Britain at the time. I decided that it was time to voice my concern about my colleagues who were still locked up in Zimbabwe. After carefully writing the latter, I gave it to Patty early one morning and asked her if she would be so kind as to type it for me. When I did not see the letter by the next day, I asked Patty if she had been too busy to type the letter. Patty looked at me incredulously and said she had never typed a letter to the Prime Minister of Great Britain. She thought that I was playing a joke on her and she had pitched the letter. Given my episode over the 'condom', I could not blame her, so we started again! This time, Patty typed the letter!

37, Millhouse Drive,
Leamington Spa,
Warwickshire. CV32 6XW.

17th November, 1983.

The Honourable M. Thatcher,
Prime Minister of Great Britain.

Dear Madam,

I have wanted to write to you since my release from prison in Zimbabwe on the 9th September, but have delayed until now in the hope that the matter would have been finally resolved with regard to the other officers who are still detained. However, as you know, this is not the case and I feel that I should not delay any longer.

I particularly wanted to thank you for your support in the fight against our unjust incarceration in Zimbabwe; your firm stand for justice and truth in our case proves to me that the Free World's much admired values are alive and well in Britain and fills me with hope for the early release of those still in detention. I know that the other officers would want me to pass on their thanks too for your interest and help.

I would like to make mention of the courtesy and help extended to me and my colleagues by Minister Rifkind and staff at the Foreign Office, including Laurence Stephenson, Roger Browne and Tessa Solesby. I am aware too of the efforts made by the British High Commissioner in Harare and Mr. Nick Elam and Hugh Samuel of his staff, but I have not written to them because of the sensitivity of the situation; their help and interest is appreciated.

I am obviously still concerned that some of the officers are still detained and secondly, that there appears to be no progress on receiving our pensions. The thought of innocent men spending another Christmas in prison, separated from their families so unjustly and needlessly fill me with sadness. If it is the intention of that Government to deliberately ignore its moral and constitutional responsibilities, then it is my duty to my family and the others to appeal to you to see that justice does prevail in all these respects.

As I am sure you are aware, claims for damages against the Government of Zimbabwe could amount to substantial sums of money. As a sign of my good faith in the outcome of this matter, I have instructed my lawyers not to proceed any further with these claims at this stage. However, if it becomes necessary to act differently at any time because of that Government's intransigence, I shall do so without hesitation. I would, however, prefer that these matters were resolved amicably, quietly and, most of all, quickly; it is in this sense that I appeal to you.

My very best wishes go to you for your forthcoming trip for the Commonwealth Conference.

I have the honour to be,
Madam,
Your obedient servant

HUGH SLATTER
(H.C.S. SLATTER) A.V.M. (ret'd)

Below is the response from the Prime Minister's office;

10 DOWNING STREET

From the Private Secretary 1 December, 1983

Dear Air Vice-Marshal,

I have been asked by the Prime Minister to reply to your letter of 17 November, which she read with much sympathy.

The Prime Minister has followed the case of the air force officers with considerable personal interest from the time of the initial arrests. The Government intervened at an early stage to urge a speedy trial and to express concern at reports of ill-treatment. Ministers also acted firmly and quickly following the re-detentions after acquittal and both Ministers and officials have been and continue to be in frequent contact with the Zimbabwean authorities. Although we have no formal standing since all the officers have Zimbabwean citizenship, the fact that many of them also hold British citizenship has, of course, given us a special interest in their case.

Your own release, and that of three of your colleagues, was extremely welcome. The intentions of the Zimbabwean Government with respect to the other officers are still uncertain. But they can be in no doubt of our concern that the officers should be freed as soon as possible.

We also fully understand your concern that the officers should receive the pensions which they have earned. Mr. Rifkind raised this matter during his recent visit to Harare and our High Commissioner is following it up with the Zimbabwean authorities.

Yours sincerely

A. J. Coles.

H. Slatter, Esq.

Hal asked me to come to his office at the end of the day. He had cleared his desk of urgent items and spent the next couple of hours giving me a very useful outline of GE business practices, from the top levels of the Company down. This was to be the work pattern for the next few months, as Hal took me under his wing and coached me on American business and GE business, in particular. That Hal gave so unselfishly of his time every evening after usual work hours was a good indicator of the man's approach to his responsibilities as my manager. I was on trial in a totally new environment and Hal was not going to let me fail.

Our New Life

Jayne, Mark and Lee's first day had also had some surprises. Since Jayne was still on crutches and there was so much snow and ice outside, it was far too dangerous for her to try and walk the few hundred yards up the road to the nearest shops. To get some lunch, and being very conscious of our money situation, Jayne gave the boys a dollar and told them to walk up the road to a 'White Castle' burger store, which our cab driver had told us was the best value around, with burgers at 25 cents each! What our cab driver did not tell us was that these burgers were mini-burgers and one would need half a dozen of them to equate to a regular burger! Mark and Lee returned to our hotel, cold, embarrassed, and still hungry and thirsty!

GE had kindly arranged the hotel for our first week and would take care of our accommodations costs for the first month. I had scouted the area for schools and for longer term accommodation when I had initially visited for interviews, and I knew that we needed to move closer to a good school that would be close to work and to our future condo. We checked out of the hotel and moved into a motel next to the highway that ran past the school, which was only a few miles from work and close to our future condo.

There was a bus to take the boys to school and return them in the afternoon, but Jayne was stuck at the motel, since I had to use the car for work every day. This was a difficult time for Jayne, being on her own in a small room all day and especially since I was always getting home late from work.

February is perhaps the coldest month in Cincinnati, with snow and ice on the ground a lot the month and temperatures well below freezing. It was too dangerous for Jayne to venture out of her room on crutches, and the days dragged interminably. At the end of the month, we moved into our condo in a large and well laid-out development, with plenty of open spaces between the blocks of condos. What a welcome change! We now had two bedrooms, two bathrooms, a combined sitting and dining area, and a small kitchen.

Since we had no furniture, we had to rent the basics from a nearby furniture store. We chose a small dining table and four chairs, a sofa, a bed for each of our sons, and Jayne and I decided on a large mattress for ourselves, because we were running out of money. Since I had lived for 13 months with no furniture at all in the various cells and prisons, this was fine for me!

Jayne had visited a specialist to continue the treatment for her leg and, in particular, her knee. While it seemed that the femur was now strengthened by the titanium insert, the knee was still impossible to bend. The specialist put Jayne in a nearby hospital for five days of extreme forced bending of the knee by a mechanical apparatus. The hospital was within walking distance of our condo and it was easy, notwithstanding the cold, for me, Mark and Lee to visit Jayne every day. Jayne, of course, insisted on reducing the rest periods between the forced bending, so she could subject her knee to the full treatment, even through the nights.

As painful as this was, her knee started to bend a little more each day. By the time Jayne left the hospital, she had almost ninety degrees of movement; a vast improvement. The doctors were pessimistic about any further improvement, but they did not know Jayne or her determination. Over the following months, she gradually increased her flexibility to some 110 degrees, by performing simple but tough and painful exercises, giving her enough motion to perform most functions.

Mark and Lee`s first day at school was another cultural awakening for us. We had bought grey slacks and white, collared shirts with black shoes in England, as was the customary dress for schoolboys. They looked tidy and sharp as they left for school, but they returned embarrassed and somewhat crestfallen. It seemed that no one wore anything except jeans and sneakers to school in American public schools! So concerned were they, and so determined not to be a spectacle on the next day too, that we took them to a thrift store that evening and equipped them with some cheap jeans and sneakers.

This did not impress Lee, who announced that the other kids wore designer sneakers and jeans, and it was hard trying to explain that we had so little money that we could barely afford the cheap clothes. While one would never be wealthy on an Air Force salary, we were paid regularly, had savings and were accumulating a pension. This was all essentially stolen by the Zimbabwe government. I realized that this is what has become of Africa, under despotic governments, and I was grateful to be in the USA, with a chance to rebuild our lives. Our lack of money would never be as important as our safety and freedom. Thank you, USA and Senator Eagleton!

These first few weeks in the USA caused us to notice some of the significant differences between the lifestyles and culture of Africans (Rhodesians) and Americans. The most obvious being the large numbers of people wherever one went in the USA. In Rhodesia, for example, a visit to Salisbury, the largest city in the country with a population of some 50,000, would probably cause one to run into half a dozen different friends in various stores, cafés or on the sidewalks. Conversely, a visit to one of the malls or anywhere in Cincinnati, for us, would yield not a single friend or acquaintance; a strange feeling of loneliness and of irrelevance.

Similarly, on a drive home in Rhodesia late at night, one might come across one or two other cars on the road, whereas in any city in the USA, the roads and highways are busy and crowded at all hours of the day and night. If you had one or two drinks too many in the evening in Rhodesia, the only car you were likely to damage was your own!

Supermarkets in America left us in awe. Even with international sanctions against Rhodesia for 15 years, we were self-sufficient in everything needed for day to day living, although the choice of products was limited. But the size, choices and selection in the USA was staggering to us. Aisle upon aisle of every product and brand imaginable, it seemed. Prices too were fair and although we had to watch our dollars carefully, we could always find good, healthy products and produce, although no Rhodesian beef! I joke about that only because Rhodesia was a major supplier of excellent beef to a lot of Europe, where it was recognized as some of the best beef in the world and priced accordingly!

Clothes, for me, were not too different, although I was no longer in uniform. Civilian work clothes were very similar, with suits and ties, slacks and blazers or sports coats being the norm for office wear. Women`s typical dress code in the USA was a disappointment to me. Often it was jeans or some sort of trouser, unless one was working for a senior executive as an aide. Not as feminine as the dresses and skirts that I was used to in Rhodesia and Europe.

Even in the normal office there was not much femininity, with only the occasional exception. I never really understood this because the selection of women`s clothes seemed vast and generally reasonably priced. When designers recognized that standard jeans could be ugly, along came the likes of Armani and others with designer jeans at several hundred dollars a pair! Being old fashioned and male, I still think that women look their feminine best in dresses or skirts.

The basic courtesies too were different. In Rhodesia, it was routine to say `please` and 'thank you', and yet it seemed not as prevalent in the USA. On the other hand, in the USA everyone would respond with a 'You're welcome' to any 'thank you' offered, not a practice in Africa. Perhaps the best example of differences in courtesy is to be found in the practice of queuing, or getting in line. Here, Americans win hands down with their orderly and disciplined approach to taking their turn, by getting in line and giving space to the person in front. In Africa and in Europe too, whoever can push their way to the front from any part of a crowd, usually does so, and it`s generally considered acceptable, albeit annoying.

When it came to meetings, I was accustomed to the discipline of the military process, whereby the senior officer would solicit the views of the most junior members first, to ensure some originality of thought. I soon learned in my business meetings in the USA that I had to speak up, almost to the point of interrupting, if I had something to say on a matter. The best opportunities for me to share my points of view usually came in the evenings, after the regular work day, when Hal would invite me to his office to discuss work. It was due to Hal`s intense and dedicated interest in my work and welfare that I was able to learn quickly about the key values and processes of business, and American business, in particular.

First Steps Up the Corporate Ladder

Hal`s interest in my advancement became more evident at the end of the year, when one of his section leaders retired and Hal put me into the position. While I was delighted with the promotion, I had mixed feelings. I was especially sensitive to the concern that long-standing members of Hal's team might have about an outsider, a foreigner at that, taking a position that perhaps one of them wanted. With this foremost in my mind, I decided to re-double my efforts to prove my worth.

It had become known that I was a dedicated and tireless member of the team, and I sensed no animosity. But now I had a staff that reported to me, as their manager, and I was determined to make this the most efficient and appreciated team in the business. My staff were all experienced and competent in their roles and I wanted to focus on strengthening the teaming efforts of the group, the understanding that we all depended on each other`s efforts and contributions. I felt that I could best do this by spending time understanding their detailed functions and helping where I could, however menial my contribution.

My group had the responsibility to provide proposals to the US Navy and Air Force for support equipment; test stands and other equipment to support ongoing operations and serviceability of US Forces. These were always required by certain dates and times and we were invariably under pressure to submit these proposals to meet the deadlines imposed by the Service requirements. Although my group had design engineers for some of the equipment, and I had control over our own input and timing, I also had to rely on other design groups for their input. This was very often at the last minute and required a lot of scrambling from my group to finalize the proposal and have it submitted on time. Obviously, if it was not on time, our proposal was not evaluated, with the associated consequences for our business.

In one particular case, we were faced with a large and detailed proposal involving the design of special test stands and tooling for the US Air Force. All the necessary data from my group was ready by midday, the day before our proposal was due, to be submitted to the Air Force who had offices in our plant. However, many of the items that were being designed by another engineering group were not ready.

I was on good terms with the head of that group and spoke to him about the impending crunch. He assured me that I would have their complete package by close of business that day. Even that would make things difficult for my group, since we then had to check the data, make the copies and assemble 50 copies of the proposal in a pre-determined format. Since the entire package would be some 300 pages, there was a lot of time-consuming work to be done before the deadline at 8 am the next day. When the data package from Engineering had not arrived by close of business, I asked the appropriate members of my staff if they could wait until it did, which they agreed to do.

The data package finally arrived, at around 6 pm, and we set to work reviewing the contents. I was fortunate that I had some very experienced and competent staff to do this, but it still took several hours before we were satisfied that we could go to print. Hal, bless him, had brought in some pizzas, knowing we would be running late, so we finished those off and then most of the team left for home, leaving me and one staff member to copy and assemble the complete set of proposals. I was determined that I was not going to let Hal down; even it meant working through the night.

Our offices had a large copying room, with three or four copiers, and we would need them all. Donna and I spent the next eight hours running those machines and assembling the required 50 copies. By 6 am, we were far enough along for me to send Donna home with my grateful thanks, and I told her to take the day off, since she had now been working non-stop for 24 hours. By 7 am, I was ready. I carried the proposals to my car, rushed home for a quick shower and shave, passing Hal on the way, and told him we would make the deadline for submittal.

I arrived at the Air Force office at 7:45 am, delivered the proposals, got proof of timely delivery and headed back to the office. I wanted to thank the team for their efforts, make sure they had all got home safely and had some rest. They were grateful for my concern and I could tell them that, due to their efforts, we had submitted the proposals on time. This was very important because it was one of our biggest proposals, worth tens of millions of dollars and included advanced test stands, much needed by the Air Force.

A few hours later, I was called to our Human Resources office where the manager informed me that I did not have the authority to give a member of my staff the day off. She was pleasant about it and explained that I would run up against the unions, if they were to find out. I was somewhat staggered, having had all the authority in the world while I was in the Air Force, but I understood her point and learned the lesson that with all the regulation in American business, I was manager in name only! However, my staff was aware of the situation. Our work through the night and word of it circulated that I was a manager who indeed 'walked the talk'. From then on, I did not feel that I was an outsider.

This first year of our new life passed quickly. So much was new to us and learning my new role, under Hal's guidance, was time consuming. Hal would usually start work around 6 am, and I liked to be at work when he arrived. After the usual work day, Hal would spend extra time, for an hour or two, answering my questions and generally teaching me about the business and what was expected. Jayne's leg continued to heal, she was no longer on crutches and was even walking without a cane after a few months. The boys were finding their way at school, catching up on the missed months while in the UK and making new friends.

The Company seemed satisfied with my performance and we were receiving regular monthly checks. On top of the regular monthly income, the Company had very generously reimbursed us for our travel expenses. This was unexpected and when I queried Hal, he simply said it was the right thing to do. We were grateful because it would allow us to look for a small house, to have enough money for a deposit and we started looking for a place we could afford. As usual, Hal came to the rescue, explaining the pros and cons of the various areas that would be safe and convenient and where we would pay less taxes!

Before we moved from our condo, we experienced an exciting day. Jayne had put our furniture in storage in Zimbabwe until we had an address in the USA that could receive the load. One day a big moving van arrived at our rented condo and off-loaded our old family furniture. It was a heart-warming experience for me. Although I had become used to minimum furnishings after more than a year in prison and various jail cells, followed by months with Bobby and Roy and the very limited furniture we had rented for the condo, it was wonderful to see our old stuff again!

It was also quite different from what I had observed at some American homes, where furniture seemed to be replaced quite frequently. In more of a designer style, our furniture was mostly old family pieces, going back to our parents and our early days together. In fact, most pieces would qualify as antiques here in America! It was a happy day and served as a very good emotional rehabilitation for me, bringing back some memories of the happier times in Rhodesia.

Upon looking into vacation time, I discovered that I would qualify for five days in my first year. I had not looked into this when I joined GE and I was to discover that American companies are not as generous with vacation as European companies or even the Air Force. However, Hal asked me what I wanted to do, and at the same time, offered us the use of his condo in Daytona Beach, Florida. It was a very kind gesture and we readily accepted.

We would leave immediately after work on a Friday and drive the 17 hours straight through to give us maximum time at the coast. Hal also spent some time telling me about the places of interest and made special mention of a pleasant beach, just a few blocks from his condo. When I asked him how we would find the special beach, he simply smiled and said:

"You will know when you are there!"

After a long, all-night drive, we arrived at Hal and Vera's condo, unloaded the car and decided to find Hal`s special beach. We had never been to Daytona Beach and we walked the three or four blocks to the ocean to be met by miles of sandy beach.

Assuming this to be Hal`s special beach, we set off walking south, along the edge of the water, with Mark and Lee making the most of the breaking waves. After walking about a half mile, we noticed a large board on a post, sticking out of the sand, and assumed it would be some sort of public warning about the beaches. However, on getting closer, the very large printing on the board read: WELCOME TO THE SLATTERS

This was Hal's special part of the beach! Hal and Vera had been at their condo some three weeks before us and I was amazed that Hal`s message was still there and untouched. It wouldn`t have lasted a day in Africa!

Our First House

Jayne had been looking at some houses that we could afford, and we settled on a home under construction in the same suburb as the GE plant. We were extremely lucky to find this home, which was the last of five homes being built along a quiet *cul-de-sac* for the families of a local business man. It seemed that the fifth member of this family had decided to live elsewhere, and this house would be on the market.

I had a difficult time getting my head around the fact that the asking price was almost $100,000! Remembering that Jayne's and my first home in Rhodesia, complete with swimming pool, had cost slightly more than $10,000! With the monies which GE had reimbursed us for our airline tickets, as well as the few thousand dollars which the Zimbabwe government had grudgingly repaid, as my contributions to an imaginary pension, we could make a minimal down payment to allow us to qualify for a mortgage.

I was grateful to the ongoing efforts of the UK government to encourage the Zimbabwe government to abide by the law and pay my full pension, but predictably, this never happened. On the bright side, we were safe in the USA, our health was good, our sons were in school and I had a job. We had much to be grateful for. Thank you, America!

Our condo lease was for a year and the house would be available when the lease was up; perfect timing! We were able to watch the last phases of construction of our new home. It was of timber construction and sat on a steep slope, with a view across the valley towards GE. The builders were friendly and Jayne and I were delighted when they wanted to talk to us so that they could hear our accents! We thought that was funny, because they were from Kentucky, with strong accents we enjoyed, although they could not understand our observation that they were the ones with an accent! It was also our first experience of having discussions with construction workers, and we loved their friendliness, calling us 'Jayne' and 'Hugh.'

This open friendliness is one of the traits that I enjoy so much about Americans. There is little, if any, of the stuffiness of the British type of formality. There was some class consciousness in Rhodesia, given its British background and ties, but this did not seem to be the case here in America. As time has passed, it`s become even more evident to me that Americans judge you by what you can do, rather than by your heritage. Perhaps that is because the USA is such a melting pot of diverse cultures and backgrounds. Whatever the reason, I like it!

A few weeks before we were due to make our move from the condo to our new home, I was talking to a friend at work by name of Nick Jones. He had recently joined GE after a career in the US Air Force, retiring as a full Colonel. We were in different sections but I was able to help show him the ropes when he joined, since everything was still fresh in my mind. He inquired when we were due to make our move; I told him the date and thought nothing more of it.

The day of our move dawned, with cold and pouring rain. I had rented a small moving van and would have to make several trips of about ten miles each time. It was going to be a long day! Jayne could help with the packing, but because of her leg, not the heavy moving, although Mark and Lee could help me with that part. Early that morning, we were still in the condo, getting things ready for our first run, when there was a knock at the front door.

It was Nick and his wife and their two teenage daughters. Mark and Lee suddenly became more interested!

Nick had brought his big truck and while Ursula (his wife) brought trays of food inside, the rest of us started loading. Jayne and I were so touched by this unexpected help and did our best to express our thanks, which were brushed aside. I`m sure the teenage daughters would rather have been in bed at that hour, rather than carrying furniture, boxes and bedding to the trucks, in the rain and wind, but they never complained and it certainly seemed that Mark and Lee needed no encouragement to impress the girls with their strength!

The result of Nick and his family`s unsolicited and generous help was that the move was completed in less than half the trips contemplated, and they were able to leave us in our new house, shortly after lunch. I had prepared to make trips with our single van until nightfall, so we were delighted! When I spoke to Nick at work about his help, he again brushed aside my thanks, but the kindness of that act has always stuck with me and Jayne. We became firm friends for years afterwards and although Mark and Lee were interested in Nick's daughters, they were at different schools and already had boyfriends!

Jayne's leg was continuing to improve and she wanted to start working. So, we looked around for an inexpensive car and soon Jayne was driving around as if she`d been driving all her life in America! Highways were a thing to avoid, in Jayne`s mind, so she learned all the back roads and was soon equipped to look for suitable work in the nearby area. Back in Rhodesia and Zimbabwe, Jayne had worked as an administrator for a local dentist, and it did not take long for her to find similar work at a large dental practice in a mall, just a few miles away. This was an excellent development for Jayne.

Back in Rhodesia and Zimbabwe, Jayne was always a busy person, working during the day in the dental office and spending time out of hours in her flower garden and running our home. Although, we had the services of someone to help in the garden, there was always planning and supervision of new plantings. Since her accident, she had been unable to work, and living in a condo, there was no garden to look after. Now we owned a property and had the opportunity to develop a garden! With her leg being functional again, she could drive, work, garden, and look after our home.

Interestingly, the word 'garden' initially caused us some confusion. In Rhodesia and in England, when one uses the word 'garden', one is referring to a flower garden. In America, it soon became apparent that the word 'garden' usually referred to a vegetable garden. When our American friends would ask us what vegetables we had planted in our garden, and we would reply 'None', we began to realize that our answer made no sense! To avoid this *cul-de-sac* in conversation, we learned to be more precise.

Jayne's work load suddenly increased and she loved it! My work load was about to increase as well, and by my own choice. GE, like most good Companies, uses an annual assessment process which allows employees to understand their strengths, weaknesses and suitability for promotion. I realized quickly that unless I wanted to remain in a low-level job for the rest of my working life, the first requirement would be for me to get an American degree.

Back To School!

GE has a great system, whereby if your managers agree to approve a course of study that would be of direct benefit in your job, the Company would reimburse you the cost of the course upon successful completion. In my first and subsequent annual evaluation documents, I had taken the time to outline my own five-year growth plan, which included specific training that would benefit me and the company. It also included minor courses that GE offered internally and at local training centers and colleges.

My bosses had liked my thinking and had no hesitation in approving the minor courses in basic finance and the like. The idea of taking on a college degree seemed like a `no-brainer` to me, but after some discussion and help from my managers, we identified a program that would lead to a Master's degree in Acquisition Management. The subjects emphasized contracts and law, especially government-contracting. This would be directly helpful in my current job and would allow me to expand into other areas later.

I did not plan to spend my life in government-contracting, but most importantly, this would give me a valuable American degree qualification, which in turn would open up many other better, more interesting and rewarding jobs. Without a recognized American degree, many opportunities would simply not be available. The classes would be on-line, by correspondence and by occasional attendance at prescribed centers around the country. I obtained my manager`s approval, applied to the college for the first set of courses and was off and running!

Taking on this degree program put a heavy, extra work load on Jayne and meant less time for me to spend with Mark and Lee. For the next two and a half years, I was to spend my evenings after dinner and my weekends studying and submitting the required papers, but I had to do it if I was to have a chance at a decent second career. At age 42 and having spent some 21 years in the Air Force, I reasoned that I had another 23 years, at least, to make a living and to help support my family.

The sacrifices made by all of us proved well worthwhile and later opened up other jobs, as I hoped it would. As promised, I was reimbursed after the successful completion of each set of courses, allowing me to advance to the next set until my final exams. The final exams took me six weeks of work, every evening and every weekend, and I was able to submit my paper in the required time. I felt confident. I had done all the required studies and I was comfortable with the exams themselves. I was delighted when I received my results, some weeks later, with a full pass and a letter of special commendation, along with my degree - Master of Acquisition Management.

Family Life

The next few years went by in a more settled manner. Jayne had found work at a florist, doing floral design. This was exactly what she needed. She had a passion for flowers and gardening and was lucky enough, like her mother, to have a 'green thumb.' Jayne`s leg was fully healed and strong, especially since the specialist had elected to leave the titanium rod inside her femur. There was no more discomfort, but the flexibility seemed stuck at about 110 degrees, better than the surgeons had hoped for, due mostly to Jayne`s very determined efforts at rehabilitation, and it was probably as good as it would ever be. At least she had a functional leg, and much better than a wooden one!

Jayne`s work at the florist meant that sometimes she would be required to work late, especially prior to special holidays and events. On such occasions, I would struggle to cook dinner. I have never had much interest in cooking, except for the good old South African '*braaivleis*' (similar to a BBQ/Barbeque). Additionally, I had never been trained in cooking and since Jayne was an excellent cook, I saw no need to try to compete.

Mark and Lee hated these evenings and would much rather have bought fast food, but I battled on, setting fire to the fries, burning the pasta and was just happy not to set the kitchen and house on fire! On one occasion, I was attempting pasta with a creamy garlic sauce, helped along with glasses of wine. Jayne`s return home kept getting later and later, but that didn`t slow down my glasses of wine. At least until the pasta resembled something that looked more like construction cement.

Finally, at around 10 pm, Jayne called to say that she was on her way. Panicked, I made a quick salad, put some flowers on the table, turned down the lighting and lit our nicest candles. As I heard Jayne pull into the driveway, I opened a fresh bottle of her favorite wine and poured glasses for us both. I had not cleaned up the cooking mess yet and soon Jayne discovered what had happened. As it turned out, she had only wanted a salad anyway and she loved the romantic setting! That night I learned that luck beats skill!

Mark and Lee's schooling continued pretty normally. However, one day I received a call from the school that Lee`s teacher wanted to see me. I should point out that this was a large school with more than 2,000 students and not much interaction between staff and parents. When I arrived, I was shown into an office where I met Lee`s teacher, a friendly African-American lady of some 50 years old, I imagined, and I liked her instantly. Lee was summoned and appeared, looking suitably surprised to see his father there too, and his teacher informed me that Lee had not been doing his homework. This surprised me because I would often ask the boys if they had homework and did they need any help. The answer was usually 'No.'

My question was,

"How long has this been going on?"

"About six weeks", was her answer.

Since there could be no motive for the teacher to lie about this, my next question, remembering similar incidents involving me at school, was,

"Have you given him a beating?"

There was a stunned silence and then the teacher said,

"Oh no, we never do that here."

I went on to say that I had not done my homework on one occasion and had received four cuts with a cane as punishment. I also explained that I always did my homework after that! Furthermore, I had suffered no long-term trauma or severe emotional distress as a result and I had no objection to physical punishment, when warranted. I seem to recall that I was asked to leave her office after that and I don`t think I was ever called back to discuss disciplinary processes again. I did, however, make it clear to Lee that I would not tolerate such omissions again.

Both Mark and Lee went on to graduate from high school and Mark completed two years of college for an Associate's Degree. Lee had little interest in academics and would learn over the next few years that a lack of useful qualification would disqualify him from any decent job. As soon as he experienced this (rather than believing Mom and Dad!), he started working on some useful and practical programs, which soon equipped him for meaningful employment. Today, he leads a group of airplane seat design engineers for a large engineering company in Cincinnati, Ohio, and enjoys the responsibility.

Mark focused on computer technology and applications and today is the number two in a growing communications company, having recently moved to New York State to take the position. When we look at our two sons and their lives today, compared to what they would have endured had they been stuck in Zimbabwe, Jayne and I feel much gratitude to those who helped with our immigration, as well as to America, for providing the opportunity to experience the American dream of freedom and to pursue one`s goals without fear of government interference.

Frustration

After several years of working and managing small groups within the large military division of GE Aircraft Engines, I found myself becoming more and more frustrated with the procurement system of the Defense Department and the Pentagon. It seemed new rules, standards and specifications were added to contract requirements on a daily basis. Even my college lecturers told me that if they could keep up with 60% of these regulations, it was not enough to avoid mistakes. Penalties for omissions or errors on government contracts could be severe and the bureaucracy was stifling.

What made it, perhaps, worse for me was the fact that I had come out of an Air Force as an operational Air Vice Marshal (equivalent to a two-star General) and was used to getting things done instantly. But now, the simplest requirement meant hours of research and analysis of specs and standards to ensure full compliance. Those who may remember the rightful public indignation over $6,000 toilet seats for the military might have been more understanding if they realized that the government procurement agency had demanded almost every specification in the book, including such expensive and unnecessary requirements as nuclear-proof, mould-proof, shatter-proof, explosion-proof, corrosion-proof and on and on!

I finally decided that I had experienced enough when I was unable to ship an urgently required spare to an operational bomber base because of a single word inversion on a government request. The defense representative insisted that I contact the requesting authority and have them amend the request before he would authorize shipment. I finally shipped the item 24 hours later, after endless scrambling, and I remember thinking to myself as I drove home late that night,

"We don`t need an enemy; WE are the enemy!"

I can honestly say that those five years were the most unsatisfying and disappointing five years of my relationship with the military, as I witnessed our proud and brave fighting forces having to deal with an acquisition process that hampered them at every turn. Speaking personally, I can honestly say that my own 21 years in the Air Force were the most rewarding years of my life. In my view, there is nothing more satisfying than knowing that one is serving one's country and its people. I was unable to do this when I came to America, but my eldest son, Mark, joined the Air National Guard and served with distinction, earning several awards and making Jayne and I very proud.

Commercial Aircraft Engines

During my years working with the military, I had kept my sights on joining the commercial engine division and I had a good friend who worked for the group. He had kept my name in the mind of the head of the division and although I had met him, I sensed little enthusiasm from him for me to join his group. That all changed one day when my friend, Chick, told me of an opportunity that would open up within the group that had responsibility for European sales. When the opening was posted, I applied immediately and shortly thereafter was invited for an interview. Here, it turns out, was the second man who was to have a major effect on me, and on my family`s life.

His name was Ray Wagner, a veteran of sales in the group. He had decided to retire at age 68, and being a man who cared about the job and his airline customers, in particular, had decided to post the job early, in order to select and train a replacement to his own standard. Ray was very interested in my background and I was impressed with his experience and successes with his airlines. I got some feedback from my friend that the interview had gone very well, but I knew this was just the start of the process within GE and did not get too optimistic.

There were many candidates for Ray's job posting. The commercial arena was much prized for its known excellence, having lead GE to be the number one sales leader in commercial aircraft engines over the years, a position that the company guarded zealously. I learned too that some of the applicants had doctorates in aerodynamics and other aviation-related disciplines, and wondered if such degrees were really a necessity for such a job. If so, I didn`t stand much of a chance.

However, Ray invited me for a second interview and I soon learned that he was a much more pragmatic man than I had realized. He actually brought up the criteria that he considered essential for the job, and happily for me, they did not include an advanced doctorate! We had a solid one-hour meeting, Ray seemed to hone in on his requirements – the ability to listen well and to be truly customer-focused.

He knew that I was not an engineer but was satisfied with my five years of experience with our military side of the engine business, as well as my Air Force technical training. I knew that if I was to get the job, I would need to spend time getting familiar with our commercial engines in some detail. Ray thanked me for my time and asked if I would drop in and speak with his boss, which I happily agreed to do. That was a short, introductory meeting and with the usual pleasantries exchanged. I knew of Ray's boss, the head of all European sales and an extremely competent man with a solid reputation.

A few days later, I got a call from Ray who invited me to come and see him. I sensed that this was either the good news or the bad news. However, Ray welcomed me with a smile and said he had a letter of offer for me. The offer was generous. It included a promotion and a raise and I had no difficulty accepting with gratitude. I had cleared the possibility of this change of job with my boss on the military side of the business (Hal had retired) and there were no obstacles in my way.

I had also spent time with Jayne, Mark and Lee, discussing this possibility, and everyone agreed that I should accept, if I got the offer. I was welcomed by the head of European sales and met his group at a staff meeting the very next day. American businesses do not procrastinate! I was mindful that I was joining a group of some of the finest sales people in the US, and possibly the world, since this was the team that had assured GE of first place in worldwide engine sales for many years. I was humbled and determined that I would make a meaningful contribution to the team. I was equally determined that I would not let Ray down.

Ray's belief was that the best training was on-the-job-training and he told me to prepare to join him for his next trip to his European airlines. Ray`s work pattern, and the reason he was so successful, was to spend as much time as possible with his customer airlines, to spend two to three weeks a month overseas while visiting these airlines. On these visits, Ray would make technical presentations on the state of our engines and our development programs, as well as consider the airline's fleet planning requirements with a view to future sales, and of course, to cement the relationships that he had built so painstakingly over many years.

I had some two weeks to get ready, and although I knew that Ray would be introducing me and doing the presentations himself, I busied myself studying our engines; performance, reliability, technical issues, fleet stats and so on. It was actually fascinating and I found myself becoming more and more interested. In addition to my studying the details of our engines, I spent time with Ray, learning the history of his airlines, what it had taken to win those airlines, what it would take to keep them and what we needed to do to capture some airlines that were not yet GE customers.

Most importantly, Ray spent considerable time outlining the main players in each airline. This was where Ray really shone. His relationships with these airlines covered some 35 years and it was clear that he cared deeply about his customers and their equipment requirements. He knew the key players in each of his airlines, from the Chairman to the head of engineering to the factory chief and beyond, and in some cases, he knew their families. I couldn`t wait for our trip to begin! Ray had outlined a three-week trip, covering some twenty airlines in Northern and Western Europe. This seemed a long time to me but I was soon to discover that no time was wasted.

We started this trip by flying out of Cincinnati to Chicago, to connect with our international flight. A distinct bonus about flying with Ray was that his airlines always upgraded him, and since I was with him and Ray would have it no other way, I got to enjoy this privilege too. We flew out of Chicago on one of Ray`s favorite airlines, KLM. The advantage of being in first class was that we had the quiet and comfort to do some more preparatory work, especially for our meetings the very next morning with the KLM Chairman, followed by two days of meetings with their operational, engineering and planning staffs. KLM was a longtime GE customer, thanks to Ray's earlier efforts, and the airline operated a large fleet of wide-bodied aircraft with our engines. Consequently, we had a large support staff on site in their overhaul facility and we would spend time with them too.

We landed, went to our airport hotel for a quick shower and shave and returned to the office of the KLM Chairman by 11 am. Suits and ties were very much the order of the day and we were promptly ushered into his office. The Chairman`s obvious pleasure at seeing Ray told me chapters about Ray's work at the airline. Ray introduced me and I was politely welcomed.

There was no prepared presentation for the Chairman; just some discussion about the fleet, overall, and any new technical developments GE was pursuing, which Ray thought would be interesting to him. We took our leave after an hour or so and I was left with the overriding impression of how much trust the Chairman placed in Ray; something that does not happen overnight.

We then spent the afternoon in detailed meetings with the engineering staffs, followed by meetings with the planning staffs. Here Ray excelled with his presentations. Although these presentations were books of some detail, Ray made them a very interactive forum, answering questions as they arose and generating new discussion where any uncertainty existed. It was clear from the questions and answers that Ray had developed much credibility with these specialists. Where there were issues, Ray did not skirt them or sugar coat them but spent time outlining our technical and business remedies. There was much to be covered and we did not finish until just after 6 pm, at which point we left for a working dinner with our own GE technical staffs.

Since Ray had taken the sensible step of inviting our chief technical manager to our afternoon meetings, we were able to cover most of these points while eating dinner, but it was clear we would need more time the next day, in a quieter environment. And then it was back to our hotel. After my first full day in my new job, I was exhilarated and excited by the intensity. I was also exhausted and went to bed, replaying in my mind the way that Ray had conducted the meetings and watching the interpersonal relationships that he had so carefully developed over the years. He was an excellent role model and I vowed to learn from his example.

The next morning, Ray, the head of our GE technical staff, and I met with the airline maintenance staffs and went through the factory, with special attention to any tooling requirements and any engines that were not meeting the usual overhaul requirements. There were no surprises and by lunchtime, we were finished. Ray and I had to catch our flight in a couple of hours and we had a quick lunch with the technical team, took some action notes and left to catch our flight to Norway, where we would meet with the Chairman of Braathens Airline and his staff the next morning.

I had not been to Norway or any of the other Scandinavian countries in my life, and I was excited to watch the landscape over Oslo unfold, as we descended into the airport. The cab ride into town was about half an hour, as I recall, and by the time we had checked into our hotel, there was time only to have dinner and go over some shared notes and follow-up items for us to transmit back to our factory in Cincinnati.

The next morning, we met with the Chairman and owner of the airline, Bjorn Braathens. It was immediately apparent that he and Ray had a long-standing relationship by their warm greeting and questions about their respective families. Ray introduced me and I felt at ease with this giant of a Norwegian business owner. He enquired solicitously about me and my family and seemed genuinely interested in my replies. I was particularly interested in the art work in his office; numerous well known works by some French impressionists and Dutch masters, which I assumed to be very good copies. Seeing my gaze, Bjorn commented,

"Yes, Hugh, they are the originals!"

I was somewhat embarrassed but complimented him, explaining that I was a bit of an art fan myself, to which, Bjorn responded,

"Then you must walk the halls of this building, each floor, because you will find many works to enjoy."

After our discussions about his airline and our engines, we did a tour of the building to see the art works. I was surprised! Every hallway had beautiful and original examples of fine European art, dating from the early masters, through the impressionists and beyond. I asked Bjorn why he did not have these priceless works in a more secure room. He stopped and looked at me in a meaningful way and said,

"These pictures are for everyone here to see and enjoy. I didn`t buy them to shut them away."

I was hugely impressed with his generosity to his staff, in this regard, but I was to learn a much more valuable lesson about Bjorn when we walked onto the factory floor. The workers on the line all knew and addressed Bjorn by his name, and he knew every one of their names and their families! We spent an interesting few hours in the factory, before meeting with Bjorn`s other staff, back in the main offices.

Braathens Airline operated narrow-body airplanes with our CFM engines, popular on Boeing 737 and Airbus A320 types. CFM is a joint company, shared equally between GE and SNECMA (now SAFRAN) of France. It is the most successful engine business in the world, in terms of numbers of engines in operation globally. Whenever we worked with CFM at our European airlines, we shared our plans and, quite often, our visits with one of our SNECMA counterparts. Ray had been doing this for so long that he always took the lead, but I started to work with a very competent and friendly young man by name of David Cook. Over the years, we did many visits and campaigns together, which David always managed to win for us.

Ray and I enjoyed lunch with Bjorn, and some of his engineering staff, and then we left for a visit to our maintenance facility in Stavanger, on the west coast. We were due in Luxembourg that evening for a dinner with the head of operations and planning for Cargolux Airlines, one Johannes Einarsson, so we were on our airplane without delay, landing in Luxembourg at around 6 pm.

Cargolux was, and still is, the largest cargo operator in Europe with 747-200 freighters, and was now looking to expand and move into the latest 747-400 freighter, with our engines; hence the sales campaign. Although Ray and Johannes knew each other, I did not sense as close a connection as that with Bjorn Braathens or the Chairman of KLM, and I surmised that we would need to conduct a concerted campaign here to convince Cargolux that our GE engines were, in fact, the best for their requirement. Our main competitor would be Rolls Royce, who also produced excellent engines, and who I felt sure would put in every effort to win such a valuable customer.

We spent the next day with Ray, making the engine presentations to Johannes, then to the engineering staff followed by the planning staffs. While this meant three different sets of presentations, it was necessary because of airline staff availability, and each group had a slightly different focus, generating different discussions. I was absorbed by the depth of the questions from these specialists of many years, and I realized that I had much learning to do.

The best thing I could do, under the circumstances, was to listen and learn as much as I could. Not having to make the presentations allowed me to observe our customer, to listen to how each one asked his or her questions and to gather a picture of their personality, since I gathered I would be spending a lot of time over the next few years with these groups.

Sales campaigns for jet engines are usually lengthy affairs, lasting some years, due to the huge investment required by the airline and the need to build the credibility required for such a long-term investment and relationship. One expects to operate airplanes and engines for at least twenty years to ensure any sort of return.

While initial purchase price was always important, it was equally important for the airline to be able to negotiate satisfactory guarantees for maintenance, performance retention, spares and so on. I was beginning to learn that there was a lot more to this business than I had initially realized, but I was fascinated and hungry to learn. On top of all this, I was impressed by the airline people that we were meeting, extremely knowledgeable, experienced and, in all cases so far, friendly! I`m sure the friendliness had much to do with Ray`s obvious ability to build long term, meaningful and valuable business relationships.

We finished our meetings, thanked our customer and since the next day was the start of the weekend, crossed the border into France and drove to Caen, in Normandy. I was to learn that Ray had been an engineer with US forces during the D-Day landings, and he had gone ashore on the second day. My respect for him rose to another level. Ray wished to visit some of the places that he had experienced under much more difficult and hazardous conditions, and I was delighted and interested to tag along.

Interestingly, the French in this region of Normandy remember the Allied forces driving the German Army from the area, and still show their appreciation and gratitude. If we were sitting at a café and locals heard Ray talking with his American accent, they would approach and offer to buy us a coffee or a glass of wine. It was heartwarming and we were able to reciprocate at some of the small villages, so very different to Paris! We spent some time at the excellent museum at Caen and were able, amongst other things, to watch live footage filmed from the German pillboxes on the coastal cliffs at the start of the allied invasion.

While the supposedly impregnable defenses of the Germans initially wreaked havoc on the landing forces, the amazing bravery and skills of the Special Forces, climbing the cliffs and destroying the pillboxes, allowed the landing craft to offload the heavy weaponry and start the real assault on the German defenses. As we know, this was the beginning of the end of World War II.

Ray and I continued our visits, meetings and presentations to our other European airlines during the following week, spending time in Sweden, Finland and finally returning to the UK. Sweden and Finland were new to me and I was excited to get my first taste of the different cultures and geography. Language was not a problem, fortunately, since everyone in the aviation industry spoke English. I had some basic French, but not enough to conduct any sort of technical discussion, and the Dutch were amused at my attempts to converse, using my conversational Afrikaans (similar to the old Dutch language).

The process was similar at all our customers; introduce the new guy (me), renew and strengthen the relationships, review the airlines' fleet plans, update the airlines on our engine developments and listen carefully for any dissatisfaction, especially on maintenance requirements. If we had no customer dinner in the evening, Ray and I would go over our notes and action items, ensuring that nothing any of our customers needed was ignored. Some of these requirements we sent to our support staff back in GE, while others would have to wait until we returned to our factory for action.

We returned home on the weekend and I was happy to have some time with Jayne, Mark and Lee again. Although my previous jobs with the military side of the business had kept me at home most of the time, I had pushed myself, working long hours and studying, as I strove to learn and start to repay my Company for their trust and support. While I slept most nights at home, there was less family time than was desirable, and the burden fell on Jayne. We all recognized that travel and time away would be a large part of my new job, but it was a much more interesting environment, I felt less stressed without a large staff to manage and the opportunities for advancement were greater.

Back in the office, I sat with Ray and we reviewed the trip, especially what I had learned. Perhaps the most important thing I learned was that I did not know enough about the commercial airline business. Ray had recognized this, even before he had hired me, but he was confident that I was a quick learner and dedicated to getting up to speed quickly. We identified some classes that GE offered, especially finance, contracts, and engine performance, so I signed up and started the courses immediately. Some of these were evening classes, leaving me the days to spend with our sales engineering group, who helped prepare our presentation material and were extraordinarily patient with this ex-pilot who knew more about breaking engines than fixing them!

Strategic Planning

One day Ray called me into his office, wanting to discuss how we would work as a team in the future. When I asked him which airlines we should consider strategic wins, which ones we must win and which ones we could afford to not compete as aggressively for, I learned another lesson.

"We compete to win all of them, Hugh," he said, "because, if you decide not to compete on some campaigns, you will obviously lose those, your opportunities are reduced and you're still facing the same competition."

Ray went on to review the airlines in Europe, for which he had responsibility. To my surprise and delight, he told me that I would assume responsibility for Cargolux, whom we had just visited and who were starting a search for engines to power their anticipated new Boeing 747–400 freighter fleet. Ray maintained full responsibility for his major airlines, of course, but allocated some important, lesser airlines in his region to my full attention. While I would still be in learning mode, Ray had, in one move, recognized and motivated me to work with his customers and to be responsible for the results. I wondered how many managers would have had the skills and trust to do that.

As fate would have it, I was to be tested sooner than I had expected! After a few weeks, Ray and I set off again to follow up on the actions and commitments from our prior visit, and to visit and be introduced at those airlines we had not had time to see on our previous trip. We had made it as far as Chicago for our international flight and were waiting in the lounge, when Ray received an urgent call from his wife, who was experiencing a personal emergency. Ray told me he must return home and that he was comfortable with me continuing and meeting the airlines and making the presentations.

He turned over his copies of the presentation books (all hard copy in those days) and caught the next flight back to Cincinnati that evening. I was thankful that I had spent my time during the last few weeks in a completely constructive manner, especially in the preparation and understanding of the presentation material. While I was a far cry from a design engineer, I felt confident that I could handle basic questions on the material and I made up my mind that if I could not answer the question, I would truthfully tell them that I did not know the answer but I would find out the answer that day for them. As it happened, this forthright approach surprised some but they always seemed satisfied, particularly when I met my commitment by giving them the comprehensive answer soon thereafter.

So, my trip unfolded. Our GE representatives at the various airlines were able to help me with the necessary introductions and the presentations were reported back to Ray as entirely satisfactory (phew!). My weekend was not as interesting without Ray and his historical background, but I was delighted to use it to visit our dear friends, Bobby and Roy, who had looked after us so caringly after my release from prison. This time, the meeting was not quite as emotional!

The trip to the remaining airlines was completed with no major surprises and I could return to Cincinnati and home on schedule. Happily, Ray`s wife had recovered and all was well. Looking back, it was a fortuitous event. The trip on my own had given my confidence a boost, it allowed Ray to get to a comfort level as to how I could perform at his airlines and everything turned out for the best.

Over the next few years, I became fully acquainted with all of Ray`s airlines and we developed a solid partnership. I was thankful to have his guidance when I ran into the unknown, which fortunately became rarer as I learned more. My focus concentrated more on the Cargolux campaign, without losing sight of the other airlines. Ray had also given me responsibility for Virgin Atlantic, who were starting to look at new 747's with our engines, and Brittania, who were looking into 767's with our engines.

Martinair was also looking to add to their Pratt and Whitney engine-powered fleet, and Ray asked me to see what we could do. Other than a very brief and uncharacteristically terse visit with their President, I knew nothing about the airline. It seemed the best way forward would be through the engineering department, and to that end, I sought the help of our senior rep at KLM, Bill Lamborn, who had met the head of engineering on some previous occasion.

After several futile attempts to get a meeting, I was finally permitted a half hour visit, arrived on time and with the support of Bill, was shown into the office of Haan Sieker. Haan was courteous but voiced his displeasure at GE`s apparent lack of interest. He was already well down the path to finalizing the deal with Pratt and Whitney and he made it plain that he had little interest in trying to build a relationship with GE. We thanked him for his time and left, offering to follow up whenever he wanted to know about our engine.

Bill and I worked hard to re-build this relationship over the following months, and we got to the stage where I could make presentations on our engine and have discussions about being able to submit a proposal. Since time was running out, I asked Haan what we could do to improve the chances for our engine. By now, Haan had recognized that we were sincere in our efforts and he responded that the engines were discussed every

Monday morning at 7 am, his time. I offered to have the latest update on our engine for him, at 6:30 am his time every Monday, and he happily accepted.

With the door slightly ajar for the next few months, I collected the latest development data from the factory and our own engineering group, set my alarm for 00:30 my time every Monday, and called Haan and briefed him. I`m not sure that he believed I would follow through on my commitment, but he soon learned he could rely on these updates for his meetings.

This continued for some months until Haan called me with the news that his airline had decided to stay with their incumbent Pratt and Whitney engine but that he had been asked to pass along their gratitude for our interest and for establishing a sound relationship. This was a significant disappointment for me and Bill, but Haan followed through and wrote a very complimentary letter to our Head of Sales, explaining that our relationship was now in good enough standing to compete fully for their next expansion and thanking us for our dedicated efforts. While this did not bring any immediate dollars into our business, it was as good a result as we could have hoped for and lessened the pain just a bit.

Since Ray was responsible for British Airways, it made sense that he asked me to look after Virgin Atlantic. These two airlines were always at loggerheads, largely due to BA`s dirty tricks campaign, which Branson, for Virgin, challenged in court and won. A nasty mark on BA`s reputation. I had been working with Virgin's engineering department and had developed a great deal of respect for their no-nonsense style of business. I spent a lot of time with Ian Taylor, a solid and likeable engineer, as we started the process to sell our engines for their new 747's.

Ian introduced me to his head of engineering, Roy Gardner, ex-Laker Airways and an extremely pragmatic, experienced engineer who asked me to visit his boss, one Richard Branson (later Sir Richard Branson). At the duly appointed time and date, I showed up at the Branson residence, in Holland Park, in what I had learned to be proper British business attire; business suit and tie, black dress shoes and leather briefcase. I refused the bowler hat! I rang the doorbell at the front door of the very beautiful looking house (Holland Park is one of the best neighborhoods in London) and was surprised when Richard Branson himself opened the door. He was dressed in jeans and a pullover. Before I could stammer a greeting, he said,

"Thank you so much for taking the time to visit and talk about your engines."

I was somewhat flustered and said something along the lines of,

"Thank you, Sir, but I thought that was my line!"

He laughed and invited me inside where I found Roy Gardner already there. We had a simple lunch of chicken, beautifully cooked by his lovely wife, a few glasses of white wine and then spent some time talking about our engines. Not a formal presentation and Roy guided the discussion. It was clear to me that Richard relied implicitly upon Roy`s guidance about engines, and the discussions flowed smoothly. I was very impressed by Richard`s easy-going, yet alert and intelligent approach to the subject and I began to understand how he had become a multi-millionaire at such an early age and without much formal education. The meeting came to an end and I left, thanking Richard and Roy for their time. I was to learn later that Richard was happy with the meeting and this was validated later by his (and Roy`s) selection of our engines.

The campaign at Brittania provided an amusing anecdote. I was having a very difficult time, not with the engineering staff, but with their Chief Financial Officer, who was obsessively relentless in his quest for more and more price concessions. I finally had to approach my General Manager, John Berten, for help. I explained the difficulty and requested that John join me on my next visit. John agreed and after some modifications to our proposal, we were ready to go.

John had agreed that he would present the proposal this time and he painstakingly walked the CFO through the changes. I could watch the CFO carefully and was not able to detect any sort of approval in his manner. Finally, he stopped John, and said,

"There is nothing in this proposal that I like."

And then, with a lot of emphasis,

"NOTHING!"

John, who had a very dry sense of humor, looked a bit nonplussed but without hesitation responded in as serious a tone as he could muster,

"Bill, (not his real name) we went to great lengths with the page numbering and we think it turned out pretty well. Don't you even like the page numbering?"

For a minute there was silence, as Bill digested this, while I tried not to laugh, and then Bill had the good grace to laugh too. However, he still did not like our proposal, but we did make enough improvements to finally close the campaign to everyone`s relief.

Engine campaigns at airlines are usually lengthy affairs, sometimes running for three to five years at major airlines, and they were always intense. Pratt & Whitney and Rolls Royce were worthy adversaries, and the competition was fierce because orders usually amounted to hundreds of millions of dollars worth of engines and spares. Since our products and support were generally superb, and remembering Ray`s admonition, we did win most campaigns.

I Become an American

A heartwarming example of the welcoming and caring example of American behavior happened to me around this same time. I was advised of the official approval of my American citizenship and I was instructed to report to the main courthouse in downtown Cincinnati, at 1 pm on the afternoon of 19th April, 1991. I explained the situation to Ray and to my general manager, John Berten, and requested an hour off work, thinking that the ceremony would be brief.

The ceremony was formal but friendly and I found it very moving, but to my dismay, there were some eighty others also to be sworn in. I determined to relish the event and to put in for a half day of vacation on my return to the office. The ceremony duly ended after about two hours and I was now an American citizen!

I could not stop smiling and I drove back to the office as quickly as possible, only to be met by one of the secretaries who told me that John (my general manager) wanted to see me immediately in the main sales briefing room. I was concerned, knowing I had been away longer than planned, but I hurried along, opened the door and "Surprise!" The room was full of the entire sales-staff. Red, white and blue ribbons hung from the walls and balloons of the same colors covered the ceiling. In the middle of the room, on a large table, sat a cake, beautifully iced and in the shape of the Stars and Stripes.

Someone turned off the lights, the screen lit up with Whitney Houston singing the National Anthem and in true American fashion, everyone sang along. This was so unexpected that I was reduced to tears, as I tried to thank everyone, but they shrugged off my thanks and welcomed me as a new citizen. I was overwhelmed!

The icing on the cake, as it were, was the following letter from Senator Eagleton:

THOMPSON & MITCHELL
ATTORNEYS AT LAW

ONE MERCANTILE CENTER
ST. LOUIS, MISSOURI 63101-1693
(314) 231-7676
FAX (314) 342-1717

THOMAS F. EAGLETON
(314) 342-1683

325 WEST MAIN STREET
BELLEVILLE, IL 62220-0758
(618) 277-4700

200 NORTH THIRD STREET
ST. CHARLES, MO 63301-2890
(314) 946-7717

700 14TH STREET, N.W.
WASHINGTON, D.C. 20005-2010
(202) 508-1000

April 17, 1991

BY FAX AND MAIL

Mr. Hugh Slatter
General Electric Aircraft Engines
Mail Drop F112
1 Neumann Way
Cincinnati, Ohio 45215

Dear Hugh:

Congratulations on becoming Citizen Slatter. We'll never have a better one! You are a thoughtful, purposeful and dedicated man. Our nation needs many more people about whom such could be said.

You cannot become President of the United States --- sorry about that. BUT you can obtain a much more important post: Commissioner of Baseball. You are much wiser about the game than Marge and her daffy dog. If you get the job, I would like to be Spring Training Investigator --- nothing big, mind you --- just lots of baseball and winter sun.

Hugh, I again congratulate you and wish you every happiness as a distinguished American.

Warm regards,

Tom

Thomas F. Eagleton

TFE/pm

(The reference to 'Marge and her Daffy Dog' refers to the owner of the famous Cincinnati Baseball team – The Reds - and their Mascot, her massive Dog.)

We had a small celebration at our home that evening. John Berten presented me with three pink, plastic flamingos to put in our garden, explaining that no true American home could be without such traditional ornaments! Don't say I didn't warn you about

John`s sense of humor! Ray, bless him, had gone overboard and presented me with a large American flag, which he had somehow arranged to have flown in my name over the Capitol building in Washington D.C.!

Adding to the occasion, my Zimbabwe prison cellmate and co-accused, Peter Briscoe and his lovely wife, Paddy, drove all the way from St Louis for the occasion. I will never forget the friendliness and the generosity of my American friends and colleagues in making this a memorable and proud occasion. Thank you! As painful as it is to be forced from the country of one`s birth, I felt that I now belonged in a new land – the Land of the Free.

Boeing Programs

Ray had decided to retire and he nominated me to take his position. I was thrilled but before he retired, with a final push from Ray, I was able to close the Cargolux campaign successfully, after some three years. This was a big deal with some 24 of our large engines (CF6s) plus spares. Ray was gracious, as usual, and gave full credit to me when I debriefed our head of sales and his full team on the success. I believe that this win cemented my promotion into Ray's job and it was hard to think that this wonderful mentor of mine would no longer be in the office next door, whenever I needed his sage advice.

Work was not the same without Ray, but life went on. Sales campaigns came and went, usually successfully. I was responsible for all of the north western European airlines, with a small sales-staff that was smart, hard working and successful, racking up many billions of dollars in export sales for GE and the US. I had kept some airlines to work on my own and found it satisfying that I was able to make some significant contributions to our group's export sales. I was beginning to feel that in this way, I could repay the investment that the Company and the country had made in me and my family, and I was grateful.

About this time, an opportunity to gain new experience presented itself. John Berten had been promoted to head the entire European sales-department, after completing a successful assignment running the GE offices at Boeing, in the Seattle area of the North West. He suggested to me that such an assignment would interest me and provide me with useful experience for later career moves. While I was definitely interested, I could not find a way to get onto the slate of candidates that our Human Resources (HR) group had drawn up. I approached the hiring general manager for the job, and although he listened to my expression of interest, he did not support my wish to be added to the slate, pointing out that there were already some thirty qualified candidates who had passed the HR screen.

As I pondered my next move, I decided to take the bull by the horns and approach the President of GE's commercial engine division, Mike Lockhart. I had worked for

Mike for a year or two, and had got on well with him. He was very disciplined and creative at the same time and he did not tolerate fools easily. Hence, he had a reputation that could scare one away, but I had no such misgivings, and held him in high regard. After one particularly difficult ongoing issue with a key airline, he had invited me into his office and asked me what I thought he should do about it. I knew something about the issue, and to me the answer was straightforward – do the right thing by supplying a new engine, even though it would cost us some extra millions. Mike was already on this path, and he thanked me, saying that he appreciated my judgment.

I knew that I could approach Mike for guidance, but I also knew not to simply dump a problem in his lap. One needed to suggest a solution as well, which he would approve or deny. It was as straightforward as that. In this case, I had a problem (I couldn`t get on the HR slate for the Boeing job), and my recommended solution was to have me added to the slate. To strengthen my case, I had gone to the trouble of researching the job and had prepared a written plan of action for my first three months running the offices.

Mike listened carefully and then said that he would support my candidacy for the job, even saying that he felt I was a strong candidate. I was delighted and thanked him for his interest. I don`t think that HR was very impressed with my approach, but I felt that I had already approached them without any response.

With that, I started the usual cycle of interviews. I went through my plan carefully in one or two of the key interviews and found I was gaining confidence along the way, although I still did not sense any support from HR. I had two strong supporters in my corner; my President and my General Manager, who had already done the job. Finally, I was called into the hiring manager`s office to be told that I was top of the list, but would still need the President and CEO's approval.

I had not had many dealings with the President, Gene Murphy, but I knew by reputation that he was a man of high integrity and deep-rooted discipline. I liked both those qualities and felt sure I would get on well with him. Gene's schedule was busy, and getting the interview proved tough. Finally, his secretary asked me to meet him at a private airport before he took off on a trip. I too was due to leave on a trip that day, coincidentally to Boeing to discuss my airlines, followed by a few days of vacation in the north-west with Jayne.

We met in a private room at the small airport and I had an hour with Gene to discuss the job. It was immediately apparent that Gene liked the fact that I had prepared a plan which clearly indicated sensible preparation. We discussed the plan at some length, with Gene adding his helpful experience and knowledge at times. Gene ended the meeting by saying,

"You have the job, Hugh, and I believe you will do it well. There is one more hurdle. You must meet the key people at Boeing. They have the power of veto. Best wishes."

I went home by way of the office to tell John and Mike the outcome, to thank them for their support and to assure them of my full commitment to the new job. I knew that their support for this new role for me was an unusual move, given the reluctance of HR, and I determined I would not let them down. I also swung by the hiring manager, my new boss, Bob Conboy, who, although I was not his first choice, was gracious and welcomed me to his group. We planned an early visit to Boeing to meet the key players immediately after I returned from my trip the following week.

Jayne and I flew to Seattle that day, and celebrated the good news that evening. This was a huge opportunity, assuming there was no veto exercised when I met with the key players. We had discussed the possibility of this major move with Mark and Lee earlier and suggested they may want to move with us. However, Mark being 24 years old and Lee 22 years old, they felt they would rather stay in Cincinnati and not have to start again with new surroundings and new friends.

'Granny' Frazier

On my return to Cincinnati, I met with my new boss, who gave me a pre-brief on the key Boeing folks we would meet. Our office was required to work with all levels at BCAG (Boeing Commercial Airplane Group), from the factory to the Chairman, but this visit would concentrate on the Propulsion Systems Division (PSD) and, especially, the Engine Management Group, led by one Granville 'Granny' Frazier. He was a legend at BCAG; outgoing, experienced, knowledgeable and extraordinarily bright. He was also a personal friend of the President (later the Chairman of the Boeing Company) and the main point of contact for our business.

Not being sure how to approach this meeting, it seemed best if I hung back a bit and watched how things developed. I needn`t have worried. For the first thirty minutes, 'Granny' and Bob held an animated discussion, using every acronym known to the aviation industry, and then some more! My concern had gone from how to start the meeting to how to get involved in the meeting! After another twenty minutes or so, things had finally got to the point where I had started to feel that perhaps this was not the right choice for me, and everyone would be better served if I simply returned to the Marketing and Sales job which I loved.

Suddenly, 'Granny' turned to me, and said,

"I know about you, Slatter." He then he proceeded to succinctly summarize my last ten years of work at GE, even going back into my Air Force career in some depth. Although I had been forewarned of his unusual abilities, I was not expecting this thorough research. He concluded his recount by adding,

"And I know that you love golf."

"Thank God," I thought, "here`s a safe subject to break the ice."

But 'Granny' went on immediately,

"I have to warn you that my golf is like masturbation!"

Never having been trained in any interview technique as to how to respond to that announcement, I did the best I could, and stammered,

"Really, Mr. Frazier, how's that?"

This was obviously the right response because 'Granny' immediately continued,

"While it gives me a great deal of personal satisfaction, it's pretty disgusting for others to have to watch!"

Again, being uncertain as to how to respond, I chuckled politely, and said,

"If you approve of me taking the job, perhaps we can enjoy a game sometime?"

The ice was very definitely broken, and the rest of the meeting went off in a robust, interactive manner. I started to feel better about the skills and requirements that he outlined and we concluded the meeting in a friendly manner. The rest of the day was spent meeting the head of the Propulsion Systems Division, although it was clear that 'Granny' was the decision maker in this process. We also had some time to meet our local office team, although without being certain of the job yet, there was not much to discuss.

I learned quickly that 'Granny' did not like to procrastinate on anything. Bob told me, as we drove to the airport for our flight home, that he had already told him he was looking forward to working with me. I was delighted and years later it would become clear to me that I had just met a man who would have a major impact on my work and on Jayne's and my life for the next ten years and beyond.

Things moved quickly and I was soon in an apartment near our offices, while Jayne remained in Cincinnati to sell the house and to make sure that Mark and Lee were settled. Jayne was able to visit and house-hunt a couple of times, before our Cincinnati home sold, and when Jayne took me to a quiet, older home in the north-west style of redwood timber and large windows on an acre, hidden deep in the woods and yet within ten minutes of the office, we were in instant agreement that we needed to look no further. While Jayne was busy with our new home, I was busy learning the culture and requirements of GE engine's paramount customer. We provided hundreds of our engines every year to BCAG, for all their airplane models, except the 757, which we had (mistakenly, it turns out) decided to avoid, not foreseeing the true market, which turned out to be over 1,000 airplanes!

It soon became apparent that our local office team was small, but experienced and effective. They decided that their new boss needed help, so they took me under their collective wing and ensured that I learned the many facets of working with BCAG at all levels. I enjoyed the added bonus of having a representative from our French side of the business, one Norbert Gaillard, and we soon developed a strong respect and friendship between us. To show you the value that BCAG attached to Norbert, he was the only non- BCAG person to ever be made the leader of an Integrated Product Team – a great honor, and well deserved.

'Granny' spent a great deal of time with me. He was and still may be one of the most interesting, generous and pragmatic intellectuals I have ever known, and I owe him much for the determination and patience he showed to a non-engineer pilot and, even worse, a salesman!

After three or four weeks, Jayne and I invited him and his wife, Geda, to dinner at our home. Jayne was and is an excellent cook and our dinner evenings were always a huge success, and I eagerly anticipated an enjoyable evening, as we got to know 'Granny' and his wife a bit better. We had enjoyed a cocktail and sat down at the dinner table with some wine, as Jayne produced one of her delicious dinners. Everything appeared to be moving along nicely when all of a sudden, 'Granny' looked at Jayne and said in a matter of fact way,

"You don`t like me, do you?"

There was a stunned silence from the rest of us and I tried to signal to Jayne to just let the remark go. But, I should have known Jayne better,

"No, I don`t," she said, in the same matter of fact way.

Now I was really concerned. I could see this escalating rapidly and my new job evaporating in front of my eyes. I tried to console myself with the thought that many of our packing cases were still in the garage, unpacked, and at least that would save some money for what was looking like an imminent move back to Cincinnati. Again, I tried to signal to Jayne but she was staring straight at 'Granny'. But 'Granny' was far from finished.

"Why don`t you like me?" he persisted.

This was getting out of control. My eyes pleaded with Jayne to make a joke of the whole thing, but no such luck.

"You`re arrogant, you're loud, you're self-opinionated, you're brash and you're superficial."

Each criticism was like a dagger to my heart and I could not believe that this was actually happening. There was a pause for a few seconds while he considered this. Then he said,

"You are absolutely right and you are the first person I've met who has the courage to tell me that. I like that. Thank you, Jayne."

The incipient crisis was over. Just like that. That was the start of Jayne's and 'Granny's' strong friendship, which they enjoyed throughout our stay at BCAG and which endures to this day. It would seem that strong characters respect and like each other.

After some weeks, we were able to have the promised game of golf. I was always learning something when I was with him and four hours in a golf cart was no exception. After our game, having a drink in the bar, I felt comfortable enough to ask him a question.

"Do you remember telling me that your golf was like masturbation?"

When he nodded, I continued,

"Well, you know, 'Granny', you were quite right!"

At that, he burst out laughing and so our friendship and respect for each other grew steadily. 'Granny', for his part, took golf lessons, became a respectable player and it was always fun to be on the course with him; a great way to discuss and resolve difficult business issues in a relaxed and helpful environment.

'Granny' had an uncanny ability to establish an immediate rapport, and I observed this time and time again, from the little old serving lady in the lunch diner to the head of GE Aircraft Engines, Gene Murphy. Gene was not an airplane man. His career had been along very different lines, but 'Granny', with his clear thought processes and ability to succinctly explain the complexities of airplanes and development strategy, in chart form, was able to keep Gene`s interest through several individual briefings that Gene and 'Granny' shared on an as required basis.

Phil Condit

It was time to meet the President of BCAG, Phil Condit. 'Granny' was the perfect one to help me with the meeting, due to his role as head of Engine Management and also because of his long-standing friendship with Phil. Phil had the well-deserved reputation of being the leading light in advancing Boeing into large, twin-engine airplanes, a major strategic shift for the industry and the key to BCAG`s amazing successes in promoting a point-to-point strategy, instead of the previously popular hub-and-spoke system.

I had prepared carefully for the meeting, aware that Phil`s schedule was always swamped, and determined not to waste any of his time. We had been allotted 30 minutes, so 'Granny' and I selected the key areas for discussion; our new engine programs to support BCAG`s new airplanes, our technology stocking process and our two companies` ability to work together for our mutual success.

We were ushered into Phil`s office and 'Granny' introduced me. I liked Phil instantly. He demonstrated a very clear thought process and had the ability to express those thoughts in clear and easily understood language. We had a rewarding discussion of well over an hour, until Phil`s secretary interrupted us for Phil`s next visitor. I learned a lot from that first meeting with this giant of the aviation industry, and quickly understood why he was leading BCAG. He was that rare combination of a visionary and a pragmatist. When you spoke, he looked at you, and he listened carefully before commenting.

Our friendship grew, due in no small part to Jayne`s ability to hold small dinners, where Phil and 'Granny' often joined us for an enjoyable and interesting evening, with drinks, Jayne`s excellent meals and aviation discussions. I had several more meetings with Phil, and then he was appointed to Chairman of the Boeing Company and moved the corporate offices to Chicago. I was able to see him from time to time and we still see him quite often, to this day. Jayne and I have remained good friends over the years with Phil and his lovely wife, and I have benefited a great deal from his generous sharing of knowledge and thoughts, as well as his unique listening skills.

New Engines

There was much activity within BCAG in the early and mid-nineties. The Next Generation (NG) 737 airplane program, with our CFM engine, was nearing completion at the Renton factory and was about to enter service. While north of Seattle, at the Everett factory, the large 777 airplane program was in its final stages of development and testing and due to enter service.

'Granny' and I spent many hours participating in engineering meetings. I was mostly in the listening mode, unless some engine-specific issue arose, but he would use all his experience and knowledge to help ensure that the program succeeded, especially the all new Extended Twin Operations (ETOPS) requirement of 180 minutes safe operation on one engine, for the large twins. This was a particularly difficult requirement for all the airplane systems, but none more so than the engines, and all manufacturers had to demonstrate reliability to unprecedented levels.

The first 777 program used engines from the three major manufacturers; Pratt and Whitney, Rolls Royce, and of course, GE. Initially, the thrust requirements of around 90 thousand pounds of thrust, some 50% more than anything else in service, were challenging, but all three manufacturers were up to it. However, GE was the only manufacturer who had the foresight, thanks to Brian Rowe, President and CEO of GE Aircraft Engines at the time, to design and build an engine for 115 thousand pounds of thrust, which actually ran at 127 thousand pounds of thrust during testing. Consequently, the GE engine was selected as the only engine to power the new, longer range and higher payload 777s, which have become the most popular large twins in aviation today.

A favorite haunt of 'Granny's' was a restaurant in Bellevue by name of 'Daniels', and one Friday evening, after a particularly long and difficult week of many program issues, we agreed to meet there for a drink and some dinner. We were well known customers and one of our favorite servers, a lovely young blonde, named Sarah, showed us to our table. While Sarah waited to take our dinner order, the sommelier came over and started to try to sell us one of his expensive bottles of wine. 'Granny' cut him short,

"We would like a Cabernet, full-bodied and fairly dry, but with low tannins and a robust yet smooth aftertaste."

I could sense the sommelier, already ringing up the cash register with one of his most expensive wines, when 'Granny' added,

"And we want it for less than $35!"

The sommelier turned on his heel and walked away, disgusted. But Sarah, bless her, said,

"Let me go down to the cellar and see what I can find."

A few minutes later, Sarah reappeared, carrying two bottles of 1986 Columbia Crest Cab, in my opinion, the most underrated wine in America, and putting them on the table, she announced,

"These are the last two, hidden in the cellar, but they are $38 each, so here`s six dollars, you cheap bastards!" Needless to say, she made up the six dollars on her gratuity!

About this time, one of life`s most joyful events occurred in our family. Our oldest son, Mark, and his lovely wife, Denise, presented us with our first grandson, Sean. Although they lived in Cincinnati and we were in Seattle, we saw as much of each other as we could. I was luckier than Jayne because I still had to travel to our headquarters in Cincinnati from time to time and always took the time to visit with them. Of course, grandchildren grow up fast, and he is now 21 – not quite as cute as he used to be, but he always introduces me to his beautiful girlfriends, so I like him!

General Manager North West Europe

In my fourth year at BCAG, and towards the end of 1997, I applied for a General Manager position, heading Marketing and Sales for Northern and Western Europe. The job was based in London, England, and would be a promotion. Jayne and I discussed the pros and cons and chatted with Mark and Lee about it. They had both acquired their US citizenship by now and would be able to travel internationally, with no difficulty. Additionally, Mark was now married with a young son, Sean, our first grandson, and had bought a house in a nice suburb of Cincinnati. Lee was gainfully employed and living in a rented apartment close to downtown Cincinnati. They both approved of the move.

There was one potential obstacle. Jayne had already applied for her US citizenship a year earlier, but in spite of trying to move the process along, it seemed that the Seattle branch of the Immigration Services (INS) was not as efficient as the Cincinnati branch. They had already lost Jayne`s papers and fingerprints once, necessitating starting the entire process again. Try as we might, we could not find out the state of Jayne`s application. If we moved to the UK, to take up the new job, and missed the citizenship hearing, we would have to start the entire process all over yet again!

Finally, and in desperation, we talked to a friend of ours who did translation services for the INS. Pravinder Vrydagh was the wife of a stalwart in our GE office in Bellevue, Jack Vrydagh, and she kindly put us in touch with a friend of hers, a lawyer at the INS who undertook to look into the matter on our behalf. A few days later, he called to say that he had located Jayne`s papers, buried at the bottom of a huge pile of other files, and he had put them into an action tray and hoped that things would happen quickly.

However, a couple of weeks later, we had still heard no more and we had to depart for England or lose the job opportunity.

And so, we made the move, and the company located us in the very nice company flat in Sloane Square, in the middle of London, while we started to look for a house. We had only been gone a week when we received notification that Jayne`s citizenship hearing was set for the very next week. The INS will not reschedule hearings, so show up or start over again! And so, we jumped on an airplane and made our way back to Seattle for the hearing.

We arrived at the appointed time and only had a short wait before being asked to enter the judge`s chambers. We were surprised to find no others waiting in the chambers, as is normal for citizenship hearings. The judge arrived promptly and proceeded to swear in Jayne, as a US citizen! Either our lawyer friend carried more power than we realized or the INS felt so embarrassed about their performance that they decided to make it right!

Whatever the reason, Jayne was now formally a US citizen and we could travel back to the UK with no further concerns about being recalled for a hearing. So, that was it. The Slatter family in the US was now officially all-American! I know that I speak for all my family when I say that we are honored, proud and grateful to be citizens of the US. Thank you, America!

Back in London, Jayne continued an unsuccessful hunt for a house, while I started the round of visits to my new team and new airlines. Totally new to me was the fact that my region also covered Russia, with the main airline being Aeroflot, who were interested in BCAG 77s with our engines. GE employed an excellent young man, Alexander Plats, in Moscow. Alexander was on my staff and was extremely helpful in setting up introductions with the key Aeroflot staff. Arriving at the main airport, I was whisked through a VIP route, with a welcoming drink, while my documents were checked and found in order.

Knowing a little bit about Russian military aircraft, I was under no illusions about their engineering capabilities, and yet their commercial engine business did not seem to have kept up with western progress in this field. Our presentations to the engineering staff were keenly followed, with considerable interest in our large GE90 engine, delivering in excess of 90 thousand pounds of thrust and 115 thousand pounds of thrust on the later versions. Our meetings were successful and after a few more visits to tie down the warranties and maintenance plans, Aeroflot placed an initial order for six 777 passenger airplanes with our engines.

GE hosted a celebratory dinner with the Aeroflot staff, in the very good hotel where we were staying. Being the host, I went to our private dining room early to check that all was in order. The staff was already waiting and insisted I have a shot of their excellent chilled vodka, along with some equally excellent caviar. I had heard of this famous Russian combination and having tried it, can vouch for the combination. The dinner continued in what I gather was true Russian style; many toasts with plenty of vodka. I amended my speech, shortening it to a few minutes only, and hoping that any slurring would not be noticed because of the language difference! I need not have worried because most of our guests decided to say something as well, and the evening ended on an extremely happy note!

We went on to enjoy a happy relationship with Aeroflot, and I would sometimes wonder, given my military background fighting against Soviet-backed forces in Rhodesia, how I now came to be working with and enjoying a culture that for so long had been ingrained in me as alien. I realized that it was really just the politics that were alien and that the people were decent.

Jayne's house-hunting continued. The hurdle was that London`s rents kept going up and our HR Department's hands were tied, by outdated allowance tables, it seemed. When my boss, a man of action by name of Herb Depp, enquired if I was making any progress, and I told him the difficulty, he was short and to the point,

"Hugh, I`m paying you to market and sell our engines, not to house hunt. Find a place that suits you and I will take care of the rent problem."

I thanked him, Jayne found a suitable house in Virginia Waters, about 20 miles outside of downtown London, and the problem was over, simply because a man-of-action boss had the sense to not allow bureaucracy to overshadow business! Although golf was not on Jayne`s mind when she chose the house, it came as a bonus that the famous Wentworth Golf Club was within walking distance. GE bought a membership for my office and we were able to put it to good use, from time to time, especially to have four hours of quiet time with a customer who might have an issue that needed thoughtful discussion. There is never a better place than a golf course to find solutions to vexing problems, particularly problems stemming from business relationships.

We enjoyed the company of many visitors while we were in Virginia Waters, including our sons and family from South Africa; the lure of London! The house in Virginia Waters was perfect for visitors. While it was quite ordinary looking from the outside, it sat on two acres of grounds, with its own little lake, complete with visiting and nesting swans in the springtime. Unlike most English homes, it had four *en-suite* bedrooms and a modern, American-style kitchen. We could reciprocate some of Bobby and Roy`s wonderful hospitality here and enjoyed many an evening in its own little pub, reminiscing about our four months in their little house with Jayne`s crutches sliding down the stairs, followed by Jayne on her bottom, and all the other challenges!

Roy loved to golf and we were able, on occasion, to have nine holes on one of Wentworth`s nearby courses. And sometimes, when the others had gone off to bed, I would sit quietly at the bar and ponder how times had changed; being banished from the land of my birth with virtually nothing to show for 21 years of service to my country, to the present, with a secure job, money in the bank and, most importantly, a healthy family, safe and secure, with an unbounded future in a civilized country. My gratitude knows no bounds.

I enjoyed being with the airlines again and was able to renew old friendships with KLM, Virgin Atlantic, BA, Cargolux, Austrian, Lufthansa, Brittania, Finnair, British Midlands and others, although my team of sales-directors was usually the prime point of interface. My office was in West London, in Hammersmith, and road traffic was always heavy, so I planned my work day accordingly, leaving home around 5 am in the morning. This would usually get me into the office before 6 am, and since most of London did not start until three hours later, this gave me a few hours of uninterrupted time to work with my staff and airlines, further east in time zones.

The days were usually spent at airlines in the UK, unless I was travelling. I would plan to leave the office at 4 pm, which would just avoid the main traffic and get me home an hour later. If, however I was late leaving the office, by even so much as half an hour, my trip time to get home could increase by as much as one to two hours, as the main traffic leaving downtown London piled up along the main roads.

Getting home by 5 pm in the summer months allowed me to take a walk on one of Wentworth`s three beautiful golf courses, for an hour or so, and I then had a few hours to connect with our offices in Cincinnati, before the end of the day in the American eastern time zone. The days were long but satisfying and my sales-directors were an experienced and successful team who concluded many major sales campaigns for the company, making it even more satisfying. Typically, and depending on fleet planning requirements, a sales campaign for an airline can take three to five years, involving much time and effort. The key to winning was to have a relationship with the decision makers at the airline that allowed one to make a winning final bid. Such relationships, as Ray had taught me, took years to develop, through honesty and trust. Selling 101!

Handling holidays proved interesting. Obviously, since I was working in the UK, I was not able to enjoy our US holidays, and likewise, since the US did not observe the UK holidays, I found myself working with my Cincinnati office on UK holidays! Again, because I enjoyed the work, this was not too much of a problem, except that the travel that Jayne and I had anticipated proved difficult. We were only able to get away on our own once, to Italy, and the wonderful Amalfi Coast, where we rented an old stone fort that had been converted into a villa, high on a cliff in Positano.

This was a remarkable spot, accessible only on foot from within the tiny village, climbing along a windy, narrow footpath for a couple of hundred yards along the edge of the cliff. The villa overhung the cliff slightly, and if one could have stepped out of the window, one would fall directly into the ocean, some 100 feet below! When the waves got big, the foundations of the villa shook – a little unnerving for the first couple of nights! The landlord, Signor Baldo, also ran one of the small restaurants on the beach in Positano, and he would prepare special meals for us in the evenings, with the usual Italian friendship and hospitality that visitors to Italy so love. Interestingly, the tiny village of Positano has two of Italy's top rated hotels, although their prices were a bit beyond our means.

The area nearby includes Naples and Pompeii, to the north, and the beautiful Amalfi Coast and town to the south, all accessible by comfortable bus service. Our week passed by too quickly and we left for London almost before we had started, it seemed, vowing to return some day.

London to Seattle

In November of 1999, exactly two years after our move to London, my boss, Herb Depp, called me on a Friday evening at home,

"Hugh," he said, "how would you feel about coming back to BCAG to run the new 777 programs with our GE90-115B engines?"

This unexpected offer surprised me for a minute. Overseas assignments were usually at least three years and we had only just completed two years. However, I was very satisfied with the team successes in Europe and I knew that Jayne loved our Seattle/Bellevue home. Furthermore, I had continued to work closely with BCAG, since most of my airlines were BCAG customers, and I had maintained strong contacts with BCAG in Seattle. I felt ready.

"Boss," I said, "the sound you hear is me running upstairs to pack. When do you want me there?"

"I need you there next week to kick off your new team. You will have an experienced and capable Marketing and Sales team to make sure this is a successful program for us and BCAG."

That was it. Jayne was as excited as I was. I booked a flight and wrote letters to my customer airlines, advising them of these developments. I would visit them later to see them on a personal basis. On Monday, I was in Seattle, meeting my new team and starting the exciting program of joint marketing and sales of these new, bigger and longer range BCAG 777s. As usual, Jayne was left with the onerous task of packing and arranging the move back to our home. Fortunately, we had decided to keep the house in Bellevue, by some strange intuition. While we were away, the price of housing in the Seattle area had shot up by some 30%!

After a week of moving into new offices within BCAG and getting re-acquainted with my BCAG customers and friends, I could return to the UK for a final round of visits to my customer airlines. It was a bitter-sweet time. I had established firm business relationships and good friendships with several of my airline customers and would miss them and my sales-team. However, I was hopeful that I would still have dealings with those who would be interested in the new 777s, and indeed, this turned out to be the case. The BCAG strategy of big twin-engine airplanes was paying off handsomely.

Back at BCAG, things were moving swiftly. Our team had established working routines with our BCAG counterparts and we were creating and sharing new marketing materials, aimed at key potential customers. The engine technology from the earlier 777s was maturing, and the component, over which industry had voiced concerns, the all-new composite fan blade, was proving to be robust, reliable and durable. This allowed us to adopt a forceful marketing position, armed with actual data to support our claims, and greatly strengthened BCAG`s case with the airlines. Our joint marketing and sales efforts started to pay off as our teams travelled the world to various airlines and presented our data and proposals. Several of the major airlines realized that this airplane was going to be a true industry leader, unique in its class and ahead of its time. A cycle of orders started.

Jayne completed the move back into our home and we were ready to start entertaining again. Jayne was particularly good at this and our customers seemed to prefer an evening away from crowded restaurants! Our home venue allowed for a quiet business dinner, with no noise from nearby tables and, more importantly, no prying ears!

I had been surprised, on occasion, at restaurants to hear obviously confidential business information being discussed loudly enough for my table, and probably for others, to hear quite clearly. Jayne had prepared dinners at home for our airline customers, starting back in Cincinnati, and had earned a justifiable reputation for being a great chef and hostess. This sometimes prompted the remark I experienced when visiting my airlines without Jayne,

"Hugh, it's always good to see you, but where is Jayne?"

I always considered that Jayne was an honorary (albeit unpaid) member of our GE marketing and sales-team and the airlines and BCAG loved her! Occasionally, we could travel together to foreign lands that Jayne would not otherwise have seen. While I was grateful for these opportunities, most of the time I travelled on my own. Hotels became my second home and I earned the title `Road Warrior`. Anyone who has had to travel a lot will recognize the embarrassment of trying to enter a hotel room, which was not yours, but had the same number as your hotel last night, in a different city and in a different country!

Halcyon Years

The late 1990's and the very early 2000's were, in my opinion, some of GE`s and Boeing`s finest years. Our GE Engines President was a remarkable man by name of David Calhoun, and BCAG's President was an equally remarkable man, Alan Mulally. David, upon taking the job as President, called me into his office and told me in very clear terms that he considered BCAG our number one customer and that he would act accordingly. He also told me that I represented him directly, as his on-the-spot man at

BCAG, and he expected me to keep him fully briefed on all issues, especially business relationships, in a timely manner.

I was also informed that while I should always keep my direct boss informed, he expected direct communication from me so that he could act quickly. David was as good as his word. I had never experienced a CEO who would respond almost instantly from anywhere in the world and if I felt that the situation warranted David`s presence, he would show up at the very earliest opportunity and even changing other plans.

David and Alan formed a remarkably effective business relationship. Although there were differences, from time to time, they were able to sit together and talk through a challenge and invariably find common ground and a solution that moved our companies forward. It was enlightening to watch.

There was considerable activity at BCAG during this time. The earlier 777s were being replaced at airlines as the newer 777s, with our very large GE90-115B engines, became available. 737 NGs were selling like hotcakes as our CFM56 engines continued to set new records for reliability. The venerable 747 was still in demand, with our CF6 engines, especially the freighter version. Production of the 767 was slowing down (except for an upcoming military tanker version) and 757 productions (not our engines) were also slowing. There was also early planning and design of a new long-range twin, the 787, expected to enter service within the next five years.

At the BCAG operation in the Seattle area, there are two main plants. Renton lies some ten miles south-east of Seattle and houses the narrow-body production facility for the 737 lines. Final assembly is completed here and then the airplanes are flown a short hop to a Boeing field for flight testing and customer delivery.

The Everett factory sits some 30 miles to the north of Seattle and houses all the wide body assembly, in different production lines under one 97-acre roof, the largest facility of its kind in the world. There is an airfield on site where flight testing and customer delivery takes place. Additionally, there are many support facilities and manufacturing sites in the area. The BCAG supply chain is immense, as is GE's, with tens of thousands of parts from a couple of thousand suppliers around the world, and in spite of the complexity of the operation, it works pretty well.

One of the more painful stories concerns the delivery of one of our very large GE90 engines. It travelled by special truck from the Propulsion System Division factory, just south of Seattle, to the Everett facility, about 35 miles to the north. Delivery of these engines required special transport vehicles on selected routes, although they still travelled along existing highways, sometimes with very minimal clearance of a couple of inches under the highway overpasses.

On this particular occasion, all was going along normally until the top of the engine on one of the special vehicles, travelling at some 40 mph, encountered the bottom lip of one of the overpasses, bringing the whole rig to a shuddering halt. Although the damage at first inspection appeared limited to the nacelle, the engine had to be disassembled, inspected and rebuilt back in Cincinnati; a major exercise.

Almost unbelievably, the reason the rig had failed to clear the overpass turned out to be that the roads department had recently resurfaced the road in that area, adding a couple of inches to the surface height and reducing the clearance to zero. Apparently, the publication of this project had not yet been promulgated. Fortunately, this was an isolated accident, necessitating daily communication with the roads department and preventing any further such incidents.

Turmoil at the Top

It was about this time that I got a call from 'Granny' Frazier. It was about 9 am on a Friday, as I recall.

"Hugh," he said, "come to the house and have a drink with me!"

I was somewhat flabbergasted and asked,

"What`s happening, Granny?"

"I just quit the Boeing Company and I`d like to see a few of my friends." he replied.

I sat for a few minutes to let this sink in and then decided that I really should go and see my wonderful mentor in person, rather than try to sift through this situation over the phone.

When I got to his home, it turned out that some disgruntled employee had filed a charge of harassment against him. As is usual in the case in big companies, the accused is under suspicion until they can clear their name. A team of lawyers had descended on 'Granny' in his office, early that morning, and had wanted to start an immediate, formal investigation. 'Granny' despised lawyers and this type of action and decided on the spot to quit. He told the lawyers he was no longer a Boeing employee and departed for the security office where he turned in his badge.

'Granny' had always told me that when he decided to retire, he would simply walk to the security office and turn in his badge, and that`s exactly what he did! Although he was happy with his decision, this was a huge loss to the Boeing Company and I cursed this process. I had seen it at work in other companies, causing misery and expense to the companies and the accused individuals, all too often caused by unsubstantiated accusations.

As the day wore on, more friends of 'Granny' arrived, all asking him to reconsider. He even had a very welcome call from our President, Gene Murphy, who held him in high regard and wondered if he could help him with his decision. But he was adamant and refused to offer his unique and valuable services with a bunch of lawyers looking over his shoulder. BCAG without 'Granny' seemed unimaginable, but that was now the reality.

Jayne and I still saw Phil Condit from time to time, but he was now Chairman of The Boeing Company and had decided to relocate Boeing corporate headquarters to Chicago. Phil was heavily engaged in the plan to merge McDonnell Douglas with Boeing; both companies` military and commercial businesses, a huge undertaking. It was a sensible fit. Boeing was very strong in the commercial business and McDonnell Douglas was particularly strong in the military business.

Understandably, there were teething problems, especially the challenge to merge two different business cultures and deciding which products would produce the best synergy. Over time, the efforts started to pay off, until a very senior executive from McDonnell Douglas, who had taken a senior position in the new company was convicted, along with a senior procurement official from the Pentagon, of criminal conduct. The reverberations were severe and caused the new company, under Phil`s leadership, to suffer serious criticism. Phil, whose own values were always beyond reproach said, "The buck stops here", and resigned.

It was a bitter blow for all of Boeing and the effects lasted years. Along with the loss of 'Granny', the Boeing Company, as I knew it, was changing. To cap it all off, Alan Mulally left to take up the CEO position at the Ford Motor Company, a huge change for Alan and one that he handled very successfully with his usual energy, skill and unbound enthusiasm. In a few short years, the top visionary and very effective leadership at Boeing had departed, leaving competent but untested new leaders to drive the Company into the future.

Joe Sutter

One of the most remarkable characters at BCAG was Joe Sutter. Joe was the original chief engineer for the 747, and due to his long-standing leadership of the program, became known as 'The Father of the 747'. He was revered around the world for his knowledge and there was hardly a question that he could not answer about his beloved 747, be it engineering or (God forbid) sales!

Jayne and I first met Joe and his lovely wife, Nancy, in Luxembourg, at the annual Cargolux airlines golf tournament. Joe was already a legend in the aviation industry and a solid golfer. He tried in vain to teach me that direction off the tee was more important than distance. He would hit his drive 150 yards into the middle of the fairway; his second shot would be the same and then a chip and a putt to finish with a par or bogey, at worst, off a 24 handicap! I would joke with him that I had seen more parts of the golf course than he would ever see and he would just smile, knowingly, and wink at me as he collected the prize for winning the tournament! We developed a firm friendship over the years and I was fortunate to learn much from him. Joe passed away in 2016, at age 94, as mentally alert and incisive as ever. Joe was one of the greatest engineers and characters that BCAG has ever known.

Perhaps a favorite story about Joe was his 90th birthday party, which Jim Albaugh, the then President of BCAG, had arranged for him. It was a wonderful party on the penthouse floor of the Columbia Towers in down town Seattle, with sweeping views across Puget Sound. Joe, of course, received many accolades from special guests who were attending, from all around the world.

Maybe the best, although I admit to bias, was when Herb Depp, in an excellent talk, announced that GE was naming one of our auditoriums in Cincinnati in Joe`s name. To some of those present, this was rather 'ho hum' stuff, until Herb went on to explain that the other two auditoriums were named after Orville and Wilbur Wright and Thomas Edison! That got everyone`s attention. It was a fitting tribute indeed.

Joe was delighted and attended the dedication, along with his family. Jim Albaugh also paid homage to Joe by telling the story about when Jim had first proposed the idea of a major celebration for Joe. Apparently, one of Jim`s staff asked whether this might not set a precedent, to which Jim replied that it might and that he would be happy to arrange such a function for any other 90-year-old icon who was still working for Boeing!

Plans to Retire

In mid-2002, I contacted my President, David Calhoun, and told him that I was planning to retire at the end of the year. I would be coming up on 20 years with GE and for whatever reason, I had a strange premonition that I was going to get ill. This was indeed strange, since I had been abnormally healthy all my life and my family had no history of health issues. However, I could not shake the feeling and I wanted to do some things with my family, especially if there was any truth to this feeling. I said nothing of this to David and I was surprised when he asked me if I would consider doing an extra year, because of the activity at BCAG. In spite of my premonition, I immediately agreed. GE had always looked after me and my family and I felt strong loyalty to the Company and particularly to David.

Jayne agreed with this decision too. We had already bought a house on the Oregon coast in 2000, in preparation for our retirement, and Jayne could move there at the end of 2002, while I would rent an apartment for 2003 in Kirkland, near our GE office. When David asked what I would need to do the extra year, I replied that I needed nothing and was very happy with the manner in which GE had looked after me and my family over the years. However, David asked me to come back to Cincinnati and chat with our head of HR, which I agreed to do.

The meeting over lunch with our head of HR was satisfying in two ways. First, because I realized that GE really appreciated my efforts on behalf of our Company at Boeing, and second, and most unexpectedly, the Company made a very generous improvement to my compensation package for the extra year. This was totally unexpected and again re-enforced my belief that GE was a company that walked the talk about putting its people first.

On the Move Again

We put our home up for sale and Jayne moved to the little fishing village where we had decided we would retire. We had found the place some years before, by driving south from Seattle into Oregon and then along the coast, looking out for suitable locations. While we both loved the Seattle area, the long, grey and drizzly winters, along with the steadily increasing traffic, made up our minds that we should be further south and in a smaller town. This turned out to be easier said than done.

We passed through many small towns along the coast, but none of them really grabbed our attention. However, as we got further south and closer to the California border, the coastline became a bit more rugged and picturesque. We passed through the little town of Bandon, with its famous links golf courses, but known for its high winds. We pressed on, past Port Orford, also very windy, and on to Gold Beach, the penultimate town before the California border, some 40 miles south. The famous Rogue River ran into the ocean here, providing world class salmon fishing and many beautiful riverfront properties, but not too many beachfront properties. We noticed that it was also windy, not unusual for the coast, but we were hoping for something a bit more protected.

As we approached Brookings, the last town before California, we noticed that the wind had all but disappeared. We had already decided that we would not live in California, due to the tax structure and over-population, and this was our last shot. Luckily, we liked what we saw. Two big rivers sandwiched the small town, with plenty of beachfront properties surrounding a small fishing and timber community. It was also known as the `Banana Belt`, because it has its own, little eco-system, created by the warm air blowing over the river, surrounded by hills and, effectively, trapping in some heat.

We spent some time looking at properties but nothing had appealed to us until we came to the very last one. This was a unique bit of land, a point, in fact, with nothing but ocean on either side, as well as in front, and a very nice house. Understandably, it was a lot pricier than the others, but it was worth a bid or two. The negotiations, directly with the owner, lasted some five months, but the result was that we became the owners of this unique and beautiful beachfront property.

This is where Jayne relocated and started the settling in process. She told me later that it was the best move ever because there was no husband in the background, haranguing her about where this picture should go, where this sofa should go or where that rug should go!

I found an apartment in Kirkland, not far from our offices, but I hadn't been in the apartment for more than a week when I got word from my brother, Don, that our mother had passed away that morning. My mother had suffered a series of strokes over a few years and was practically bed-bound in the last year. Jayne had become quite fond of my mother, and we agreed we would visit as often as possible, while she was still fit enough to know what was happening around her.

Although her death was not unexpected at that stage, it is always a blow to lose one`s mother, especially if one has already lost one`s father. While naturally saddened, I could take comfort knowing my Mother`s strong belief in the spiritual life as a normal conclusion to physical death. The realization comes quickly that one needs to remember all the lessons and values imbued by one`s parents over the course of their lives. There will be no more loving parental guidance.

Kirkland is a quaint little village on Lake Washington, with excellent amenities, plenty of good accommodation, restaurants and a happy vibe. Properties were priced accordingly and although it would have been a fun spot to retire, we would have faced the same problems of weather and traffic in Seattle. For me on my own, it was ideal. My apartment was close to the waterfront and comfortable. I could probably have settled anywhere for the year, since I planned to spend practically all my waking hours with my customers. And that is what I did.

Our engine programs with BCAG were in full swing, with production rates increasing rapidly as BCAG sold more airplanes in the market than ever before. David Calhoun and Alan Mulally continued to strengthen the business relationship between our two companies, and the orders for airplanes kept coming. The demands on the supply chain and on our factories increased almost daily. The challenge became production and deliveries, particularly as BCAG`s large twins gained prominence in the market.

Orders for narrow body airplanes, especially BCAG`s 737 family, were also increasing, putting further strain on suppliers. And yet, the systems and processes which had been tried, tested and improved over many years, held steady as the airplanes and engines rolled out of the factory doors and were delivered to Paine field and Boeing field for flight test and customer delivery.

Another Attempt to Retire

My time with GE Aircraft Engines and Boeing Commercial Airplanes was coming to a close (or so I thought!). Just before my retirement date, Jayne and I were invited to a farewell dinner, hosted by Alan Mulally. This was a kind gesture from Alan and his staff and was totally unexpected. Jayne flew into town for the evening and my GE President, David Calhoun, with some of his staff, were also invited. The dinner was held at the Newcastle Golf Club, a beautiful club, set high above Seattle, with sweeping views of the city, Puget Sound and beyond.

We were seated in a private room, which had a small stage for presentations. Jayne and I were seated at the front and Alan got on stage to welcome everyone. Jayne was already nervous about the event and when Alan invited her onto the stage, she clutched my hand and hesitated. Knowing Alan and his unique ability to relate to people, I encouraged her.

"Go on," I told her, "Alan will look after you."

Jayne went onto the stage and in just a few minutes, Alan had her chatting away, as if she had spent her life on the stage! It was a wonderful few minutes of fun and Jayne came back and sat down, utterly charmed.

Then it was my turn. Alan was very gracious and said many kind things about my work with Boeing, especially my dedication to the `Working Together` concept, which Phil and Alan had always championed. `Working Together` did not mean that one always had to agree with each other, but it did mean that you always found a solution by open and frank communication to achieve the best results for the program – no secrets. If there is any principle in business that enables different companies to succeed in joint projects, it is this one. It allowed David Calhoun and Alan Mulally to achieve total success, where others might have failed.

The truth is that it had never felt like work to me, not in the usual connotation, anyway. I had enjoyed the opportunity to work alongside the best minds in the industry, mostly listening, of course. Above all, I had enjoyed the people around me who made it a pleasure, and even fun, to get up really early in the morning for program technical reviews! No one had made meetings at BCAG more interesting than Alan, and I always left his meetings feeling energized and looking for a dragon to slay!

Before he left the stage to allow me to respond, Alan asked one of his staff to come up on the stage with something that BCAG wanted me to have. Some weeks before, I had been chatting with Larry Dickenson, Head of Sales for BCAG, and an avid golfer. We played golf with airline customers on a regular basis, and Larry was on the Callaway golf club test panel. I happened to ask him what driver he would recommend for me, since I was struggling with my game off the tee. Larry didn`t answer me right away, and then he said I should hold off on buying a new driver for a while.

I admit that I thought at the time that it was not the most helpful answer, but standing on stage now, I put two and two together and figured that BCAG had bought me a new driver for my game. And they had, but they had also included 12 other matched Callaway clubs, along with a putter, a bag and a gross of Alan Mulally special logo golf balls! I had played golf since I was nine years old and knew that good clubs could not fix one`s game, but they could certainly make a very positive difference. I was a bit overwhelmed, but very appreciative, and I managed to blurt out my thanks to Alan, his staff and especially to Larry!

The remainder of the evening revolved around an excellent dinner, wine and many stories of GE and BCAG programs, the good, the bad, and even the ugly! Jayne and I left the club that evening with very strong emotions, not actually happy about retiring and coming to the end of the work that I loved, and really sorry to be leaving so many good friends.

Jayne flew back to Brookings, her home and what was to become my home. The next few days were spent clearing out my office and visiting the many friends who had made Jayne and I so welcome to the Seattle area.

Norbert Gaillard, my close friend from SNECMA and CFM engines and team member on our staff, arranged a farewell party for me with some of SNECMA`s top management. He had earned himself a position of complete trust with BCAG, and CFM owed much to him for his solid and valuable work.

Finally, it was farewell to my special team who had taken me under their wing on day one and worked so hard to ensure that the GE/Boeing relationship was always one of a genuine 'Working Together' process; partners, rather than simply supplier and customer. David Calhoun`s and Alan Mulally's example had been a successful model to follow.

Arriving to replace me and to run the GE office for BCAG was my ex-boss, Herb Depp. Dave Calhoun, in his usual and thoughtful manner, had been courteous enough to call me some months earlier and ask my opinion about such a move. I remember telling Dave that in my opinion, it was a stroke of genius. Herb was well versed with Boeing worldwide, in his job as Head of Sales for GE, and was a known and respected figure at BCAG. Herb and I had spent several days together in the final weeks of my tenure and I felt entirely comfortable that our number one customer was going to be in good hands.

On the morning after my final day, I climbed into my over-loaded car at 3 am and started the ten-hour drive to my wife and our new home in Brookings, Oregon. The first half of the drive is along the I-5 freeway, which travels from the Canadian border south to the Mexican border and is heavily trafficked. By leaving at 3 am, I missed the heavy rush hour traffic areas of Tacoma and Portland. Before 6:30 am and after an hour or two more on I-5, I turned off the freeway onto State Route 38, a picturesque drive along the Umpqua River to the coast.

This route intersects with Highway 101 at Reedsport, and I then followed 101 South, along the coast for about 125 miles into the little fishing village of Brookings. After a couple of stops for gas, food and a couple of view sites to enjoy the magnificent scenery along the spectacular Oregon coast (surely one of the most beautiful coastlines in the USA and perhaps in the world), I was home at around 2 pm.

Jayne had done a wonderful job of setting up our new home and I had to promise not to change any of the furniture or art arrangements without having a discussion first! Jayne had the distinct advantage of being the first permanent resident, and as such, had full rights to arrange the furniture and art as she saw fit. Jayne has a good eye for interior decorating and the only thing that was apparent was that we needed some extra furniture, since this was larger than our house near Seattle.

Retirement

The first year of retirement passed quickly, due to the novelty of living in a new area and especially living by the ocean. It had always been a dream of ours to live next to an ocean one day, but realistically, we had considered it only a dream, especially from a prison cell in Zimbabwe! But here we are and our delight in watching the ever-changing Pacific Ocean and beach is unbounded. There is ample sea life, from otters to pelicans to crabs to seagulls and more.

The Oregon coast is the first coast in the USA that we had seen that is unspoiled, probably because of the light human population of the state. The tidal pools are pristine, with starfish, urchins, crabs and minnows, just as I remember the South African coast when I was a child. The beaches in Oregon are public, although one owns the land/beach from the mean high tide level, in theory, but not in practice. The coves around our beach are impassable after mid-tide, and since there is no public access for a mile in either direction, our beach is private for all intents and purposes.

Although Jayne had accomplished much in her first year of getting settled, there was a never-ending list of things to be done; both on the grounds and in the house. The landscaping had been designed by the original owner to be minimum maintenance, with mostly low evergreens and ground cover, but with several high-maintenance lawns! Jayne, having a green thumb, wanted many flower beds and shrubs and a good deal of time and effort was spent starting to clear as much of the low evergreens as we could achieve on our own.

The house, too, required endless maintenance, being right next to the ocean and because of its unique location on a point, totally exposed to the winter storms. The huge glass windows facing the ocean would flutter in the high winds associated with storms passing through, sometimes packing 90 mph winds and dumping up to 10 inches of rain in a night.

I Get Restless

After it became apparent that getting the property in the condition that we wanted was going to be an ongoing exercise for several years, at least, and since my premonition about getting ill had not materialized and I was becoming tired of `honey-dos`, I decided that I must look for something to challenge my mind and to take some advantage of my 40 years in aviation, in one form or another.

My thinking was to see if any aviation firm would be interested enough in my experience and background that they would consider using my expertise in a consulting role. As a courtesy to my former President of GE, David Calhoun, I decided to call him and let him know that I was planning to start looking around within the industry. To my great surprise, David told me he thought that was a great idea and he asked if I would consider doing some work again for GE.

Specifically, he wanted me to help sell our all-new CFM LEAP engine to BCAG, for their new 737 MAX airplane, due to enter service in 2017. Since I already understood much of BCAG`s requirements with their airplane family, and I knew that I would be able to help with communications and relationships between the companies as we progressed through the campaign, I was delighted! The stakes were high, since the market was forecasting anywhere between 3,000 and 5,000 new 737's, which meant up to 10,000 orders for the winning engine.

Our competition would be Pratt and Whitney (PW), with their all-new Geared Turbofan (GTF) engine. We had looked at geared turbofan technology before but had concluded that we could achieve the same, or better, performance with more standard and reliable engine architecture. Pratt had not had an engine on the 737 for decades and they were putting considerable effort into this new venture and were not to be underestimated. However, our CFM engines were and are the most popular and trusted in the world, having sold more than 30 thousand to date with the best reliability rates in the industry.

The necessary legal documentation was completed to finalize my contract with CFM, detailing my responsibilities on the LEAP engine program for the 737 MAX airplane and '*voila*', I was a consultant and raring to go! The plan was for me to work closely with the CFM office in Cincinnati, as well as the GE/CFM office in the Seattle area. It was clear that constant co-ordination would be necessary, so as not to duplicate work or tread on each other`s toes. This was not difficult because I planned to work with a different set of people at Boeing, including the past Chairman, the best strategist and clearest thinker that Boeing has produced. Other BCAG icons like Joe Sutter, John Roundhill and 'Granny' Frazier, amongst others, sat on the Senior Advisory Group, but with whom our offices had no dealings.

There were always different viewpoints that came out of my contacts, since they felt no need to always agree with the party line. These discussions usually offered more creative, or in some cases, simpler ideas than the official, decision-making chain of command. The particular advantage that these long-standing business relationships offered was the credibility and trust that each side offered to other. We had all worked together over many years and through several different programs had developed a comfort level with each other that allowed for frank and open discussion to resolve issues and to develop plans together for the benefit of both of our companies.

One of the distinct advantages of working as a consultant is the freedom to choose which meetings add value, and which do not. Gone is the requirement to sit in huge meeting rooms with multitudes, working through lengthy and not always relevant agendas. Instead, meetings can be smaller and in more convivial surroundings, with smaller, focused agendas. Working breakfasts or lunches/dinners usually provide such forums for amenable discussions, and golf course meetings are notorious for achieving breakthroughs on issues that have thwarted closure in more formal venues.

Senior Golfer

Since my retirement from full time work with GE and Boeing, our local office in the Seattle area has always been kind enough to invite me to play in the annual Senior PGA Pro-Am golf tournament. GE sponsors two teams, and the Boeing organizing committee, in conjunction with the outstanding golf club committee at TPC Snoqualmie, and others, determines the mix of professional golfers and business teams. We would mix our GE teams with GE and Boeing players, since the time on the course provided us with an excellent opportunity for business discussions, as well as golf lessons!

As luck would have it, the first time I played with a GE team at this Pro-Am, our team was paired with Nick Price, my long-time friend from my Rhodesian Air Force days, and world number one player in 1993 and 1994. I suspect that my good friend and head of the Boeing organizing Committee, Larry Dickenson, had something to do with this arrangement, but I could never figure out what, and I was grateful. Nick and I had maintained our friendship since 'Operation Thrasher' in 1977, when Nick was still a teenager and I had followed Nick`s remarkable golf career through all this time.

The Pro-Am was run over two days, with 18 holes being played each day. The format was Best Ball Nett Stableford, which meant you had to score a birdie or better to register a score. A birdie would get you one point; an eagle would get you two points, and so on. Our team played some solid golf on the first day, but the tournament was cancelled after 13 holes due to heavy rain. Never the less, our team had put together 13 points, as I recall a respectable total for 13 holes. The next day we could complete all 18 holes and I seem to remember that our team scored 19 points, a decent score. When we finished the round, Nick went to sign our card and then to sign autographs for the many fans waiting to chat with him.

After about an hour of this, I suggested to Nick that we should perhaps go along to the prize-giving in the clubhouse. Nick however had already noticed a wounded veteran in his wheelchair, walked over to him, sat down on the grass next to him and started chatting. I was by now even more impressed with my friend, Nick, and his caring thoughtfulness. But he was not finished. He found a golf ball, signed it and handed it to the surprised veteran, put his hand on the vet`s shoulder and said farewell to him. One happy vet!

Now I felt we should get along to the prize giving, as a courtesy to the organizers, but Nick had a powerful thirst for a quiet beer.

"Let`s go back to town, Hugh", he said, "and we can have a couple of beers and some Thai dinner".

"But what about the prize giving, Nick?" I persisted.

"We should go", said Nick, "but we`re not in the running to win anything, so I think beer is the priority."

I assumed that Nick had played enough Pro-Ams in his life and therefore must know what he was talking about, so I stopped arguing, we got into my car and set off for town and beer. We had probably gone about 15 miles when my phone rang; it was Larry Dickenson, the tournament organizer.

"Hugh, where are you guys? You`ve won the tournament and there`s no one here from your team to accept the first prize!"

Nick and I looked at each other. We were too far on our way into town to turn around, but we felt terrible.

"I'm so sorry, Larry", I apologized, "It would take 30 minutes for us to turn around in the traffic and get back. Would you be kind enough to accept the prize on our behalf?"

Larry graciously agreed and I was glad that I had not explained our overwhelming thirst for a beer! The first prize was not insignificant; an all-expenses paid trip for four to the Super Bowl, the American equivalent of the Rugby World Cup, in terms of numbers and dollars! It was a big deal and a very generous first prize. Nick was not eligible and I gave my ticket to a fellow team member, so he could take his wife. One of my other team mates did the same thing and two happy couples had a great trip to the Super Bowl. I told Nick that my child-like faith in his judgment had suffered a bad knock!

Jayne Diagnosed With Cancer

Two years after retiring from full-time work, my premonition about developing some serious illness had still not manifested, but suddenly, Jayne became seriously ill with cancer. As is sometimes the case with cancer, Jayne felt healthy, but her careful doctor did not like some signs evident at Jayne`s annual medical and referred her to an excellent local specialist who confirmed our worst fears. Our thoughts of going to a major center for her surgery were dispelled by several local friends who explained to us that a local surgeon was known for his excellence in this type of cancer surgery.

Interestingly, he was a retired Air Force surgeon who wanted to live and serve in a small community. We both liked him immediately and the reports of his abilities were quickly proven correct. After some serious surgery, he nursed Jayne to health after a tough initial period of a week, when Jayne had a deathly white pallor and could only swallow melted ice cubes between her lengthy and frequent sleeps.

I would visit Jayne three times a day, making the 60-mile round-trip early in the morning, at midday and again in the late afternoon. Our wonderful friend and next-door neighbor, Beth, would often beat me to the hospital in the early morning, and I would find her sitting quietly next to Jayne, watching caringly while Jayne slept. If I had not arrived, Beth would have stayed there all day without disturbing Jayne! After the first week, Jayne could start on liquids and I could push her around the hospital corridors in a wheelchair to give her back a rest from the hospital bed.

After a few weeks, I could take her home, weak as a kitten but surviving, thanks to our wonderful specialist`s skills and caring. Before Jayne became ill, we had booked an Alaskan cruise and had considered cancelling it when Jayne was diagnosed. However, after discussion with our specialist, he was of the opinion that it would do her some good, and a month after the surgery, we went off on our cruise, along with my brother Don, who had come to the US from South Africa (his home) to be with us.

I knew Jayne was getting better when she started to act in her usual feisty manner, telling me that her cooking was much better than anything onboard and that she would rather be working in her flower garden than cooped up on a cruise liner. Such gratitude! At the end of our trip, I still felt that the cruise did some good in taking our minds off what was yet to come - six months of chemo.

The chemo treatments necessitated a 250-mile round trip drive, twice every 11 days, to a treatment center in Medford. Jayne`s oncologist turned out to be of South African birth and after the seriousness of the first few visits, the mood became lighter. We would usually discuss the major South African topics of rugby, *braaivleis* and biltong (jerky/dried meat) for the most part of the meeting and until the oncologist would say,

"Okay, Jayne, jump up on the bed and let`s have a look at you."

He was extremely competent and had clearly diagnosed the chemo treatment correctly, because after the six-month course, Jayne was deemed cancer free. He also had a great sense of humor. One month while checking a bill from his office, I found a $50 charge for `smoking counseling`! When I questioned him about it, he said, "Hugh, when Jayne tells me that she is still smoking, even when I have begged her to stop, you will see this charge every time!"

He did get Jayne to stop for three months, but only because Jayne realized that he could not analyze her results accurately, due to her smoking. After the treatment, Jayne went straight back to smoking!

For those who have been or have friends or family who have been subjected to chemo, you will know that it is no fun at all. Jayne had a port in her neck so that she didn`t end up looking like a pin cushion. The long, winding drive after the chemo treatments really caused her to feel ill. She would have a three to five hour infusion of chemo in Medford and we would then drive home with a two-day steady infusion attached to her, before driving back to Medford on day four to remove the attachment.

She would feel pretty grim for the next four or five days and then start to feel better on about day five, before we had to drive back to Medford for a repeat performance. This pattern continued for six months and through it all, I never heard a word of complaint or self-pity. On Jayne`s final appointment with our wonderful South African oncologist, and after studying her results, he said, "Do not darken my doorway again, Jayne! Go home and watch rugby, enjoy your *braaivleis*, make some biltong and have fun!"

We were indeed fortunate with our fine surgeon and our oncologist, without whom my beloved wife might not be with me today. As it turned out, my premonition was partly right. I just got the wrong person but I was glad to be at least semi-retired and in a position to provide all the support necessary.

We were touched when our friends from Australia, the former Commander of the Rhodesian Air Force, Norman Walsh and his lovely wife, Merilyn, as well as our longtime friends from New Zealand (also ex-Air Force), Charles and Sandy Connolly, visited us to be with Jayne as she battled her way through the chemo treatments.

Charlie himself had been battling cancer for some time, but one would never know it from his wonderful, always happy attitude. I couldn`t help thinking that if I did ever get really sick, like Charlie or Jayne, I hoped I could portray the same strong and positive attitude to the world. Charlie finally succumbed to the dreadful illness after a long and brave fight, an example to all who knew him. Go well, our friend.

Also visiting us during this time were my ex-Station Commander and boss from the Air Force, Tol Janeke and Anne, his beautiful wife and long-time good friend of Jayne`s. They came all the way from South Africa to give support, love and strength through the difficult times. Our little Air Force was always known as a family, and these acts proved it. Thanks to all of you. I`m happy to report that Jayne has gone from strength to strength and today, 11 years after her treatment, is still cancer free and we are grateful for each and every day.

More Bad News

Then I suffered a series of bad news. Within a span of some three years, around 2010, I was dealt some devastating blows. First, my wonderful mentor, who had hired me into GE Commercial Engines, Ray Wagner, passed away due to cancer. It was Ray who had given me a start into his side of the business and had trained me tirelessly. His guidance encouraged and equipped me with the interest and skills to make the commercial aviation industry my life for the next 25 years. When he retired, he selflessly recommended and ensured that I took his position. He was an expert in his field, a true gentleman, and I am grateful to this day for his guidance and help.

Then, out of nowhere, my trusted friend, fellow officer and prisoner, Pete Briscoe, developed a brain tumor and died within three months, in his home town of Saint Louis. Pete and I had been through a lot together over our Air Force careers, finally sharing a cell and a bucket in the various prisons where we spent time, and then coming to America to start our lives again. This just did not seem fair to me, especially after we had both survived the Zimbabwe ordeal.

Jayne and I were shocked. We had visited Pete and his family in Saint Louis as often as we could, when he was diagnosed, but his condition deteriorated rapidly and the recovery we all prayed for was not to be. We are as close to Pete`s lovely family today as we have ever been. In some ways, they are our second family and we love them dearly.

Not long after Ray`s passing, Jayne and I lost the person who was primarily responsible for clearing a path for us to immigrate to the USA; Senator Tom Eagleton. Tom never faltered in his dedicated quest to get entry into the USA for me, my family and for Pete Briscoe and his family. It is fair to say that without Tom`s support, we may never have made it into the USA. He was a man of absolute principle and he was determined to rectify the injustice we had suffered and give us a chance to start a new life in a safe environment in a civilized country. Tom passed away from complications after a severe bout of pneumonia, which he had contracted, ironically, while on a trip to South Africa. Not what we wanted for you, Tom.

Then, that brave man who did all he could to keep us prisoners safe and alive until our trial, often at great risk to his own safety, passed away in his adopted country of Australia, after complications from an old injury. Air Marshal Norman Walsh had the unenviable task of trying to work with some radical Ministers of the new Zimbabwe government, who seemed hell bent on destroying the country`s own Air Force, especially after the false accusations against his own senior officers. Norman`s only concern was for his men and he would not leave the country until he was sure we would be safe.

Jayne and I had visited Norman and his wife, Merilyn, in their home in Australia before Norman became ill and were delighted to see them so happy and settled. Merilyn had been the leading light in raising funds from many sources for our defense lawyers and shepherding the wives of the prisoners through those long and worrisome months of imprisonment.

As if this was not enough, Hal Balo, my first GE manager and mentor passed away after a lengthy illness. It was Hal who had patiently coached me, after normal work hours, about GE and American business practices, and it was Hal who trusted me enough to give me a lead position in his organization after only one year on the job. He was a man of absolute integrity and loyalty to the Company and to his country. Hal was a Navy man, he knew of my Air Force career and we both recognized each other`s love of serving our country. We visit Hal`s wonderful wife, Vera, whenever we are in Cincinnati. She is a loving and caring lady of Italian heritage and she makes the best stuffed shells on the planet! Go well, Hal, and thank you.

Amongst all this bad news, there has to be some good news. Actually, some really good news! I happened to be in Seattle on consulting business when I got a call one evening from our youngest son, Lee.

"Dad," he said, "my girlfriend is pregnant!"

I paused before replying, determined not to play the part of a Victorian parent, and then was able to say calmly,

"Congratulations, Lee! That`s terrific news!"

"But Dad", he went on, "what do I tell Mum?"

I demurred, knowing that Jayne had very strong views about this sort of thing, but then I said,

"You have a problem there, Lee, and I can`t help you with it. Just be honest and take your beating!"

I said no more and when I got home and asked Jayne if Lee had called her, I got the reaction I expected. I told Lee that he would just have to tough it out and maybe Mum would come around later. Coincidentally, I was in Seattle some four months later when I got another call from Lee.

"Dad", he said excitedly, "we had a sonogram today and it`s a girl!"

I heaved a sigh of relief and said,

"Call your mother right now! You are home free!"

I went straight to the bar for a celebratory martini!

Our first granddaughter, Kaylee Jayne, arrived on the 4th July, 2011, an auspicious day, indeed! She has just turned six and is the light of our lives. Thank you, Lee and Chelsie.

New Engine on the 737

Back at BCAG and after several years of negotiations, we (CFM) won the competition to put an engine on the new 737 MAX. This was an enormous success, against a very worthy competitor, but there was no time for much celebration. While the technologies for our new engine components were understood and tested, through GE`s unique `technology stocking` process, there was now the major requirement to blend these all into a whole new engine alongside SNECMA`s (SAFRAN`s) new components. At the same time, we would be working with BCAG to understand the new requirements from the airplane side.

New airplane and new engine programs are always exciting, and this latest program is no exception. Given the history of these two companies and the known process of working together, we have overcome the expected and unexpected hurdles, usually in a timely manner. The program to stay on track, for deliveries of new airplanes to airlines and entry into service in May 2017, is a tremendous success! A remarkable achievement by all concerned, given the rapidly growing production rates to support the growing order book.

While this has been a team effort, with many contributors, I believe the strong and tireless leadership displayed by David Joyce and Bill Fitzgerald, of GE / CFM, who, like David Calhoun, promote the essentials of solid engineering and tireless customer support have been key. With similar strong and experienced leadership from industry giants like Ray Conner at BCAG, this team has been the glue needed to keep the program on track.

The aviation industry never stands still. BCAG and Airbus continue to do battle, in every segment of the airline business, and air traffic continues to grow at about 5% per year. BCAG is far advanced into the new and larger 777 program, with our new GE90 engine, and is already well advanced on a study for a new mid-range airplane, to fill the market space between the 737 and the 787.

This business is not for the faint of heart, requiring huge capital investments, along with carefully considered risk taking, but it is always exciting and requires constant cutting-edge technology to stay ahead of the competition. It is exactly this approach that has kept GE and CFM the number one commercial airplane engine manufacturer and supplier in the world, with Rolls Royce and Pratt and Whitney constantly driving competition with their good products.

For my part, I will continue consulting as long as I add value for my company and the Industry, and as long as my health permits. Aviation has been my life since I was 19 years old and I just hit 75! I have indeed been blessed.

PART SEVEN

Reflections on Life

REFLECTING ON LIFE, *the most intriguing thing is how much my life has changed, driven in the first instance by the radical change of government and their unwarranted actions against me and my Rhodesian Air Force colleagues. While many would say that those events were predictable, I was prepared to give the new government a chance. After all, this was the land of my birth, and while I did not relish the change, I had met the new Prime Minister, Mugabe, on several occasions and I was encouraged by his then conciliatory and sensible approach to the future.*

While I recognized we would all face challenges, I felt that if I and others remained to keep the Air Force viable, we could play a constructive role for the good of the country. Several of our good friends decided to leave the country, a huge challenge in itself, and I was saddened to see them go. To a man, they told me I was being naïve, and in hindsight, they were right.

The events leading to my arrest, torture, trial, total acquittal and, finally, eviction from the country of my birth, are still fresh in my mind. They were clearly the biggest life changing events that I have ever experienced or would ever want anyone to experience. And yet, when I consider the outcome today, I feel strangely fortunate.

Even if events in Zimbabwe had been different, and if I had, indeed, assumed overall command of the Air Force that year, I would have been faced with obligatory retirement after four years, at age 46; a four-year maximum term as Commander. It`s likely I would then have lived on my deceased father`s fruit and timber farm, at Inyanga. That farm would probably have been seized by the government, for redistribution to some favored Minister, leaving me reliant on a small, government pension, which very rapidly would have become totally worthless, leaving me and Jayne destitute and effectively financial prisoners in Zimbabwe.

This is the fate that befell most of the people and friends that we left behind in the country. Instead, and as a direct result of that government's actions against me, I live with my family in a civilized country that respects the rule of law. I have a roof over my head, food on the table and I`m in a position to assist some of those less fortunate. Most of all, my family is safe and I feel blessed. Thank you, America.

But what is to become of Zimbabwe, South Africa and, indeed, the whole of Africa? The continent is rich in resource but plagued by corrupt and incompetent governments. Much of the problem in Southern Africa and Zimbabwe, in particular, lies with the original colonizing power, Britain, who did little to help develop the country that was then Southern Rhodesia. They (Britain) hastily abandoned Northern Rhodesia and

Nyasaland to incompetent governments, and then interfered with the successfully developing Rhodesia.

The result, in the case of Rhodesia, was a war leading to a government that has proven to be one of the most corrupt and incompetent in the history of Africa. At one point, some 20 years after inheriting the jewel of central Africa, a record inflation rate of one quadrillion percent was set! Not the sort of record to aspire to! And today, the jewel of Africa is no longer the jewel. Severe poverty, massive unemployment, illness and hunger are everywhere.

Jayne and I are still in regular contact with our wonderful ex-cook and housemaid. We are able to provide money for her, as well, so that she has a house and food and can survive, since the unemployment rate is somewhere around 90%! The relationship between employer and employee in Rhodesia and Zimbabwe, in our day, was often misstated and usually, for political purposes. My family and most of our farmer friends enjoyed life-long relationships with their employees. Sadly, a lot of that changed, due to the war and the inability of the new government to attract and even retain investment. The result is a broken infrastructure, few jobs, and badly failed agricultural, mining and commercial businesses.

The massive and impressive infrastructure which the Mandela government inherited in South Africa will take longer to collapse, but there are warning signs everywhere and unless the people of the country can somehow find better government, and quickly, they too will be faced with a future resembling Zimbabwe. Perhaps the current rising tide of the peoples' criticism of the corrupt and incompetent ANC government, led by a crooked President, will galvanize the electorate to seek a better government.

As for Africa, the continent has a history of turbulence, driven in most cases by greed. Governments have effectively emasculated their peoples, so that they have no say in matters and are rendered harmless and without a voice. Perhaps the point of no return has already been reached? While I miss the country of my birth, its wonderful warm peoples and our long-time friends and families, it's difficult to hold much hope for any early improvement in the situation. Oh, Africa!

I reflect too on those intangibles, absorbed unseeingly, at the time; the fine values inherent in my parent`s everyday lives; the discipline, love of country inculcated by the Air Force, the association with our Army and Police Forces and the comfort of finally gaining an understanding of some of Jesus' words that I felt I could trust.

I have avoided any religious discussion deliberately because it is such a personal matter. In my case, it was my Mother, a woman with the unusual combination of intellect and wisdom who introduced me, at a late stage of my life, to the readings of one Mary Baker Eddy. This, in turn, caused me to realize that our Creator has made us spiritual, rather than simply physical beings. That has become a source of great comfort to me and I hope it is to others who feel the same. It is of interest that all the people that I have met, who have suffered near-death experiences or tragedy, have sought comfort in a better understanding of our Creator.

Finally, I reflect on the love and support of my family, through tough times. Where lesser mortals may well have `cut and run`, my wife stood her ground firmly, against the radical elements of a government hell bent on executing her husband and destroying the Air Force, as a viable and essential component of the country.

And my sons, whose emotional feelings about the entire fiasco, I later realized, I had badly underestimated. This really became clear when I was finally released from prison and my older son, Mark, told me that he and his (also 12-year old) friend had planned to 'eliminate' the 'Mad Minister' who kept locking me up!

No book that mentions the word `Rhodesia` should do so without paying tribute to the men and women, black and white, who fought to save Rhodesia as a civilized country, capable of sustaining and protecting all its peoples. I pay solemn tribute to the courage of all those who fought for a just and decent cause, but who were duped by the hypocrisy and chicanery of a highly-politicized western world and the greed of the resulting government. Thank you all for your service and your sacrifice. To those who lost loved ones, I offer a special prayer of comfort. "No greater love hath man..."

While that war is over, I am very much aware of our American soldiers and our allies who fight each and every day to protect our lives and allow our countries to remain civilized and sustainable. Freedom requires constant vigilance, courage and sacrifice against the ongoing forces of evil, and I pray for all our soldiers` lives and safety. Thank you and your families for what you do so selflessly and bravely. All who live in the Free World owe you a huge debt of gratitude.

THE AUTHOR

Hugh now lives with Jayne, his wife of 50 years in a small fishing village on the Oregon coast in the USA. He still consults for General Electric Aviation and its subsidiary CFM, focusing on new engine programs for Boeing Commercial Airplanes. His interest in aviation spans some 60 years, including both military and commercial fields.

His sons and grandchildren live in Ohio and New York, and he has a brother in South Africa.

Writing this book had been on his mind for many years. Friends and family eventually prevailed upon him to sit down and write this so his side of the saga would be known and a piece of the country's history would be on the record.